Improving
Adolescent Literacy

Improving
Adolescent Literacy
Content Area Strategies at Work

Third Edition

Douglas Fisher

San Diego State University

Nancy Frey

San Diego State University

Boston   Columbus   Indianapolis   New York   San Francisco   Upper Saddle River
Amsterdam   Cape Town   Dubai   London   Madrid   Milan   Munich   Paris   Montreal   Toronto
Delhi   Mexico City   São Paulo   Sydney   Hong Kong   Seoul   Singapore   Taipei   Tokyo

Vice President and Editor-in-Chief: Aurora Martínez Ramos
Editorial Assistant: Meagan French
Project Manager: Barbara Strickland
Marketing Manager: Danae April
Production Editor: Janet Domingo
Editorial Production Service: S4Carlisle Publishing Services
Manufacturing Buyer: Megan Cochran
Electronic Composition: S4Carlisle Publishing Services
Interior Design: S4Carlisle Publishing Services
Photo Researcher: Annie Pickert
Cover Designer: Elena Sidorova

Credits and acknowledgments borrowed from other sources and reproduced, with permission, in this textbook appear on appropriate page within text.

Library of Congress Cataloging-in-Publication Data
Fisher, Douglas
  Improving adolescent literacy : content area strategies at work / Douglas Fisher, Nancy Frey—3rd ed.
    p. cm.
  Includes bibliographical references.
  ISBN-13: 978-0-13-248712-2
  ISBN-10: 0-13-248712-8
  1. Reading (Secondary)   2. Content area reading.   I. Frey, Nancy   II. Title.
  LB1632.F57 2011
  428.4071'2—dc22

                                                                        2010050630

10 9 8 7 6 5 4 3 2 1 [EDW] 15 14 13 12 11
ISBN-10:   0-13-248712-8
ISBN-13: 978-0-13-248712-2

www.pearsonhighered.com

Brief Contents

Contents

Chapter 6: Picture This: Graphic Organizers in the Classroom   **101**

Chapter 7: Getting It Down: Making and Taking Notes Across the Curriculum   **121**

Preface

Middle and high school teachers across the curriculum face the challenge of helping their students comprehend their subject area texts, which can be particularly difficult for those students who lack the literacy skills to succeed academically. This urgent challenge means that reading, writing, and thinking must be developed in every middle school and secondary classroom. We believe that it's you, the middle school or secondary teacher, who can make a difference in student success. For this reason, we offer this concise text with key strategies that will allow you to develop the literacy skills students need to comprehend course content, no matter what content area or elective you teach.

New to This Edition

This decade has been an exciting one for those interested in adolescent literacy issues. The field emerged in the 1970s with the work of Hal Herber and his associates, who developed the field of content area reading and writing. In its early days, content area literacy was conceived as an approach that infused specific strategies into instruction when possible. In turn, this was expanded through the Writing Across the Curriculum movement that began in colleges and filtered to middle and high school classes. What has become clear in this decade is that adolescent literacy is not an add-on to content instruction, but is central to learning. This edition seeks to incorporate this stance. Here are changes that you can look forward to in this book:

1. *Guidance for developing literacy skills with English learners.* In addition to specifically identifying why a specific instructional routine or procedure would be helpful for English learners, we have added new scenarios to profile students developing proficiency in English.

2. *Focus on readers who struggle.* In each chapter, we call out specific information about readers who struggle. Taken together, these key points help teachers consider the perspective of readers who struggle and what can be done to accelerate their achievements. In addition, each of the classroom examples were tested and validated with students who struggle with school.

3. *New classroom examples.* In each chapter, we have new examples from our own teaching and our co-workers' teaching at Health Sciences High School. These examples include the use of technology and media.

4. *Updated research base.* Although the tried and true structure of this book remains the same and we continue to focus on the same core ideas that were presented in the first edition, we have updated the research base for each of the chapters, providing readers with current sources of support and additional reading.

5. *Assessment chapter revisions.* We have also revised the assessment chapter to provide readers with additional information about the current state of formal and informal assessments and how they can be used in the classroom. Specifically, we have added a section on feed forward, which provides information about using assessment information to guide instruction.

Text Organization

This book is organized into nine chapters. In chapter 1 we introduce critical goals for adolescent literacy and a rationale for your involvement in improving adolescents' access to literacy. We also introduce a number of grouping and instructional strategies useful in engaging all students in their own learning.

Chapters 2 through 8 present sound, core instructional strategies that develop lifelong literacy skills and allow students to access text. The purpose of each of these key strategies is to enhance students' comprehension of the content—the ultimate goal of all educators—and develop students' access to vocabulary.

The core strategies covered in chapters 2–8 include:

- Anticipatory activities
- Vocabulary instruction
- Read alouds and shared reading
- Questioning
- Graphic organizers
- Notetaking and notemaking
- Writing to learn

Each of these chapters opens with a vignette, modeling how the instructional strategy is implemented in an actual adolescent classroom. These scenarios are followed by a rationale for each strategy as well as the research base that supports its use. Each chapter ends with an example of the strategy being used in English, science, social studies, mathematics, and elective classes.

Chapter 9 is a capstone chapter offering guidance and insight into the standards and assessments that hold middle school and secondary teachers accountable for student proficiency.

New! CourseSmart eTextbook Available

CourseSmart is an exciting new choice for students looking to save money. As an alternative to purchasing the printed textbook, students can purchase an electronic version of the same content. With a CourseSmart eTextbook, students can search the text, make notes online, print out reading assignments that incorporate lecture notes, and bookmark important passages for later review. For more information, or to purchase access to the CourseSmart eTextbook, visit www.coursesmart.com.

Acknowledgments

We have had the opportunity to learn alongside a number of skilled teachers as they delivered their content in ways that have increased their students' literacy learning. We thank all of the teachers who invited us in and provided us with detailed information about their practice.

This book would not have been completed without the support, assistance, and encouragement of several key individuals: Rita Elwardi, Tom Fehrenbacher, Christine Johnson, and Lee Mongrue have been with us every step of the way. Their contributions have been invaluable. Our current work is influenced by the amazing teachers at Health Sciences High & Middle College. From people starting their careers (such as Dominique Smith and Sarah Soriano), to people consolidating their practices (such as Ben Teichman, Lucas Staker, Javier Vaca, Jo Schaefer, Adam Renick, and Randy Conrad), to veteran teachers (such as Kelly Johnson, Dina Burow, Aida Allen, Heather Anderson, John Goodwin, and Jeff Bonine), we are lucky to work alongside a group of content teachers as they develop students' literacy and love for learning.

We would also like to thank the reviewers who offered their thoughtful comments as this work progressed. Their feedback made this a better book and we thank them. These reviewers include Linda Cole, The Barrie School; Karen Ford, Ball State University; Gay Ivey, James Madison University; Courtney Kelly, Manhattanville College; Margot Kinberg, National University; Valerie Kinloch, The Ohio State University; and Scott R. Popplewell, Ball State University.

Douglas Fisher & Nancy Frey

Chapter **1**
Ensuring All Students Read, Write, and Think

*A*s your eyes pass over these little squiggle marks, consider the amazing feat you're accomplishing. Small ink marks are being transferred from the page, through your eyes, to your brain. Once there, your brain makes a series of connections such that you make sense of the ideas on the page. It's amazing really, and it's how we learn. Humans learn through language. When we read, write, speak, listen, and view, we learn. It's really that simple. It's why we wrote this book. We want to ensure that middle and high school students have opportunities to use language to learn the amazing content introduced to them in school. Whether that content be in the form of a 15th-century sonnet, an experiment in physics, the analysis of a jazz composition, or perfecting a free throw, language is involved in learning.

As a case in point, let's venture into a social studies classroom. As you read about Ms. Johnson's class, think about the reading, writing, speaking, listening, and viewing students do, all in service of learning history.

The students in this 11th-grade social studies class are studying the rise of industrialization and immigration at the turn of the 20th century. These dual trends intersected tragically in the sinking of RMS Titanic on Sunday, April 14, 1912. Christine Johnson is using documentary film clips as well as key scenes from the popular movie Titanic (Landau & Cameron, 1997) to help students understand the event. She uses reproductions of newspaper accounts from the era, including the St. Louis Dispatch and the New York Tribune. Students will also read modern accounts of the event and an article on the recovery effort.

Ms. Johnson asks the class, "After seeing the video presentation of the Titanic accident, what are your thoughts and feelings about this tragedy? Write all you know. You have 5 minutes." Time is called and the students share their thoughts and feelings. They begin to brainstorm prior knowledge using the K-W-L strategy to focus on the assigned text. Ms. Johnson follows with the question, "What would you like to know about the Titanic?" The students write their questions and hold them aside for later inquiry after reading the newspapers. She asks the students to share their questions as she writes some of them on the board. The students seem eager to respond as well as to question.

Anna reads, "Why didn't they listen to the warnings? Why didn't they look hard enough for an iceberg?"

Isaac asks, "What did they do to the ship that made them think that it was unsinkable? How long does it take an iceberg to disappear?"

"I want to know, why didn't they have enough life boats for everyone?" asks Cesar.

Marco adds, "Who were some of the people in first class? I would like to know about them in more detail."

Latasha wonders, "Who were the survivors and are they still alive? Are they scared to go on trips in a boat?"

"Whose fault was it?" asks Josie.

Ms. Johnson identifies each question as either literal or interpretive level. She challenges the students to extend their thinking as strategic readers and to answer their own questions in the final step of the K-W-L strategy.

Next, Ms. Johnson introduces relevant vocabulary, including **steerage, disaster, panic, transmit, SOS,** and **dispatch,** all of which appear in the news articles. She constructs a concept map to visually represent both the definitions and relationships among the target words. She also reviews the organization of the texts they are about to read. "We will read and question the text, so that we can build an understanding of the human experience in this tragic event." She adds, "Newspaper text is often organized in a temporal sequence that tells a chronological description of events. We will pay close attention to see how this structure is used in our articles." Two other articles analyze the event from the research conducted on the wreckage site. She explains that these texts are organized for cause and effect. To help students differentiate cause from effect, Ms. Johnson points out that a cause may have one or more effects and an effect may have one or more causes. She emphasizes, "The cause must always precede the effect. The following signal words will help you identify the cause and effect pattern: reasons why, if . . . then, as a result, therefore, because." She writes the signal words on the board.

Then she posts springboard questions taken from student K-W-L charts to stimulate predicting, searching, and verifying information:

- Why didn't Captain Smith want the crew to announce that the ship was sinking?
- Why did Jack Phillips, the radio operator, think the disaster was his fault?

- *What does SOS signify? What signal did it replace? Explain.*
- *Why did it take so many years for anyone to reach the wreck of the* Titanic?
- *What have you learned about this disaster?*

Ms. Johnson reads aloud the first news report, titled "'Save Our Souls' Was Titanic's *Last Appeal." She encourages her students to follow the way she constructs meaning using the three central DR-TA questions:* What do I think about this? Why do I think so? How I can prove it? *She guides the students with her questions and think-aloud responses through the reading process. Systematic questioning helps structure thinking in a manageable order so parts of the new text fit together with their prior knowledge. Using a step-by-step questioning procedure, she helps the students understand the organization of the text. "What are the 5Ws (Who? What? Where? When? Why?) and How? These are questions we ask ourselves to find the information. Let's also think about what happened first, second, third?" "What is the result of these events?" This directed questioning guides the students for their independent reading and leads them toward higher-level thinking.*

After her guided preparation, the students participate in a pair-share reading of their assigned news articles. Chunks of text on the same topic will be interpreted using the DR-TA and springboard questions. Ms. Johnson monitors the students as they read to achieve individual levels of understanding.

Shifting Responsibility From Teacher to Students

Over time, her teaching role will shift from generating questions to coaching students to generate and respond to their own questions. She advises them to use a time line or graphic organizer to show the sequence of details and again directs the students to the posted springboard questions. The students are alerted to read between the lines because the answers are not explicitly stated. She informs the students that some of these questions require thinking and searching because the text information is implicit. She reminds them, *"Implicit* means you have to link main ideas with supportive or specific details to arrive at an answer. When you connect ideas with details to find the answer, you become a critical thinker."

After reading, the students review their answers to verify their understanding and accuracy. Their responses are shared in a whole-class discussion. Ms. Johnson reviews the learning processes they used, including mapping, questioning, reading, and writing. Then she summarizes the events of the tragic voyage of the *Titanic*. The students are asked to reread, this time skimming and scanning, in order to write more extensive responses to the springboard questions. The readers revisit their selections to link information acquired from their video observations, questions and answers, and discussions.

The guided discussion focuses on the participants' roles. Ms. Johnson points out that the common link—human behavior—connects the series of events that led to the sinking of the *Titanic* and its aftermath. Students support their statements

Struggling Readers

ARE A DIVERSE GROUP

Students who struggle to read in middle and high school are a diverse group. Some have learning disabilities, others have motivational issues, and still others have been undertaught. Creating or reviewing a literacy profile for each struggling reader will allow you to make instructional decisions based on student performance data. One student in your class may need help with vocabulary knowledge, whereas another student may need guidance in paying attention and organizing his or her instructional materials. Some students may need significant modeling of comprehension—as is done in a read aloud or shared reading—to begin to integrate these strategies into their personal habits. Regardless of their areas of needs, remember that adolescents who struggle to read often have very complex thoughts that are based on their understanding of the world (Ivey & Fisher, 2006). As such, wise teachers remember to activate and build background knowledge with their students knowing that every one of them has lived experiences.

with evidence from the texts, and their written responses serve as talking points for their conversations.

The final stage of the DR-TA is the postreading and Ms. Johnson requires the students to apply what they know. She assigns them the role of newswriters. As reporters, the students are to write a news article on the effects of the *Titanic*'s sinking on the world today. In applying what they learned to a new situation, the students develop an extended perspective of their knowledge.

Having read about the students' experiences in Ms. Johnson's class, think about how their understanding would be different—compromised even—had they simply been told the information, rather than experience it through all of the various aspects of language. Listening is one aspect of language, but not the only one. If students are to reach high levels of achievement and understanding, both in terms of literacy and content knowledge, they have to read, write, speak, listen, and view on a daily basis. And that's what this book is about. Over the course of the nine chapters, we will introduce you to the various ways that students can use language to comprehend the curriculum.

If you are not an English teacher, you might be asking yourself why the English teachers can't just take care of this instructional need. It's a good question. After all, English teachers work with language extensively. But that's not the only place where students need to use language. As we saw in Ms. Johnson's classroom, language is used throughout the school day. But even more importantly, the types of texts and activities students do differ across content areas. In other words, reading like a scientist isn't the same as reading as a historian or art critic. Students are expected to read for information and use that information while writing, speaking, and listening.

Venezky (1982) estimated that by the time students reach sixth grade, 75% of their school-based materials were informational in nature. This has undoubtedly increased in the ensuing decades, especially with the rise of digital forms of texts. It appears that informational texts are more difficult for students—even those at or above grade level—as measured by their ability to recall and retell (National Center for Educational Statistics, 2001). Romero, Paris, and Brem (2005) found that this difficulty was due to the challenge of monitoring the text globally; that is, they must monitor and integrate ideas that arc over a large amount of cognitive territory.

But narrative texts are not without their challenges. Students in middle and high school must also read increasingly complex narrative and poetic forms, especially in English courses. Much of the content of English courses is derived from the so-called canon of literature. These works are predominately in the form of novels, plays, and epic poetry, most of which were written decades or centuries before these students were born. The need for background knowledge is high, especially for historical events, and the vocabulary and syntax is often arcane, if

not archaic. Knowledge of story elements such as character, setting, and plot will take a reader only so far. Students must recognize complex literary devices such as mood, tone, allegory, paradox, and symbolism.

As students begin to use more complex reading materials, their need for additional comprehension strategies increases, as well. Although students are more comfortable using narrative texts, especially stories and chapter books, they are often less adept at using informational reading materials such as textbooks, reference materials, and nonfiction books. Informational text contains "ideas, facts, and principles related to the physical, biological, or social world" (Fountas & Pinnell, 2001, p. 399). Lack of instruction using informational texts may explain why even at-grade-level readers in middle school score a full year level lower on comprehension of informational texts when compared to their narrative reading levels (Langer, 1985). The range of types of informational texts challenge adolescent readers, as well. Thankfully, each content area has some common text styles that can be used.

Common Text Styles

Each content area uses some common styles that students should understand. In English courses, for example, fiction is the most frequent text students encounter. Teachers can help students understand fiction by providing them with ideas about how this genre is structured. For example, students should understand character development, setting, and types of conflict, including human versus self, human versus human, human versus circumstances, and human versus society. In addition, they need to recognize the common structures of literature—introduction, rising action, climax, falling action, and denouement.

As you can imagine, this categorization system does not work for a science book. Science texts are often organized using introductory thesis paragraphs, followed by supporting details in subsequent paragraphs. Vocabulary is essential to the field of science and is frequently introduced through a bolded word and an example.

However, students may find this format frustrating because an explicit definition may not be found in the body of the text. Pictures and charts, not surprisingly, are used to illustrate phenomena and offer more details about the topic. Although many text structures may be used throughout the science book, cause and effect is the most common.

On the other hand, history texts use a more journalistic style. Journalistic style is common in newspapers—the main ideas are presented first and then explained or explored in subsequent paragraphs. Narrative text may be embedded, particularly in sidebar features about interesting people or events. Readers can expect that the chapters and headings will be organized by concepts, and this may prove confusing at times. For instance, a chapter titled "Setting Sail for New Lands" is more ambiguous than one that reads "How European Exploration Changed the Americas." Prior knowledge is critical—and often assumed—in many history texts. Gaps in a student's experience or prior knowledge may derail his or her ability to comprehend the passage. Consider the prior knowledge required to understand the following example from a 10th-grade world history textbook:

> The era from the beginning of the Sui Dynasty to the end of the Song Dynasty lasted nearly 700 years. During that period, a mature political system based on principles first put into practice during the Qin and Han Dynasties gradually

emerged in China. As in the Han era, China was a monarchy that employed a relatively large bureaucracy. Beyond the capital, government was centered around provinces, districts, and villages. Confucian ideals were the cement that held the system together. (Spielvogel, 2003, p. 105)

Beyond the content directly related to this passage (Chinese dynasties from 581 to 1279), the reader must understand political systems, monarchies, the hierarchical nature of human settlements, Confucian philosophy, and the idiomatic use of the word "cement."

Photographs are more frequently used in historical materials to illustrate important people, places, and events, unlike diagrams in science books that are usually conceptual in nature. Like all textbooks, history texts rely on a variety of text structures, although cause and effect is dominant within a chronologically arranged format.

Mathematics texts are distinctly different from those encountered in other content areas. Each chapter follows a predictable pattern, usually an introduction of a concept or algorithm, followed by an explanation, an example, and then a problem. The main idea appears in the chapter title or headings and features comparatively little extended text passages. Instead, extensive amounts of symbols and numbers communicate complex concepts. In addition, unique technical vocabulary such as *Cartesian graph* and *sine* are used. Students, particularly those who are English language learners, are likely to be confused by mathematical words with multiple meanings such as *set, function,* and *operation.* The text structure is almost always sequential and structured to explain a procedure.

Although physical education, art, and music classes rely less on traditional textbooks as a source of information, they do exist. Students' use of these texts may be complicated by the amount of prior knowledge necessary, as well as the amount of content-specific vocabulary needed. A positive is that these texts tend to use a great deal of primary source information, including newspaper and magazine articles, film, slides, and CD-ROMs and other electronic media. Using these materials requires a great deal of visual literacy, or the ability to think critically about information presented in graphic forms. This type of literacy mirrors the changing modes of information retrieval and interpretation in our society (Bruce, 1997) and is increasingly common in informational texts.

Developing Comprehension

Although comprehension is not necessarily "taught" in the sense that it occurs in the mind of the reader, intentional instruction still plays a key role. Reading comprehension does not simply happen through lots of reading; it is developed through activities designed to teach students about what good readers do. In particular, good readers are purposeful in reading and they use strategies to extend their understanding (Paris, Wasik, & Turner, 1991). Three approaches are essential in developing reading comprehension:

- Building metacognitive awareness by teaching students what to do before, during, and after the reading
- Developing their ability to formulate questions as they read
- Providing intentional instruction in using strategies to support their comprehension

Building Metacognition to Develop Reading Comprehension. Metacognition is often described as thinking about one's thinking; it is also being aware of what one knows and does not know. For instance, readers use metacognitive skills in reading when they:

- Develop a plan of action
- Maintain/monitor the plan
- Evaluate the plan (Kujawa & Huske, 1995)

As we described earlier, reading comprehension is an active process undertaken by the reader. Therefore, the reader approaches text with a plan, uses the plan, and then checks to see if the plan worked. This metacognitive awareness can be modeled through instruction using questions before, during, and after the reading.

- *Before the reading—developing the plan.* Before beginning any reading, discuss questions such as the following:
  - What is my purpose for reading?
  - What do I already know about this topic?
  - How long do I think it will take for me to read it?
- *During the reading—monitoring the plan.* While reading, pause occasionally to ask these questions:
  - Do I understand what I'm reading?
  - If not, what can I do to help myself?
  - What do I already know that I can connect this information to?
  - Do I need to change my pace?
  - What are the important ideas?
- *After the reading—evaluating the plan.* Once the reading is finished, revisit the plan by asking questions such as:
  - How did I do?
  - Did the reading meet my expectations?
  - Did I understand?
  - Do I need to revisit any part of the text? (Kujawa & Huske, 1995)

Kujawa and Huske's (1995) model is based on the mind of the reader and emphasizes what good readers do to prepare to read, to monitor understanding while reading, and to reflect and extend their knowledge after they have completed the reading. However, students need modeling and scaffolding to achieve this level of independent and effective reading. This is accomplished through the use of research-based instructional strategies that mirror the cognition of effective readers.

The model of before, during, and after in reading instruction is useful because it provides a template for the instructional intentions of the teacher as well as the cognitive ones of the learner. We will extend this useful model throughout the text, describing specific instructional strategies that support children as they read for information. Learning to use the before, during, and after reading model will serve as a cognitive guide for the teaching and learning that occurs in classrooms committed to instruction in reading for information.

Conversations: Structures That Support Adolescent Literacy Development

The influence of the classroom and school environment on instruction is significant. A number of meta-analyses and research reviews have confirmed that when teachers and students have opportunities to collaborate with their peers, learning occurs (e.g., Calweti, 2004; Marzano, Pickering, & Pollock, 2001). Learning is a community function, not an isolated one, and the conversations that occur between learners foster growth for all involved (Vygotsky, 1978).

We will consider a number of structures that ensure students have opportunities to engage in conversations with their peers. As part of these collaborative learning situations, students consolidate their understanding and improve their understanding of the content (Frey, Fisher, & Everlove, 2009).

Think-Pair-Share

One of the most transportable teaching strategies is *think-pair-share* (Lyman, 1981). Think-pair-share introduces an intermediate stage between when the question is asked and when the answer is delivered, and serves as an important strategy for developing accountable talk (Resnick, 1995). After asking the question, the teacher invites the students to think about the possible answers. When a short amount of time has elapsed (30 seconds or so), the teacher then instructs students to turn to a partner and discuss their answers. After allowing a few moments for discussion, the teacher then invites students to offer answers. Invariably, more hands go up because they have had some time to consider their answer, listen to someone else, and refine their response. In addition, the answers are likely to be rich and detailed because of this intermediate step. Figure 1.1 shows a classroom poster for think-pair-share.

THE BENEFITS FOR ENGLISH LANGUAGE LEARNERS

Adolescents who are English language learners face two challenges: learning the content while simultaneously learning a new language. We know that language and learning are inexorably bound; thus, their ability to understand and produce the academic language needed is essential if they are to learn the content standards of the course. It is this production of academic language, both verbal and written, that English language learners need to engage in throughout the lesson. Peer learning arrangements that require language learners to discuss content are of benefit because they allow them to listen to, ask questions about, and furnish explanations of concepts being learned (Fu, 2004; Vandergrift, Goh, Mareschal, & Tafaghodtar, 2006). The integration of peer learning practices in content area classrooms has been shown to be an effective tool for increasing learning and achievement among English language learners (Echevarria, Vogt, & Short, 2004).

Flexible grouping arrangements mean that the teacher must have a repertoire of instructional strategies to ensure that students have many opportunities to work with one another. These strategies include think-pair-share (Lyman, 1981), learning stations (Diller, 2003), jigsaw (Aronson, 1978), and reciprocal teaching (Palincsar & Brown, 1986).

Learning Stations

An optimal time for students to work collaboratively is during *learning stations*. Students work in small heterogeneous groups (three to four students) on tasks designed to consolidate concepts and skills previously taught. These stations are usually related to one another in content and are designed to create a cohesive learning experience. For example, Soto (2005) described the use of stations to introduce concepts about the Human Genome Project to students. A learning station arrangement is ideal for WebQuests, which are Internet-based inquiry projects, because small groups of students can work collaboratively on a single computer. Stations offer another advantage as well. They allow the teacher to provide direct instruction to small, homogeneous groups of students who have been chosen according to similar instructional needs while other students are working at stations. Students move in and out of learning stations using the Center-Activity Rotation System (CARS) (Lapp, Flood, & Goss, 2000).

The success of these learning stations is dependent on each student's ability to work with others. As you can see from the graphic in Figure 1.2, the majority of students are engaged in heterogeneous small-group learning stations while the teacher meets with specifically selected groups of students for teacher-directed instruction. These lessons can last between 15 and 30 minutes, depending on the levels of the students, so the teacher can meet with several groups during the class period.

Figure 1.1 Think-pair-share.

Think about the question:
What do you know?
What experiences have you had?
What connections can you make?

?!?!   **Pair** with your partner:
Listen to ideas.
Share your ideas.
Create new ideas together.

Share your ideas with others:
Listen to ideas.
Share your ideas.
Share your partner's ideas.
Create new ideas together.

Jigsaw

Whole-class instruction for informational reading often involves a single text, as when the teacher reads an article during a shared reading. However, there are occasions when students need to analyze multiple texts at the same time. When a group of readers is presented with information from several texts, the readers are more likely to make connections between those readings, a phenomenon referred to as intertextuality (Bloome & Egan-Robertson, 1993). However, it can be difficult to organize multiple readings for use in a discussion. One instructional arrangement for doing so is a *jigsaw* (Aronson, 1978).

The readings used in a jigsaw may be chosen because they each offer similar perspectives of the same concept or event (*complementary*), or because they present very different views (*conflicting*) (Hartman & Allison, 1996). A third arrangement divides a concept or idea into smaller elements so that the topic is fully understood only after all the readings have been discussed (Aronson, 1978). Examples of these types of text sets appear in Figure 1.3.

The jigsaw is accomplished through two types of groups—the home group and the expert group. First, members of a home group divide the task of reading multiple texts among themselves. Each reader is responsible for identifying the important elements of the text to report to the home group. Students then meet in an expert group of students reading the same text to discuss the reading and take notes for use in the home group. Finally, students reconvene in their home group

Figure 1.2   Center-activity rotation system.

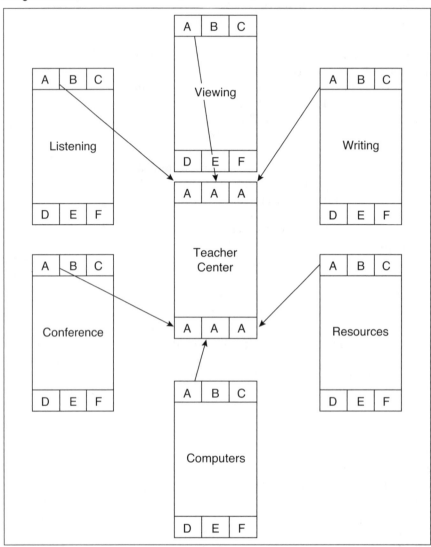

Source: Adapted from "Desks Don't Move—Students Do: In Effective Classroom Environments," by D. Lapp, J. Flood, and K. Goss, 2000, *The Reading Teacher, 54,* pp. 31–36. Used with permission.

to learn and share information from each of the readings. A procedural map for jigsaw is illustrated in Figure 1.4.

Reciprocal Teaching

Teachers wishing to move instruction from delivery to discovery are wise to consider reciprocal teaching in their repertoire. Reciprocal teaching is used in student-directed groups of four to jointly understand a common piece of text (Palincsar & Brown, 1986). The text is segmented into smaller chunks, allowing students to check their understanding periodically throughout the reading. This

Figure 1.3   Text sets for jigsaw.

TYPE	PURPOSE
Complementary	Texts focus on single concept
Example: Who was Vincent van Gogh and why did he have a significant impact on the art world?	A & E Biography. (1997). *Vincent van Gogh: A stroke of genius* [VHS]. Greenberg, J., & Gordon, S. (2003). *Vincent van Gogh: Portrait of an artist.* New York: Yearling. Metropolitan Museum of Art. (2005). *Vincent's colors.* New York: Chronicle. *Vincent van Gogh Museum,* http://www3.vangoghmuseum.nl/vgm/index.jsp
Conflicting	Texts focus on divergent perspectives of a concept
Example: What were the benefits and costs to exploration of the New World?	Maestro, B. (1997). *Exploration and conquest: The Americas after Columbus: 1500–1620.* New York: HarperTrophy. Prescott, J. (1996). *100 explorers who shaped world history.* San Mateo, CA: Bluewood. *Visions of the Caribbean: Exploration and Colonization,* http://www.historical-museum.org/exhibits/visions/ec.htm Yolen, J. (1996). *Encounter.* New York: Viking.
Divided	Concept is divided among texts
Example: Why are the planets in our solar system so different from one another?	Cooper, H., & Henbest, N. (1997). *Big bang: The story of the universe.* New York: Dorling Kindersley. Redfern, M. (1999). *The Kingfisher young people's book of planet Earth.* New York: Kingfisher. Ride, S., & O'Shaughnessy, T. (2003). *Exploring our solar system.* New York: Crown. *The Online Planetarium Show,* http://library.thinkquest.org/3461/

is accomplished using a structured discussion format and is performed several times until the piece is complete. The teacher may create the stopping points for discussion in advance, or the group may decide how best to break up the text. At each stopping point, students use four kinds of comprehension strategies to understand the text:

- *Questioning* the text by asking literal and inferential questions of one another
- *Clarifying* understanding through discussion of how a confusing point might be cleared up (for example, using a dictionary, checking the glossary, asking the teacher)
- *Summarizing* the main ideas of the passage
- *Predicting* what the author will discuss next, based on prior knowledge

The strength of this approach is in the consolidation of sound comprehension practices used during the reading process. These four steps do not need to be performed in a fixed order, but can be discussed in the order the group decides.

Research on Reciprocal Teaching. The use of this instructional strategy is widespread in schools; thus a considerable number of studies have been conducted on the effects. As a student-centered process, this strategy has been

Figure 1.4   Jigsaw.

Phase One: Home Groups

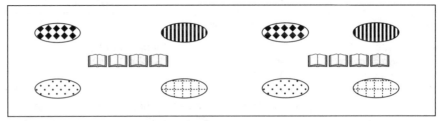

Students meet in home groups to divide the readings among themselves.

Phase Two: Expert Groups

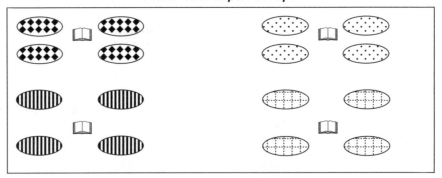

Students meet in expert groups to discuss one of the readings.

Phase Three: Home Groups

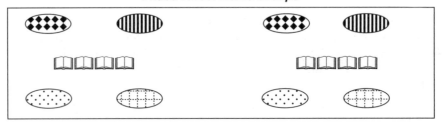

Students reconvene in home groups to discuss all of the readings.

found to be motivating to students considered to be at risk (e.g., Carter, 1997; Palincsar & Herrenkohl, 2002). Rosenshine and Meister (1994) reviewed 16 separate studies on reciprocal teaching and found the strategy to be effective in a wide range of classroom settings. In particular, they noted that reciprocal teaching was found to positively impact standardized testing results on reading comprehension (Alfassi, 1998).

Introducing Reciprocal Teaching. As with the other peer strategies, the techniques used in reciprocal teaching must first be taught so that students are comfortable using them in collaborative groups. Each role is modeled until all have been introduced. We advise practicing each role separately until students are ready to use all the strategies together in a group meeting. This means that there is a series of lessons where everyone in the group uses prediction, followed by a series on summarizing, and so forth.

Role Sheets. Many teachers use role sheets in the beginning of the year to support student dialogue within the group. Because the text is not read in advance, but rather is chunked, read, and discussed in the same sitting, these question stems can be useful when group members are at a loss for what to say next. These role sheets are shown in Figure 1.5.

Ultimately, students become proficient at reciprocal teaching by doing it. An example from a high school English class illustrates the level of comfort students can reach after several opportunities to engage in this strategy.

Reciprocal Teaching in the English Classroom

Groups of four students band together across Lisa Douglas's American literature classroom. Each student in the group has a role to play. Brightly colored cards of different hues sit on desks, each indicating a distinct role for its student owner. Today, Audrey will be the predictor, José the questioner, Beth the clarifier, and Ben the summarizer. Students' roles change regularly, either daily or with the introduction of a new text. Before Ms. Douglas has finished moving through the room, Audrey starts her group.

"Do you guys remember where we were?"

"Look at the wall, Audrey. We've already summarized three parts." Beth refers the group leader to the wall behind her where the class has posted summaries from yesterday.

"Yeah. Okay. So we are here on page 6. Right? So, Ben, could you please read for us?"

Ben reads a passage from *"The Yellow Wallpaper" and Other Stories* by Charlotte Perkins Gilman (1997). The short story tells of a woman in the late 1800s who has a mental illness and becomes more obsessed each day with her bedroom wallpaper.

As Ben concludes his passage, Audrey quickly inserts her opening remark. "Boy, I feel so sorry for that woman. No one seems to be able to help her. I predict that she is going to get worse and worse. They may even have to move her away somewhere to a hospital or mental person's home."

"No. I think she is going to get better. All she has to do is get rid of that ugly wallpaper."

"You've gotta be kidding, José. No way. I agree with Audrey."

"Me, too. Except maybe she will attack her husband or do some other crazy thing before they take her away." Each of the group members contributes a prediction to the discussion. Audrey moves her group along.

"Okay. I'm the predictor, so I want you to write down my prediction."

"And, that is?" remarks Ben.

"She is going to get worse," Audrey states with authority. She continues, "Let's see, José, you are the questioner. So what question do you have?"

"What's her problem? I mean, is she suffering from depression or what?" José asks.

The discussion continues around different questions posed by the group members. In the end, José determines the question to be used. The group work in

Figure 1.5 Role sheet for reciprocal teaching.

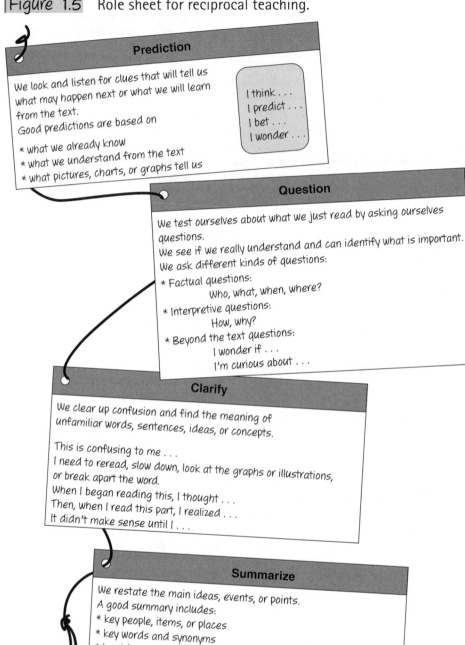

Prediction

We look and listen for clues that will tell us what may happen next or what we will learn from the text.
Good predictions are based on

* what we already know
* what we understand from the text
* what pictures, charts, or graphs tell us

I think . . .
I predict . . .
I bet . . .
I wonder . . .

Question

We test ourselves about what we just read by asking ourselves questions.
We see if we really understand and can identify what is important.
We ask different kinds of questions:

* Factual questions:
        Who, what, when, where?
* Interpretive questions:
        How, why?
* Beyond the text questions:
        I wonder if . . .
        I'm curious about . . .

Clarify

We clear up confusion and find the meaning of unfamiliar words, sentences, ideas, or concepts.

This is confusing to me . . .
I need to reread, slow down, look at the graphs or illustrations, or break apart the word.
When I began reading this, I thought . . .
Then, when I read this part, I realized . . .
It didn't make sense until I . . .

Summarize

We restate the main ideas, events, or points.
A good summary includes:
* key people, items, or places
* key words and synonyms
* key ideas and concepts

The main point is . . .
If I put the ideas together, I now understand that . . .
The most important thing I read was . . .

Ms. Douglas's room continues through the next step of reciprocal teaching, clarification, in much the same way as predicting and questioning steps were accomplished. However, when Ms. Douglas's students reach the summarizing stage, each is asked to write a summary sentence that is shortened several times when the students pass their statements around the group. Then, the shortened versions are discussed and compared; a final product is produced using the best from all the versions. This is especially useful because students are often required to write summaries for standardized tests. After this final summary is written down, students rotate their role-indicator card. Each group member has a new role to play in the reciprocal teaching process, a new passage of text is read, and the cycle continues.

Struggling Readers

REQUIRE LITERACY INSTRUCTION ACROSS CONTENT AREAS

Students who read and write below grade level are not confined to low-performing schools, and comprise a significant portion of the secondary school population nationwide. The National Educational Assessment of Progress (NAEP), commonly called "the nation's report card," tracks achievement among a representative sampling of students from across the United States. The 2008 test results were analyzed for long-term changes dating back to 1971. Reading scores of 9-year-olds in 2008 were the highest thus far, and 13-year-olds had no growth between 1999 and 2008, but were still higher than those reported in 1971. However, there has been no measurable change in the reading scores of 17-year-olds in over 30 years (Perie & Moran, 2005). Clearly, if secondary students who struggle to read are to make any gains, then secondary educators must look beyond the English classroom as the place where they will "catch up."

Ms. Douglas uses assigned roles when her students are learning about the reciprocal teaching process. As they become more proficient, the student roles will expand to facilitate the assigned component rather than serve as the sole individual responsible. For example, the student assigned to questioning will not have to contribute all the questions, but will facilitate a discussion in which questions are generated.

Teaching That Is Transportable and Transparent

The strategies outlined in this book are designed to fit easily into the school day. Although we identify them as "literacy strategies," most could really be called "content area instructional approaches." The strategies in this book have a research base and a practical foundation for ensuring that students understand the content that they are being taught. Students need guidance through informational texts, not simply an assignment to "read pages 118 to 132 for homework tonight." We like to think of these literacy strategies as being transportable across content areas. What we mean is that each is flexible enough to be applied to a variety of learning situations. For example, a strategy is transportable for a student when she uses vocabulary skills learned during a history lesson on the Antebellum South to understand antecedents in her psychology class.

Another important goal of a schoolwide approach to instruction is that, over time, these strategies become transparent to learners. As teachers, we are thrilled when we hear students murmur in recognition when we speak of graphic organizers or anticipation guides. It tells us that our colleagues have done a great job in creating a common vocabulary across the grade levels. It also means that when we collectively teach these strategies, we end up spending less time mired in the mechanics of getting the lesson under way. Setting up a graphic organizer becomes an instructional routine that takes seconds, rather than half the morning. In other words, it allows us to use an instructional shorthand that gives us more time to actually teach the content. Ultimately, we hope that these strategies are transparent in our students' learning lives as they become aware of how they learn.

We concur with this approach and see the evidence in our own school experiences. We believe that it takes time and collegial conversations to develop a shared vocabulary of teaching and learning, and these conversations spring from a habit of reflective teaching. In other words, it is not a program, a set of books, or a box of materials that creates a high-achieving school. It is always teachers who matter, and what they do that matters most. And a teacher's ability to teach reflectively ensures continued professional growth.

Reflective Teaching

When we use the term "reflective teaching," we are speaking of the habits of mind of effective educators who practice a recursive cycle of self-questioning and self-assessment to improve teaching and learning. Reflective teachers take the time to stand back from the fray and ask:

- How effective was I today?
- What can I learn about my teaching by looking at today's lesson?
- How can I improve my teaching?

Teaching is both an art and a science, and each of these perspectives requires that we take a step back from what we have been doing to analyze the efficacy of our practice. At best, teaching is inexact because the context keeps changing—student needs never remain static and always demand shifts in how we create meaningful learning opportunities for them. Therefore, it's impossible to replicate the same lesson exactly. You need only look to your own variation in teaching the same lesson content in two class periods. We often hear teachers remark that they taught a small-group lesson more effectively for the second group. This is reflective teaching in action, because these teachers are self-questioning and self-assessing. This applies across lessons and entire years as well, and we believe that a strong repertoire of strategies for your instructional tool kit can help you arrive at solutions to these reflective questions.

A Professional Invitation

The point is simple, but often overlooked in the busy world of a teacher: To enjoy and flourish in your job, you can never stop learning.

It is ironic that those of us in the business of learning, caught up in the delivery of information and the orchestration of the classroom, have little time left to engage in our own learning. After all, the teacher is the oldest in the room and, by tradition's unspoken and timeless decree, the one who is supposed to know what he or she is doing.

The remainder of this book focuses on instructional strategies and planning tools that you will find useful in ensuring that your students can read for information. Note that specific instructional strategies are highlighted in different grade levels and in different content areas. That does not mean that the strategy would fail to work in another content area or grade level. For example, word sorts are highlighted in a biology class while studying molecules of life. Of course, word sorts can be used to teach vocabulary in other grades and with other content areas.

This holds true for all of the major strategy chapters—the specific examples in this book are not tied to a specific content area or grade level.

We provide examples across the content areas and grade levels for the following strategies:

- Anticipatory activities (chapter 2)
- Vocabulary instruction (chapter 3)
- Read alouds and shared reading (chapter 4)
- Questioning (chapter 5)
- Graphic organizers (chapter 6)
- Notetaking and note making (chapter 7)
- Writing to learn (chapter 8)

In addition to these specific strategies, we provide information on assessing students on their progress as part of chapter 9. In chapter 9, we also address the ways that teachers prepare students for standardized tests. In particular, we will discuss how the literacy practices profiled in this book better prepare students for such tests.

Conclusion

To be successful in middle school, high school, college, and their adult lives, students must learn to read for information. There are a number of informational texts—with their accompanying text structures and features—that should be used in secondary classrooms. Guiding readers through texts in order to understand content is an essential responsibility of every teacher.

We invite you then to consider the flexibility and applicability of these research-based literacy strategies in a variety of content areas. Peer learning strategies such as think-pair-share, jigsaw, learning stations, and reciprocal teaching are viable in an algebra class, or a 2–D art course. The purpose of these is to give students the opportunity to use academic language in purposeful ways. However, if we are to expect our students to learn collaboratively, then we must do so as well. The schoolwide conversations that encourage colleagues to think together produce innovative practices that are unlikely to be developed within a single department.

Chapter 2

Setting the Stage: Building Background Through Anticipatory Activities

Ten images of war are displayed around the 10th-grade world history classroom. As teacher Stephanie Jordan speaks, she moves to one of the memorable photographs of Robert Capa, one of the 20th century's most notable combat photojournalists. "Imagine how war was viewed before his work appeared. It wasn't common to see violent images because there weren't many places to show them," she explained. "But imagine what it was like to get your copy of Life *magazine and see this," gesturing to Capa's* Falling Soldier. *The photograph of a Spanish Civil War soldier at the moment he was struck by a bullet is chilling, even 70 years later. "It would get people talking," remarked one student. "Exactly," replied Ms. Jordan. "Images of the Spanish Civil War brought the conflict to the doorsteps of Americans, and got them to pay attention to this conflict. In this unit of study, we're going to see how media played a role in setting the stage for American involvement in international conflicts."*

One of the most influential contributions to 20th-century educational theory was the development of the field of cognitive science. Before the advent of cognitive studies, the prevailing learning theory was behaviorism, which concentrated on the role of outside stimulus as a mechanism for learning. The publication of *A Study of Thinking* (Bruner, Goodnow, & Austin, 1956) led the way for exploration of what happens inside the minds of learners and how they organize and use information. Over the course of the next 50 years scientists, psychologists, and educators have examined memory, emotion, schema, and experience as essential components of learning. In fact, the influence of cognitive science is so profound that it now may be difficult to conceptualize how the process of learning was perceived in the first half of the century. This book, for instance, is replete with learning approaches that reflect our profession's roots in cognitive science—scaffolding, metacognition, accessing background knowledge, and transferring of learning—to name a few.

Types of Anticipatory Activities

One aspect of learning theory that has received a great deal of attention is (please pardon us now) "attention." Anyone who has ever faced the task of teaching a group of people can appreciate the importance of attention as a factor in learning. After all, if students aren't paying attention, how can they process new information?

When we speak of attention we are not referring to behavior management, but rather to practices that elicit curiosity, provoke questions, and evoke recall of newly learned information. In addition, attention also means activating students' background knowledge about the topic. This is really the very beginning of the learning process, although it is not bound in time to the beginning of a course, class, or lesson. Therefore, anticipatory activities should be tied to the introduction of new concepts, and not simply to the first 5 minutes of a class period. Good and Brophy (2002) remind us that effective teachers create memorable events throughout their lessons to capture student attention, not unlike the teacher in the opening vignette for this chapter. However, it is essential to note that gaining attention through anticipatory activities is not intended to provide entertainment for students, but to scaffold learning so that the cognitive responsibility for learning shifts to the student. A primary goal of classroom instruction is to move from teacher-directed instruction to student-centered learning. Anticipatory activities can ground new learning in meaning-based inquiry because the student's attention has been gained through an event connected to the purpose for studying the topic.

These memorable events may also use drama, humor, movement, or emotion to make an impression on learning.

Eggen and Kauchak (2001) suggest four instructional routines for gaining student attention:

1. demonstrations,
2. discrepant events,
3. visual displays, and
4. thought-provoking questions (p. 271).

We will discuss each of these in detail and then take a look inside classrooms to see how teachers across the content areas are using these anticipatory activities to stimulate curiosity,

Struggling Readers

HAVE RICH BACKGROUND EXPERIENCES

As Broaddus and Ivey (2002) noted, knowing students as readers, maintaining a wide range of reading material on topics under investigation, and allotting time for reading in every class can support readers regardless of motivation, interest, or ability. An important way of knowing students and connecting them with reading material is to activate and build background knowledge. Quick writes, for example, allow the teacher insight into students' thinking. Classroom discussions using K-W-L or other language charts provide information about students' background and prior knowledge such that the teacher can find reading material that students can and want to read. Visual displays also help struggling readers develop their understanding of the content as they discuss this type of information with their teacher and with one another.

build background knowledge, and promote learning. But first, let's consider the use of anticipatory activities for English language learners.

Demonstrations

Classroom demonstrations are typically performed to display a theory, concept, or phenomenon. A demonstration of gravity is likely to involve dropping objects from a height; a demonstration of fractions and decimals might include several apples sliced into equal parts. The use of demonstrations is critical in the field of mathematics (Lee, 2000) and is associated with higher levels of learning in science (Beasley, 1982). Don't overlook the availability of technology to enhance demonstrations of complex phenomena (Brooks & Brooks, 1996). We particularly like Web sites that portray scientific concepts. For instance, students can watch how an earthquake occurs, see the phases of the moon change, or dissect a virtual frog. One of our favorites is VisualThesaurus.com, which displays a semantic web of related terms organized by meaning and usage. The use of demonstrations to illustrate and augment lecture and readings is particularly effective for students with disabilities (Janney & Snell, 2000) and English language learners because it is enhanced by physical and kinesthetic involvement.

Demonstrations should be used judiciously in order to prevent confusion. In particular, a demonstration is likely to fail if it is not grounded in the theoretical framework. In other words, an interesting demonstration does not replace the need for deep exploration of concepts. Also, don't overlook the importance of telling students that the demonstration is important to remember, and why. These simple statements of emphasis have been shown to be effective when coupled with demonstrations (Eggen & Kauchak, 2001; Larsen, 1991).

Discrepant Events

Discrepant events are those demonstrations that involve a surprising or startling occurrence designed to command the students' attention. A performance may be staged—for instance, another teacher may be recruited to rush into the classroom to hand the social studies teacher a copy of a newspaper dated December 7, 1941. Hurst (2001) suggests that attention-grabbing events are a key element to content area lesson planning, along with mini-lessons and comprehension instruction. She and others (e.g., Anderson & Pearson, 1984; Smith, 1998) remind us that attention is directly related to schema, the knowledge structure used to comprehend. Events such as these can assist students in organizing new information, integrating it with prior knowledge, and increasing their ability to retrieve it later (Landauer, 1975).

THE BENEFITS FOR ENGLISH LANGUAGE LEARNERS

The use of anticipatory activities is especially helpful for English language learners as they activate background knowledge. Background knowledge is related to the unique experiences that each student has, such as living in places where it snows, the look of a wheat field, or what it feels like to surf. It is also the formal learning that students are expected to have. Anticipatory activities help activate this knowledge for students by providing them ways to connect their experience and new information. As Rothenberg and Fisher (2007) note, building background knowledge is critical if English language learners are to be successful in academic classes.

Discrepant events also access a powerful aid to memory—emotional connection. As humans, we have a tendency to remember episodes connected to our emotional memories, such as a favorite birthday party or a first kiss. The associations may be negative as well—most readers will recall where they were when they found out about the terrorist attack on America in 2001. Whereas discrepant events in the classroom are unlikely to be connected to such intense emotions as these, it is important to recognize that they tap into the same neural pathways (Metzloff, Kuhl, Movellan, & Sejnowski, 2009). Integrating music, art, and dramatic play can provide a means for accessing students' emotional memory and increase their ability to retrieve the information at a later time (Sprenger, 1999). Jorgensen (1998) calls these events "grabbers" because they command student attention and capture the imagination.

Visual Displays

Because visual displays such as graphic organizers are more thoroughly presented in chapter 6, we will confine our discussion to what Hyerle refers to as "visual tools for constructing knowledge" (1996, p. 1). The rise of information technology in the last quarter of the 20th century has fundamentally changed the way information is generated and shared. These same technologies—computers, CD-ROMs, Web-based resources, iPods, and digital cameras, to name a few—are becoming an increasingly common means for classrooms to access information. Unlike earlier classroom technologies such as televisions and video recorders, these newer advances are interactive and require the active participation of the learner. No longer is visually presented information viewed as a passive experience to be absorbed by the learner. Rather, it is seen as a generative processs in which the learner influences and changes the information. This is at the heart of visual literacy—it is the ability of one to interpret, analyze, and create visual displays of information that are accurate and complete. Students need exposure to, and experiences with, visual displays of information in order to develop these abilities.

Interactive whiteboards are a part of many secondary classrooms, as they allow teachers to display and manipulate visual information in innovative ways. Of course, what makes the board "smart" is the user (Somyürek, Atasoy, & Ozdemir, 2009). It is important to remember that interactive whiteboards are a tool, not an end unto itself. When using presentation tools such as interactive whiteboards and document cameras, keep the *function* in mind. These functions, whether print-based or digital, include interpreting, analyzing, locating, producing, and sharing information (Frey, Fisher, & Gonzalez, 2010).

WebQuests are one way to gain attention and support long-term learning. A WebQuest is "an inquiry-oriented activity in which most or all of the information used by learners is drawn from the Web" (http://edweb.sdsu.edu/news/webeye) and is used to guide students in an investigation of a topic. The teacher plans the WebQuest in advance, and students are typically given a series of questions to guide their search. Specific Web sites may be identified and bookmarked by the teacher to provide some frame for the learners to follow, much like lily pads strung across a pond. The good news is that you don't have to create your own WebQuest (although you may choose to do so later). Topics as varied as polar ice caps, eating disorders, and paper airplane design are only a click away.

In addition to electronic sources, many print-based visual displays are readily available for classroom use. For example, many textbooks feature four-color images of places, people, and objects. Select some of these powerful images to display on an overhead projector and invite students to discuss their impressions. Photographs from picture books and photoessays can help students understand information to be learned in the unit of instruction. *Through the Lens: National Geographic Greatest Photographs* (Val, 2003) offers arresting images from the last 100 years. Teachers of American history can find an archive of little-known images in *African American Vernacular Photography* (International Center of Photography, 2003). English teachers might use *Stranger in the Woods* to teach foreshadowing (Sams & Stoick, 2000). Science instructors can use visual images from the illustrated edition of *On the Origin of Species* (Darwin & Quammen, 2008) or *The Hubble Space Telescope: Imagining the Universe* (DeVorkin & Smith, 2004).

Source: Unidentified photographer, [11th Patriarchie Regiment Band, GUOOF], ca. 1990 © ICP/Steidl.

Thought-Provoking Questions

Thought-provoking questions are intended to assist students in organizing new information. Like discrepant events, they are meant to appeal to the emotional channels of learning. The use of a provocative question, particularly one that defies a simple answer, has been recognized as a method for promoting interest and sustaining learning by inviting students to formulate an understanding of the material (Brandt, 1992; Muncey, Payne, & White, 1999). These questions may be of a general investigatory nature, as in the K-W-L technique (Ogle, 1986). K-W-L stands for "What do I **know**? What do I **want** to know? What have I **learned**?" This organizer mirrors the process of scientific inquiry inherent in any investigation. Typically, a teacher will arrange these questions into three columns and then prompt discussion about the new topic of study. Student responses are recorded and then become the guide for subsequent study. This technique has been modified in a number of ways, including K-W-L-Plus (Carr & Ogle, 1987) which adds summarization and K-W-L-H (Wills, 1995) that adds "**How** do I know?" to focus on sources of evidence. The recursive nature of inquiry is emphasized through K-W-L-Q (Schmidt, 1999) when a fourth column for further questions is added at the end of the unit of study.

Other thought-provoking questions might be more specific to the unit and are likely to encourage an interdisciplinary study. A question like "What is a hero?" is far more interesting than a unit titled "Heroes of the 20th Century" and is likely to promote greater student interest. Jorgensen (1998) refers to these as "essential questions" because they are so difficult to answer succinctly. An example of an essential question discussed by Jorgensen is "Can you truly be free if you're not treated equally?"—an invitation to examine the U.S. civil rights movement of the 1950s and 1960s. Other essential questions used by educators include:

- What is the human need to celebrate?
- Is there an art to science? Is there a science to art?
- Mark Twain said, "History is lies agreed upon." Was he right?
- Does an apple a day keep the doctor away?
- Probability and Pop Culture: Are you more likely to hit the lottery or get hit by lightning?

When curriculum units are organized around thought-provoking questions, it provides the teacher with a means for establishing relevance. Learning is enhanced when the relevance of the material is made clear. In fact, information that is not attached to any larger meaning is likely to be quickly forgotten (Donovan &

Bransford, 2005). And remember that relevance is in the mind of the learner, not just the teacher. We know from our own teaching experience that we believe everything we teach is relevant, otherwise we wouldn't bother to talk about it. However, we can also appreciate the importance of relevance from our students' viewpoint. Therefore, it is up to us as instructors to make the relevance explicit. When a curriculum unit is organized around an essential question, and that question is then connected to the assessments and culminating projects of the unit, students can begin to make meaning of the information. After all, when students understand that the information they are reading and writing about will ultimately be used to answer the question, they can then appreciate the value of their inquiry.

We've discussed the importance of gaining and sustaining student attention to promote and extend learning. Now let's take a look at how teachers are using anticipatory activities in their content area classrooms.

Strategies at Work

Anticipatory Activities in English

Visual Displays Through Virtual Interviews. Justin Phillips sometimes teaches by talking to the past. In his ninth-grade English classes he uses creative means to build ideas, information, and historical context that may be absent from his students' frame of reference. Instead of assuming his students have the required background information for a unit of study, he assesses what they know about the main ideas of the unit and fills in the missing links. Making these links interesting, informative, and memorable is one of the tools in Mr. Phillips's teaching repertoire. He combines a home video camera with simple costumes and props to create a "virtual interview" with historical and contemporary figures, thereby introducing them to his class. This technique serves as an inventive visual display of information to assist his students in fleshing out the details of both historical and fictional characters.

To introduce a group project on biographies, Mr. Phillips assumed the identity of Lech Walesa, founder of the Polish Solidarity Movement and 1983 Nobel Peace Prize winner. He scripted a mock interview and then filmed himself in costume. Later, he told his students that they would be seeing Walesa courtesy of a satellite broadcast. Mr. Phillips asked "Walesa" a series of questions timed to coordinate with the tape. He later remarked, "I decided that staging a mock interview would surely get their attention, especially if they realized I was the man behind the fake facial hair. It proved to be a success, and I still find myself introducing characters that access students' prior knowledge or build new knowledge on what they already know. I believe I engage students by tweaking the usual. I purposefully complicate what students may expect."

Mr. Phillips has some advice on how to create a successful virtual interview. In addition to the video equipment and costumes, a willingness to engage in a bit of acting is also necessary. The taping, of course, must happen before the class period begins. Prior to the taping, the teacher must select a character and write out a dialogue no longer than a couple of minutes. The conversation should be natural, original, and based on texts. Mr. Phillips uses this opportunity to "drill the character" on some difficult questions. He is always sure to include questions students might ask.

The timing and logistics of the interview are important in establishing its believability. When you film the "interviewee," be sure to leave enough time for asking the interviewer questions live. Shake your head in approval of the "question" being asked and send nonverbal signals, including a few "hmms and ums." Don't worry if you veer from the exact words you composed while writing the dialogue. Mr. Phillips has found that the interview is more natural when you get the gist of the response and not focus on the exact words. Remember only the "interviewer" questions are time sensitive, not your taped responses. Once you have signed off, keep the dialogue and practice by reviewing the tape for the in-class performance.

Once you are in class and the students have been prepared, it's show time! Inform the students that the focus character has taken time to join the class live via satellite. Students tend to believe the setup is true, if only for a few seconds, and then go along with you. After the satellite interview and while enthusiasm is still high, be sure to transition to a focus on the text. Copy the video and put it on the school server to allow students to replay the video.

Thought-Provoking Questions Through Quick Writes. We refer to brief timed writing activities intended to activate background knowledge and personal experience as *quick writes*. Students seem to like the term because it connotes an event that is limited in duration, and teachers appear to honor the spirit of this anticipatory activity by indeed keeping it brief. We like the key contrasts that Daniels and Bizar (1998) offer between this type of writing event and other process pieces:

- *Spontaneous* vs. planned,
- *Short* vs. lengthy,
- *Exploratory* vs. authoritative,
- *Expressive* vs. transactional,
- *Informal* vs. formal,
- *Personal* vs. audience centered,
- *Unedited* vs. polished, and
- *Ungraded* vs. graded (p. 114).

Quick writes are frequently used in English classrooms at the introduction of a new reading to tap into background knowledge through reader-related experiences, as well as to initiate a reading–writing connection. The choice of text is crucial, too. Reading multicultural literature can build confidence in fledgling second language readers and writers. When students relate to good literature on a personal level, they discover a purpose for reading and response, and begin to find their writer's voice. Before reading *The Circuit: Stories From the Life of a Migrant Child* by Francisco Jiménez (1997), the students in Rita Elwardi's English as a second language (ESL) class participated in a number of anticipatory activities focused on thought-provoking questions related to a quick write designed to accomplish these objectives.

In order to establish a personal connection with the character and the central conflict in the story, students were asked to write about a moment they remembered well; a moment when they had to say good-bye. Because English language learners need structured support in writing, Ms. Elwardi created a list of guiding questions to help even the most reluctant writers begin to recount such an experience. She reminded her students that these questions are there to provoke thought and should not all be answered. To introduce this activity, she recounted an unforgettable moment when she also had to leave a place and a group of friends. Using the questions as her guide, she modeled how these questions could structure a response. Her questions included:

- Where and when did this take place?
- Who was with you and why?
- Why did you have to leave this place or say good-bye to this person?
- What did you say, and what did the others say to you?
- What did you do during this time?
- What were you thinking before, during, and after this moment?
- How did you feel during and after you had to say good-bye?
- How do you feel now that you are looking back at the moment?

While the class began the 10-minute quick write, Ms. Elwardi walked about the room and spoke to students not yet putting pencil to paper. After asking these students a number of questions from the list and making notes, she had gathered enough information to ask them to now write what they had just said to her, and to continue writing down their thoughts, one after another, from that point on. Circling the room again, Ms. Elwardi scanned the responses of students who had stopped writing and asked them a clarifying question that could lead to more writing. Below is an example of one student's response (we've included irregularities in grammar):

> On November 15, 1996, it was winter and too cold. At that time I was so sad because I was coming to America. I think I couldn't see anymore my country, my cousins and relatives, my country's church, also my mother. One word was hard to say, for my mother. It was Good-bye. Because I never left my mother for a long time or few days before I came to United States. My feeling was bad like a sad for two weeks before I came to U.S.A. I was counting each day and I thought how do I say good-bye for my mother, cousins, relatives and my country? I was looking all around and I was crying. At last the day, November 15, 1996 came. But at that time I was not sad and I was well. I thought, "Now I can to say good-bye for my mother," and I told to myself. Each minute and hour were decreasing. I was ready and I went to my mother and I hugged. I was looking at the ground and I couldn't say good-bye. Both of us were crying. I remember that time. I never forget I couldn't say good-bye.

With quick writes completed, the class then participated in a collaborative oral language building activity called the Three Step Interview (Kagan, 1992) that encourages students to become active, responsible listeners. In this activity, students are placed in groups of four (Students A, B, C, D), and partner up within their group (A with B, C with D), so that there are two partners in each group. We've included a chart of this activity in Figure 2.1. Using their quick writes as material, each group of four followed these three steps:

Step 1:   Student A recounts her or his "good-bye memory" to student B, while student C recounts the same to student D (2 minutes).

Step 2:   Partners switch roles, and B recounts his or her "good-bye memory" to A, while D does the same with partner C (2 minutes).

Step 3:   The four members of the group come together in a circle. Now student A must retell his or her partner's memorable moment to

Figure 2.1   Three-step interview chart.

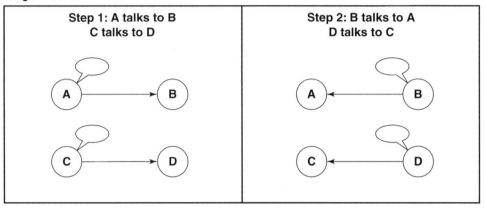

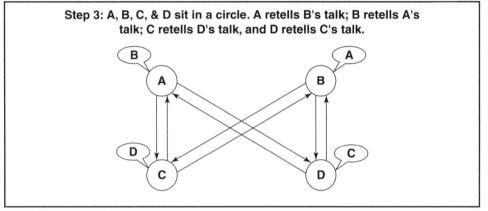

students C and D. Student B then does the same for student A. Then student C retells partner D's memorable moment, and D follows suit (5 to 6 minutes).

The final anticipatory activity to lead into the reading of *The Circuit* came the following day. Ms. Elwardi displayed her own quick write from the previous day on a doc camera as a way to demonstrate a writing activity called "found poems" (Dunning & Stafford, 1992). Students used words and phrases found in their quick write to compose a poem. She modeled these steps to the class:

Step 1:   Read your quick write aloud from beginning to end.

Step 2:   As you reread the quick write, begin to underline important words and phrases that convey sensory details and express the tone of your writing. (The use of the doc camera helps students see exactly what they will be asked to do.)

Step 3:   Now read only the words and phrases of your found poem—a poem you found within your original writing.

Step 4:   Finally, rewrite your poem using an open verse structure.

The students used their own quick writes as the teacher gave individual assistance to a number of students and encouraged others who were attempting to "find their poems." The example below shows the found poem that came from the previous student quick write. One can see from both the writing and the poem that this student has made a personal connection to a conflict central to the story, even before having read it.

> Winter
> too cold, so sad,
> coming to America.
> one word was hard to say—
> Good-bye.
>
> How do I say it
> to my mother,
> cousins, relatives,
> and my country?
>
> I was counting,
> the last day came.
> I was counting
> each hour, each minute
> decreasing.
>
> Looking at the ground,
> crying,
> I hugged my mother.
>
> I remember that time,
> I couldn't say
> Good-bye.

Ms. Elwardi strung together several anticipatory activities that had their genesis in one quick write. Her purpose extended beyond activating background knowledge to prepare them for the book they would be reading. She explained that the author was a member of a family of migrant farm workers. She recounted his struggles to learn to read and write, and read aloud the picture book *La Mariposa* (Jiménez, 2000), based on one of the chapters in the book they were about to read. "Francisco Jiménez 'found' his poetry in the words he wrote for *The Circuit*," she told them. "Just as you have found your poetry as well." With that, Ms. Elwardi's students opened the first page of their book and began to read.

Anticipatory Activities in Social Studies

Demonstration Through Guest Speakers. Many educators acknowledge the role of experience in learning, especially for adolescents (Dewey, 1938/1963). The transformative nature of experiences can assist learners in connecting knowledge to its application and variation in the larger world. Experiences can also provoke reflection as students begin to understand that knowledge is not fixed and static, but is constantly tested by new experiences (Kolb, 1984). This theory, called experiential learning, has its roots in the work of John Dewey and has been extended by the educational research of the past decade. Internships and community service hours are common examples of experiential learning in high school. However, teachers can also use the tenets of experiential learning in the classroom by introducing students to community members who apply the topics of study to their own work. This can be considered a unique form of demonstration through the experiences of others, while serving as an interesting means of introducing a course of study. When the experiences offered through guest speakers are introduced to the classroom, students can clarify their understanding through the eyes of another.

The use of guest speakers in social studies courses is very popular, perhaps because the study of the past and present often converge in the living examples of members of the communities. Historical study of war has been a particularly rich field for guest speakers. A Vietnam War veteran can speak to the experience of being 18 years old and drafted (Poling, 2000). Students can begin to glimpse the meaning of 6 million dead when they can talk with a Holocaust survivor (Glanz, 1999). Attitudes can change when students meet a citizen of a foreign country (Giannangelo & Bolding, 1998). Guest speakers can also contribute to the understanding of students when they are experts on a topic.

Tom Fehrenbacher's world history class had been studying the role of the arts in both reflecting and driving political events. Their inquiry included *Uncle Tom's Cabin* by Harriet Beecher Stowe (1852/1983) and Pablo Picasso's painting *Guernica*, an indictment of the 1937 Nazi bombing of a small Spanish town. He wanted to include a study of the "Ring" cycle of operas by Richard Wagner and their influence on Adolph Hitler, but knew that this form of music was unfamiliar to his students. He contacted the local opera society and arranged for a guest speaker to share information on this operatic music form. Mr. Fehrenbacher knew that he would need to prepare his students for their visitor, so he established the purpose and introduced technical vocabulary like *aria, leitmotif,* and *soprano,* and then posted them for easy reference so that these would not be unfamiliar when the guest speaker used them. He also created a form for his students to use during the lecture and charted some of their questions for use during the visit (see Figure 2.2).

When the representative from the opera society arrived, he was delighted to find the students primed for his visit. He gave a brief presentation on the origins

|Figure 2.2   Student form for guest speakers.

Name of Speaker: Arthur Reed	**Topic:** The Opera	**Date:** 10/9

Purpose of Visit: To learn about the opera as an art form

Unique Experiences:

Mr. Reed has been director of the opera company since 2008
He went to his first opera when he was 10
His grandma loved opera and was always playing the records
Mr. Reed plays the viola and has performed in non-singing roles in lots of productions
He wishes he could be a bass, because those seem to be the fun parts, like being the villain or an interesting character

Connections:

It's like musical theater because it is a blend of drama and music
The lyrics and the music tell the story
People a long time ago liked operas about love and war, just like today

Questions:	**Answers:**
1. Are operas still being written today?	1. Yes, but they sound different from classical operas. Most interesting new opera? One about Moby Dick
2. What's your favorite opera?	2. Favorite is Cosi Fan Tutti because Mozart is the best

of opera in Italy and explained the differences between operas and musicals. He then played excerpts from a selection of operatic works to give the students an idea of the range of the art form, from the light comedies of Mozart to the dramatic works of Bizet. He also included samples of *Porgy and Bess,* a 20th-century opera by George Gershwin. Students were able to ask questions and clarify their understanding of the general knowledge of opera. Mr. Fehrenbacher later described the visit as a success and attributed the preparation of the class to the success of the discussion. He also offered advice to ensure a successful visit with a guest speaker:

- *Discuss the purpose and audience in advance.* Furnish specifics in writing about the objectives for the visit—guests welcome this level of detail because it helps them prepare. Make sure that you have discussed any technology needs, including visual and audio displays. Discuss the number of students involved, and don't surprise the speaker with a few "extras" on the day of the presentation.

- *Prepare the students as well.* A guest speaker who appears unrelated to the current unit of study may be viewed as a "filler" and not central to their understanding of the course materials. Make sure they are familiar with the work of the guest, and have an adequate command of vocabulary and terminology the speaker is likely to use.

- *On the day of the visit, have the room and students organized for the presentation.* Don't waste time with moving furniture and students while the guest stands by.

- *Be an active participant in the presentation.* This is not the time to grade papers—ask questions and make connections for your students. You are modeling the behavior you expect from your students.

- *Have a backup plan in case the speaker is unable to show.* Emergencies happen and you don't want to be left with lots of down time.

- *Write a note of thanks after the visit.* Your mother would be proud. If the speaker is representing a place of work, copy the letter to his or her supervisor.

Thought-Provoking Questions Through Anticipation Guides. An anticipation guide is a teacher-prepared list of statements that connects to a passage of text. The purpose is to activate prior knowledge, encourage predictions, and stimulate curiosity about a topic (Head & Readence, 1986). These guides are usually constructed for use with texts that are controversial or commonly misunderstood, such as sharks, slavery, or the legal age for drinking alcohol. These guides are useful for promoting class discussion as well, because they can spark debate and foster the inevitable need to consult other sources of information (Fisher, Brozo, Frey & Ivey, 2011). In addition, they provide a visual record of student learning, as it scaffolds their increased understanding of the reading.

Helen Arnold used an anticipation guide in her history class study of the Los Angeles Zoot Suit Riots of 1943. These violent clashes between Mexican American youths and American servicemen brought in from Southern California military bases are now understood to be racially motivated, but at the time of these events, the Mexican American community and "zoot suiters" in particular, were blamed for the riots. Ms. Arnold prepared an anticipation guide like the one in Figure 2.3.

Many of the statements do not appear in the text, but rather are inferred from several places in the reading. Some are "think and search" questions that are intended to give students experience with putting together answers from more than one sentence (Raphael, 1986). Others require both information from the text

|Figure 2.3| Anticipation guide.

Discuss each statement with your group. Mark your opinion and then read the assigned Web site to check your understanding.

BEFORE READING			AFTER READING	
True	False		True	False
		1. When bad times came, Mexicans who had been encouraged to come to Los Angeles were now seen as "job stealers."		
		2. Thousands of Mexicans, some with children born in the United States, were sent back to Mexico.		
		3. Mexicans were the only group to suffer from discrimination and injustice.		
		4. Headlines in newspapers disapproved of the attacks.		
		5. The servicemen who took part in the attack were prosecuted.		
		6. Eleanor Roosevelt blamed discrimination as a root cause of the riots.		
		7. Today, there is more anti-immigrant sentiment in California.		

After reading the assigned text, discuss your answers with your group. Identify whether you believe the statement is true or false in the "After reading" columns.

as well as their personal experiences—so-called in the head questions that often demand more complex answers.

Perhaps the most challenging part of developing an anticipation guide is identifying a provocative text that will motivate your students to discuss, debate, disagree, and confront their own misconceptions. Once that is done, the steps to creating a guide are fairly simple (Head & Readence, 1986):

Step 1:   *Identify the major concepts in the reading.* What are the main ideas in the passage? Keep it to two or three so the guide won't be too long.

Step 2:   *Consider your students' prior knowledge.* What are they most likely to hold misconceptions about?

Step 3:   *Write 5 or 10 statements pertaining to the reading.* Don't make them all factual—be sure to create open-ended statements as well. Look again to your major concepts to make sure you are creating statements that relate to larger concepts rather than isolated facts.

Introduce the anticipation guide and ask students to complete it before the reading. Encourage small-group discussions of the statements, then invite them to read the text passage to confirm or disconfirm their beliefs. Let them know they can change their answers while they read, then follow up the reading with a class discussion of the items and the broader questions generated by the reading. This is an ideal opportunity to connect this activity with a strategy employed by critical readers—the self-assessment of beliefs and assumptions that may be supported or disputed by a reading. After all, it is this cognitive dissonance that challenges all of us to continually refine what we know.

Anticipatory Activities in Mathematics

Advance Organizers in Algebra. Secondary students are often required to read extended passages of text containing complex ideas and concepts. A challenge for content area teachers is that the very reading materials essential to learning the content may be too complex for students to process. One method for scaffolding comprehension of text passages is through the use of an advance organizer (Ausubel, 1960). There are two types of advance organizers—expository advance organizers, meant for use with texts containing new material, and comparative organizers, which link new knowledge with previously learned material (Ausubel, 1978). These are not just summaries of the passage—they are meant to contain more complex information than the reading alone offers so that students can gain a sense of how the information is associated with other concepts and ideas. The use of advance organizers with young adults enhances student recall and understanding of the material (Thompson, 1998).

In their study of specific reading strategies useful in mathematics lessons, Carter and Dean (2006) noted that vocabulary instruction, questioning, and anticipatory activities such as using advance organizers and guides improve students' comprehension of the mathematical text.

In order to prepare his algebra students for an end-of-course test, Aaron Sage chose a shared reading of poems from *Math Talk* (Pappas, 1991). These unique poems are designed to be read by two voices, or groups of voices. After modeling the performance of one, he assigned a poem to each small group. Their task was to perform the poem for the class and explain the mathematical concepts contained in the poem. The purpose of this lesson was to give students a creative means for reviewing the major mathematical concepts featured on the upcoming test. In addition to the poem, their textbooks, and mathematics notebooks, the groups were given a comparative advance organizer on their assigned poem's topic. For example, one group was given a poem on imaginary numbers. Their advance organizer appears in the box below.

This advance organizer made connections between the information contained in the poem and knowledge learned from earlier in the year. It is important to note that the advance organizer contained more complex information than the

---

IMAGINARY NUMBERS

This poem discusses imaginary numbers and uses humor to remind us how odd it is to have numbers that "don't exist." Of course, they do exist because they help us solve equations. An imaginary number is the square root of a negative number. It is called "imaginary" because any number that is squared results in a positive number. It is written as "i" and is defined as $i = \sqrt{-1}$. They are used in physics and engineering.

poem itself contained—a hallmark of the strategy. In this case, the advance organizer was a bridge between the poem, the textbook, and the students' notes. With advance organizers like these, the teacher can consider both the information contained in the text and the prior knowledge and experiences of the students to create a higher order of associative learning than the text alone can offer.

Anticipatory Activities in Science

Demonstrations in Chemistry. Perhaps there is no content area more perfectly suited to classroom demonstrations than science. A jaw-dropping demonstration can provoke wonder and inquiry and establish real purpose to subsequent study of a scientific concept. These memorable occasions can also be considered discrepant events because they use the element of surprise to motivate (Wright & Govindarajan, 1995). They may be considered visual displays as well because they activate memory and retention through motion and light. We suspect that inside every good science teacher there is a young child who was mesmerized by a dazzling display of a mysterious scientific concept. In his autobiography *Uncle Tungsten: Memories of a Chemical Boyhood,* Oliver Sacks (2001) recounts life in a household surrounded by parents and siblings deeply involved in the sciences. In a chapter titled "Stinks and Bangs," he writes of a demonstration he performed as a 10-year-old with his two older brothers:

> Attracted by the sounds and flashes and smells coming from my lab, David and Marcus, now medical students, sometimes joined me in experiments—the nine- and ten-year differences between us hardly mattered at these times. On one occasion, I was experimenting with hydrogen and oxygen, there was a loud explosion, and an almost invisible sheet of flame, which blew off Marcus's eyebrows completely. But Marcus took this in good part, and he and David often suggested other experiments. (p. 77)

Chemistry teacher Robert North uses the "stinks and bangs" of science to motivate and stimulate interest in chemistry. A member of the local American Chemical Society, he recruits eighth graders from middle schools to foster their interest in science. He brings a "day of magic" to each feeder middle school and proceeds to dazzle them with a range of demonstrations of chemical wonders, always connecting to the scientific concepts that explain the phenomena.

Many of these same students sign up for chemistry when they reach 11th grade, enticed by the memory of amazing demonstrations and plenty of stinks and bangs. On the first day of the course, he sets a tone for the "Cardinal Chemists," his nickname for those enrolled in his course. While he introduces the rules of the class, he pours a small amount of isopropyl alcohol (2-proponol) into an empty 5-gallon water cooler container. Without explanation, he lights a match at the mouth of the jug and a loud "boom!" results, along with startled gasps and squeals of his new students. He then instructs them to quickly write about what they have just witnessed. After inviting responses from the students, he prompts a discussion on the difference between an explosion and a burn, terminology many of them have just used interchangeably. Mr. North then gives them a few minutes to revise their writing using accurate vocabulary and reviews the rules again, reminding them that they exist for the safety of all. Finally, he moves in for the final point— "Chemistry is a bomb!"

It is important to note that Mr. North's teaching is not all "stinks and bangs." He pairs writing with the demonstrations to give students an opportunity to clarify their understanding and support their inquiry of what is still unknown to them.

He is also careful to ground his work in the theoretical underpinnings of each demonstration. Indeed, without this careful attention to the scientific concepts, students are likely to form misconceptions about what they have seen (Li & Li, 2008). But the powerful responses to anticipatory activities like this one are always part of the instructional repertoire of this teacher. "Science is fun," says Mr. North, "and there's a reason why it should grab their attention."

Freedman (2000) recommends several principles for designing effective science demonstrations:

- *Establish a clear purpose.* The demonstration must be directly related to the scientific concepts being studied.
- *Plan the demonstration carefully.* This is more than just assembling the materials. What other learning experiences will the students have in order to understand the theoretical basis for the demonstration? Plan the related lessons to support student connections to important concepts.
- *Plan for repeatability.* Students may need to see the demonstration again. Be sure to have extra materials on hand for this possibility. Also, be sure that the demonstration you've selected yields reliable and consistent results.
- *Plan for safety.* Although discrepant events like science demonstrations can enhance learning, your students don't need to witness you getting hurt.
- *Consider visibility.* A crowded classroom can make it difficult to see and fully appreciate the demonstration. It can become a safety issue as well for your students if they are jockeying for position. If the sight lines are obstructed in your classroom, consider dividing the class in half and performing the demonstration twice. If the phenomenon you are demonstrating needs to be seen from close range, then perform the demonstration with small groups of students.
- *Don't discount the importance of showmanship.* The literal and figurative "stinks and bangs" of science demonstrations can intrigue your students. Don't be afraid to play it up—your enthusiasm is infectious.

Thought-Provoking Questions in Physics. Hal Cox, physics teacher, uses thought-provoking questions to follow demonstrations and lab experiments. During a unit on waves, students worked in small groups to complete a lab using slinkies. With slinkies stretched across the floor and a lab sheet to structure their inquiry, they performed a series of experiments to make predictions about wave behavior by manipulating length and tension. During another lab, they used string instruments to study the effect of these variables on sound waves. The following day, they arrived to find a question posted on the overhead: What would happen to the pitch of a string if you changed both the length and the tension on a string?

Students discussed this for a few minutes with their lab groups and then wrote their responses in their science journals. Most of the students were able to connect the concept of wave frequency with the variables. However, he was delighted to see that some of them had also understood that the same pitch could be obtained by manipulating either variable. He then reviewed the lab from the previous day and led a discussion on the successes and challenges the groups had in completing the lab sheet. One of the things we admire about Mr. Cox's approach is the efficiency of this instructional strategy—the entire review process took only 10 minutes. By beginning his class with a thought-provoking question, he activated his students' prior knowledge and gave them an opportunity to make connections to newly acquired knowledge.

Visual Displays in Earth Science. Maria Grant used a picture book, *Galileo's Universe* (Lewis, 2005), to introduce her students to Galileo Galilei's thinking about the world. She selected this book for its interesting use of pop-up pages. Like books for very young readers, this text literally has pop-ups on every page that help explain the content. In addition, the text is written as an informational poem about Galileo's life and his discoveries. Further, the text has short pieces of informational text to further students' understanding of things such as the compass and hydrostatic balance. Ms. Grant used this book as a visual display, reading aloud the text while displaying the pop-up pages on her document camera and LCD projector.

Anticipatory Activities in Electives

Thought-Provoking Questions Through K-W-L in Art. As we discussed earlier in this chapter, a popular and effective anticipatory activity is K-W-L (Ogle, 1986). Remember that K-W-L (know/want to know/ learned) is a method for activating prior knowledge and formulating questions to guide inquiry (see Figure 2.4). Teachers across content area subjects have confirmed the usefulness and flexibility of this technique for introducing a unit of study. Buehl (2001) identifies it as one of the instructional strategies essential in the repertoire of every secondary content area educator.

Jeremy Merrill's art students are required to conduct in-class research every 2 weeks on an artist of their choice. Mr. Merrill introduces research methods early in the year and models the first project on a single artist. He shows them a selection of slides featuring the artist's work and invites questions about the paintings. Subsequent research projects are student directed and encompass every era from medieval to postmodern. K-W-L charts are the initial component of any inquiry, and are expected with every research report. Hayna researched the life and work of Leonardo da Vinci. (We've included irregularities in grammar.) Her K-W-L chart is displayed in Figure 2.5.

Mr. Merrill's emphasis on the history of art, as well as its execution, connects past works to the students' original compositions. He has found that using K-W-L charts

Figure 2.4   K-W-L chart.

What Do I Know?	What Do I Want to Know?	What Have I Learned?

Figure 2.5   K-W-L art inquiry chart.

What Do I Know?	What Do I Want to Know?	What Have I Learned?
He was an artist He was famous He's dead	Why was he famous?	He painted <u>Mona Lisa</u> and <u>The Last Supper</u>
	Does he use the elements of art in his work?	He used line, hatching, shadowing, 3-dimensional shading
	When was he born?	Born 1452
	Where was he born?	Born in Italy
	When did he die?	He died 1519
	What influenced him?	Imagination and creativity
	Was he only an artist?	He was an inventor, scientist, and city planner
	What were the names of his famous works?	<u>Mona Lisa</u>, <u>The Last Supper</u>
	What material did he use for his work?	Red chalk (sanguine) finely sharpened
	What kinds of things did he paint?	In early career, he drew/designed military arms Left-handed

supports the development of research and inquiry skills among his students while giving him a way to prompt discussion about works of art and their creators.

"It's really the basis for what we do as artists. 'What has been done by others?' 'Where do we want to go with our own art?' 'Now that we've attempted it, what have we learned?' That's the artistic process in a nutshell."

Conclusion

Anticipatory activities can enhance the learning and retention of students in content area classrooms. They can also serve to motivate and stimulate curiosity about the topics being studied. Demonstrations, discrepant events, visual displays, and thought-provoking questions are examples of the types of anticipatory activities used by effective teachers.

Demonstrations are typically used to display a theory, concept, or phenomenon. They are a staple of science instruction, but can be used in any content area. Demonstrations are particularly useful for English language learners because they foster mental models for concepts. It is important to remember that a demonstration does not replace the need for the theoretical basis for understanding the phenomenon. Discrepant events are useful for gaining attention and creating a lasting impression. These events are characteristically described as surprising or startling. Teachers have found success in using costumes and props to illustrate a character, setting, or era. In addition to picture books, the growing availability of technology makes it possible to include novel visual displays for illustrating an idea or concept. Web-based programs are a particular area for resources on a variety of phenomenon. Thought-provoking questions are a primary tool for teachers to create anticipatory activities. Examples of thought-provoking questions in this chapter included essential questions, quick writes, found poems, anticipation guides, and K-W-L charts.

Chapter 3
Word for Word: Vocabulary Development Across the Curriculum

*D*avid is sitting at a computer working on a poem that is due as part of his response to the essential question, "Who am I?" He has an idea for the word he wants to use but can't think of it. He calls his teacher over, saying, "I know there's a word for it, the things that get in your way, but I can't think of it." Mr. Goodwin asks if he has tried to insert a common word and then use the thesaurus, which David shows him he has done. Mr. Goodwin says, "I think you might be thinking about the word obstacle. Take a quick look at MW.com and see if I'm right. If I am, remember to add it to your electronic vocabulary journal."

David opens another browser window and looks up the word obstacle. Realizing that this is the word he was looking for, David closes the window and opens his Google Docs page. He finds his electronic vocabulary journal and adds the word, its definition, and a reminder about the word's meaning.

When David finishes his first draft of the poem, he file transfers it to a friend for review. As Russell reads David's poem, the two students instant message each other. Russell asks a lot of questions about the poem and makes some suggestions about word choices. David's final version of his poetic response to the essential question reads:

I am David; this is my image.

I am from extreme physical dedication
I am from confused mazes of reality
From daydreams and nightmares of hope and failure

I am Superman, creating and destroying obstacles of doom and love
I have a shield pierced only by those determined and close
I wear a mask to cloak my sly image
I dress to impress
  And fit the part
    Of athlete and lover
      Like Tiger Woods (but a faithful version)
I use my powers to take care of others
I mentor and help
I run interference, on the court and off.
My extreme physical dedication is more than sports.
It's also about me, friends, and family.
I am David; this is my image.

The vocabulary demands on students skyrocket during the secondary school years, ballooning to an estimated 88,500 words (Nagy & Anderson, 1984). Although academic language demands are high, it is estimated that everyday speech consists of only 5,000–7,000 words (Klein, 1988). Therefore, it is unlikely that conversation and discussion alone can compensate for a limited command of the academic vocabulary. Taken together, these two figures demonstrate what most secondary teachers already know: The vocabulary gap for many students is so large that it is difficult to identify where to begin. In addition to vocabulary instruction, which is the focus of this chapter, it is important to recognize that students acquire word knowledge from the wide reading they do and from teacher read alouds and shared readings, especially when teachers contextualize vocabulary in their think alouds.

Struggling Readers

DO NOT SIMPLY NEED MORE BASIC SKILLS

It is tempting when working with struggling adolescent readers to revisit basic skills—after all, if one can only fill in the gaps of knowledge, these students will be able to catch up. Unfortunately, decades of remedial and basic skills instruction have not fulfilled this promise. An adolescent who reads on a fourth-grade level is not the same as a fourth grader, and using materials and approaches effective at fourth grade will not yield positive results. Many struggling readers use what Thorkildsen and Nicholls (2002) describe as a performance goal orientation, meaning that they compare their reading competence to others, resulting in a competitive learning environment and decreased reading motivation. It is essential for these students to develop a task value orientation, wherein they see worth in the task they are attempting. Students who feel they are being taught a "watered-down" version of the curriculum will not value the tasks. Wigfield and Eccles (2000) explain that task value is further influenced by the degree to which an individual is able to exercise choice, and then persists with the task to completion. Curriculum and instruction that are rich in content and oriented toward the sophisticated thinking of adolescents will result in higher degrees of motivation. Differentiated instruction provides struggling readers with the necessary supports they need to accomplish those tasks so that they are able to persist in their learning and fulfill their goals.

The Importance of Word Knowledge

This gap in word knowledge is problematic because of its impact on content learning and reading comprehension (Fisher & Frey, 2008). Mastery of the technical language has long been recognized as a predictor of success in any field. For example, in a study of 184 secondary students, Espin and Foegen (1996) found vocabulary to be an important predictor of content area performance. Vocabulary knowledge can also have a profound influence on reading comprehension, as evidenced in a 1992 study by Farley and Elmore. They examined the achievement of struggling first-year college students and discovered that vocabulary knowledge was a stronger predictor of reading comprehension than cognitive ability. In addition to vocabulary, comprehension is also influenced by prior knowledge, fluency, text difficulty, and interest.

Given the academic vocabulary demands of the secondary school curriculum, it would seem logical to first identify and then explicitly teach the necessary words until the gap has been bridged. Indeed, vocabulary research through much of the 20th century consisted of lists of words, such as *McGuffey's Eclectic Spelling-Book* (1879), Dolch's sight words (1936), and Thorndike and Lorge's (1944) *Teacher's Word Book of 30,000 Words*. In this stance, vocabulary was viewed as a subset of either comprehension or spelling, but was rarely examined closely in its own right. Instead, emphasis was on teaching individual words, and these lists guided teachers in making word selections. Instruction often relied on rote memorization of definitions followed by weekly vocabulary tests. Words were rarely derived from texts the students were reading.

Vocabulary Acquisition

Research in language acquisition in the 1980s had an important effect on trends in vocabulary instruction. Along with the studies about academic language demands and everyday usage, it was reported that students learn an average of 3,000 new words per year (Nagy & Herman, 1985), hardly an adequate pace for closing the vocabulary gap. Indeed, it appeared that teaching words in isolation exclusively was an inefficient way to foster word knowledge. At the same time, instructional approaches were influenced by a growing understanding of meaning as a component of vocabulary acquisition. Practices shifted to culling vocabulary words from narrative and expository reading selections used in the classroom. Many teachers and educational researchers expressed dissatisfaction with this method as well, because of the hodgepodge nature of the word selection.

THE BENEFITS FOR ENGLISH LANGUAGE LEARNERS

Adolescents who are learning English as a second or third language are often challenged by curricular demands that accelerate rapidly in middle and high school. Teachers sometimes misjudge language proficiency because they attend more closely to the social uses of language, rather than a student's cognitive academic language proficiency (Cummins, 1980). Linguists describe this range of levels as language registers. For instance, Cuervas (1984) discusses the notion of a "mathematics register" for vocabulary that describes "the meanings belonging to the natural language used in mathematics" (p. 136). Therefore, systematic instruction in academic vocabulary is critical for English language learners because their knowledge of the content is linked to the academic language registers of the subject (Fitzgerald, García, Jiménez, & Barrera, 2000; Shanahan & August, 2006). Consideration of the developmental needs of the young adult must be considered in this instruction. There is evidence that vocabulary and literacy instruction that addresses the need for psychologically safe, motivating environment leads to increased levels of learning (Taylor & McAtee, 2003).

A complicating issue regarding vocabulary acquisition is *word schema*. This term is used to describe the complex web of knowledge of a word, including metalinguistic (inferring meaning through context), morphological (prefixes, suffixes, and roots), and patterned (understanding the plausibility of a meaning) (Nagy & Scott, 1990). Stated another way, "knowing a word" involves more than definition; it also means understanding its use in relation to the context, its permutations (*port, airport, portly*), and your ability to make accurate predictions about the meaning based on these elements. Nagy and Scott liken this to walking into an unfamiliar restaurant. It would be inefficient to begin ordering at random. Instead, you would consider the type of restaurant (fancy? truck stop?). You would expect certain constants, like being required to pay, and sitting at a table. By the time you looked at the menu, even an unfamiliar item wouldn't be utterly unknown to you. Based on your schema, you would be able to hazard a pretty good guess about the item. Likewise, memorizing a single definition is likely to fall short of usefulness. To "know" a word, you must understand its context and morphology and hypothesize its meaning based on these elements.

Vocabulary as Concepts or Labels. More vexing issues in vocabulary word selection concern the usefulness of the word and its relation to the curriculum. Some words are concepts, whereas others are labels. Given that students need to acquire a tremendous volume of vocabulary words each year, it seems careless to squander valuable instructional time on words that function only as labels in a particular reading. For example, in Lois Lowry's story *The Giver* (1994), a boy is faced with the challenge of confronting truth in his "perfect" community. The word *utopia* is a concept word, for it is central to the understanding of a society with no illness or poverty. On the other hand, the word *tunic* is a label describing the type of clothing worn by the characters. *Utopia* is well worth the instructional effort for students to think deeply about the complexities represented by this one word; *tunic* is a word that can be inferred through context clues and is not essential to comprehension. Students also benefit from instruction on the differences between concept and label words because it can prevent them from getting bogged down in minutia at the expense of big ideas.

Self-Assessment of Current Knowledge. Teaching vocabulary is further complicated by the varying word knowledge levels of individual students. Even when the core reading is held in common, students bring a range of word understanding to the text. Rather than apply a "one size fits all" approach to vocabulary instruction, it is wise to assess students before the reading. This awareness is valuable for the student as well, because it highlights their understanding of what they know and what they still need to learn, to comprehend the reading. One method for accomplishing this is through Vocabulary Self-Awareness (Goodman, 2001). Words are introduced at the beginning of the reading or unit, and students complete a self-assessment of their knowledge of the words (see Figure 3.1). Each vocabulary word is rated according to the student's understanding, including an example and a definition. If they are very comfortable with the word, students give themselves a "+" (plus sign). If they think they know, but are unsure, students note the word with a "√" (check mark). If the word is new to them, they place a "−" (minus sign) next to the word. Over the course of the reading or unit, students add new information to the chart. The goal is to replace all the check marks and minus signs with a plus

Figure 3.1 Vocabulary self-awareness chart.

WORD	+	√	−	EXAMPLE	DEFINITION

Procedure:

1. Examine the list of words you have written in the first column.

2. Put a "+" next to each word you know well, and give an accurate example and definition of the word. Your definition and example must relate to the unit of study.

3. Place a "√" next to any words for which you can write only a definition or an example, but not both.

4. Put a "−" next to words that are new to you.

This chart will be used throughout the unit. By the end of the unit you should have the entire chart completed. Because you will be revising this chart, write in pencil.

Source: From "A Tool for Learning: Vocabulary Self-Awareness," by L. Goodman, in *Creative Vocabulary: Strategies for Teaching Vocabulary in Grades K–12* (p. 46), by C. Blanchfield (Ed.), 2001, Fresno, CA: San Joaquin Valley Writing Project. Used with permission.

VOCABULARY

Figure 3.2 Vocabulary self-awareness example.

Word	+	√	–	Example	Definition
prejudice	+			Not hiring a person because of their color, religion, or gender is a form of prejudice	A bias, usually not based in fact, against a person or group
civil disobedience		√		Disobeying a law	
transcendentalism			–		

sign. Because students continually revisit their vocabulary charts to revise their entries, they have multiple opportunities to practice and extend their growing understanding of the terms. An excerpt of one student's vocabulary chart for *Civil Disobedience* (Thoreau, 1849/1965) can be found in Figure 3.2.

Vocabulary Instruction

Current practices in vocabulary instruction seek to integrate these varied methods. Word selection is essential for content area language growth, and a growing number of teachers are identifying grade-level words for explicit instruction. However, reinforcement of understanding through meaning is also seen as critical to student learning. Blachowicz and Fisher (2000) identified four principles for effective vocabulary instruction. They advise that students should

- be actively involved in word learning,
- make personal connections,
- be immersed in vocabulary, and
- consolidate meaning through multiple information sources.

The authors note that whereas these principles apply to all learning, their experience has shown that these conditions are vital for vocabulary acquisition and retention.

Secondary teachers must also consider the type of vocabulary used in their instruction. Vacca and Vacca (1999) suggest that there are three types of vocabulary to consider—*general, specialized,* and *technical*. General vocabulary consists primarily of words used in everyday language, usually with widely agreed upon meanings. Examples of general vocabulary words include *pesky, bothersome,* and *vexing*. The meaning of these three words tends to be consistent across contexts, and the appearance of any one of these words would signal the reader that the subject of these adjectives would be annoying. In contrast, specialized vocabulary is flexible and transportable across curricular disciplines—these words hold multiple meanings in different content areas. For example, the word *loom* has a common meaning— an impending event—as well as a more specialized definition in textile arts—a device for weaving thread or yarn into cloth. Finally, there are technical vocabulary words that are specific to only one field of study. *Concerto* in music, *meiosis* in

VOCABULARY

science, and *abscissa* in mathematics are all examples of technical vocabulary specific to a content area. These words can be more difficult to teach because there is little association with previously known word meanings. In addition, they tend to be "dense" in meaning; that is, the level of knowledge necessary to fully understand the word is directly related to the content itself. Technical vocabulary, in particular, tends to be vexing for secondary content teachers because the fallback system for acquisition is often rote memorization. Let's look inside classrooms to see how teachers address vocabulary teaching and learning across the curriculum.

Strategies at Work

Vocabulary Instruction in English

English classes are the primary location for teaching language skills and strategies that are transportable across the learning day. Therefore, vocabulary instruction sometimes focuses on analysis of familiar words through word study. Even a cursory review of the English language arts content standards for middle and high school would reveal a significant focus on vocabulary and word analysis. For example, in ninth grade in California, students are expected to focus on the following skills:

> *Vocabulary and concept development*
> 1.1 Identify and use the literal and figurative meanings of words and understand word derivations.
> 1.2. Distinguish between the denotative and connotative meanings of words and interpret the connotative power of words.
> 1.3. Identify Greek, Roman, and Norse mythology and use the knowledge to understand the origin and meaning of new words (e.g., the word *narcissistic* drawn from the myth of Narcissus and Echo). (California State Board of Education, n.d.)

In many English classrooms, word walls are prominently displayed.

Developing Familiarity Through Word Walls. Word walls (Harmon, Wood, Hedrick, Vintinner, & Willeford, 2009) are alphabetically arranged (by first letter) high-frequency words displayed in a manner to allow easy visual access to all students in the room. However, it is essential to "do" a word wall, not merely display one. For example, during a study of *The Grapes of Wrath* (Steinbeck, 1939), a teacher may include words like *Dust Bowl, Okies, drought*, and *migrant* on the word wall. These English teachers "do" the word wall through brief (10 minutes or so) daily instruction around a particular set of words. Typically, five words are introduced and located on the word wall display. Novel games such as Guess the Covered Word (Cunningham & Allington, 2003), where a word is revealed one letter at a time, may be used. It is important that the words, once taught, remain in the same spot so students can reliably locate them.

Expanding Student Vocabulary. Another popular method for expanding written vocabulary is through specialized word lists, thesauri, and dictionaries. Many English teachers have experienced the overuse of terms like "said" in their students' writing. This may occur because students have not explored how writers convey the way a character speaks a message to illuminate the action. Teachers can adopt the "said" word list to assist students in using more descriptive terms instead. Called "Said" Is Dead (Peterson, 1996), students in

VOCABULARY

writing and drama courses post a list of words to help them use more interesting terms like *confided, quipped*, and *scoffed* in place of the aforementioned term when writing dialogue (see Table 3.1). Similarly, these same students also have a wealth of reference materials available to them to support their word choices. Student thesauri are useful for budding writers struggling to find the perfect word, but other specialized materials like a slang thesaurus, rhyming dictionary, and books of quotations are also popular with students.

Developing Structural Word Analysis. The ability to deconstruct words to ascertain meaning is directly related to a student's knowledge of root words and affixes. Root words are morphemes (units of meaning) that compose the foundation of all words. Affixes (prefixes and suffixes) are attached to the root word in order to modify the meaning. For example, the word *dictionary* comes from the Latin *dictum* meaning "to speak." Other root words are derived from Greek words, such as *phonogram* from *phono* meaning "sound." Still other root words are free morphemes, meaning that they can stand alone as a word. For

Table 3.1 Expanded Vocabulary Word List

"Said" Is Dead	
Enrich your dialogue writing with more descriptive terms like these:	
added	moaned
advised	mumbled
allowed	objected
babbled	parroted
barked	pronounced
begged	protested
blurted	quipped
cajoled	reported
complained	scoffed
confessed	scolded
confided	simpered
demanded	snapped
dithered	swore
droned	stuttered
gasped	taunted
groaned	teased
howled	wailed
interjected	whimpered
interrupted	yammered
jabbed	yapped
jeered	yelled
leered	

Source: From *The Writer's Workout Book: 113 Stretches Toward Better Prose*, by A. Peterson, 1996, Berkeley, CA: National Writing Project. Used with permission.

example, *port, form,* and *act* are important common root words that also serve as a platform for activating word knowledge through the addition of a variety of affixes. By closely investigating the parts of a word, including root words, derivations, and affixes, students can acquire tools for use with unfamiliar words, thus expanding their general and specialized vocabularies.

Word study often begins with free morphemes like *port* because their meaning is generally more accessible. After discussing the meaning of *port* as a Latin word for "carry," and the common definition of the word as "a place where ships can safely dock," word extensions become more apparent. *Porter* means a person who carries an object; *airport* means a safe place for airplanes, and *import* means to carry something into an area.

In addition to root word analysis, instruction about prefixes and suffixes also occurs regularly. Understanding of the morphological basis of affixes is critical to word knowledge. Cunningham (2002) estimates that "re-, dis-, un-, and in-/im- account for over half of all the prefixes readers will ever see . . . [and] -s/-es, -ed, and -ing account for 65% of all words with suffixes" (p. 4). Coupled with root word and derivational knowledge, students who understand common affixes possess a powerful set of skills for taking words apart and reassembling them to extract their meaning. This level of word analysis also appears to support reading as well because learners who can extract the morphological characteristics of the word will process and analyze across morphemes rather than syllables (Templeton, 1992).

Focusing on Words With Multiple Meanings. Confusion about words with multiple meanings can also confound English language learners. For example, the word *run* has 69 meanings, as defined by the *New Webster's Dictionary of the English Language* (1981)! This small word can refer to a rapid form of ambulation, entrance into a political contest, or a migration of fish, as well as dozens of other meanings. Interestingly, teachers report that it is often these humble words, not just those glamorous polysyllabic darlings strung like a necklace with multiple affixes, that interfere with reading comprehension. In order for students to correctly interpret which definition should be applied, instruction must include pointing out such words and then using them in a variety of texts. English language learners can build their specialized vocabulary through semantic instruction of multiple-meaning words like *run* and *bear.* By examining both the rules and the fluidity of meaning in language, students are positioned to make increasingly finer distinctions between words. After all, Mark Twain once said, "The difference between the right word and the almost right word is the difference between the lightning and the lightning bug!" (Twain, 1890).

Noticing Subtle Differences in Meaning. Relationships between words can be particularly challenging when discussing synonyms. The difference between *annoyance* and *harassment* is a fine but distinct one. The ability to discern between these gradients of meaning is a skill tested on the Scholastic Aptitude Test and other college board exams. Truly "the difference between the right word and the almost right word" can impact the ability of the student to use precise language. These "shades of meaning" can be taught in an imaginative way using paint chip cards from the local hardware store (Blanchfield, 2001). Students attach a paint chip card containing shades of color to notebook paper to illustrate a string of synonyms. Definitions are written to the right of the paint chip card on which the word has been written. For example, Bridget created the card in Figure 3.3 to illustrate synonyms for the word *fear.*

VOCABULARY

Figure 3.3 Shades of meaning.

SHADES OF MEANING	DEFINITIONS AND SENTENCES
fear	a feeling of anxiety because danger is nearby I have a fear of getting a shot at the doctor.
dread	a great fear mixed with awe or respect The girl dreaded moving to a new school.
terror	an intense fear and shock I saw terror in the driver's eyes right before he crashed.
panic	a sudden fear that might cause the person to collapse My mother panicked when she saw the cut on my face.
phobia	a fear that doesn't make sense My friend has a phobia about roller coasters.

Learning Vocabulary as Parts of Speech. Dana Kuhn's ninth-grade English class studied parts of speech as a method for understanding vocabulary in the context of its appearance in a sentence. Mr. Kuhn used his own version of "Vocabulary Jeopardy" to engage students in cooperative learning activities while building their understanding of the language. Words were selected from a cross-matched list of vocabulary identified by the ninth-grade English department and readings that had been discussed and studied during recent lessons. He used the game as a formative assessment of student learning of words introduced the day before. Heterogeneous groups of four or five students competed as teams to provide questions that accurately matched the prompts displayed on the familiar game board constructed through a PowerPoint display. The categories Mr. Kuhn used on a recent afternoon were Nouns, Adjectives, Verbs, and Spelling Required, a particularly challenging category for most students, especially his English language learners. The captain of each team chose the category and dollar amount while Mr. Kuhn read the prompt. Teams had 10 seconds to consult before answering. The prompt "plentiful" appeared in the $400 Adjective slot. After consulting for a few moments, Haley's team rang in with "What is *abundant?*" Mr. Kuhn finds these team competitions to be useful because they "encourage students to teach other students." He does caution, however, to use games such as this judiciously—"have fun, but don't kill the game with overexposure!"

Vocabulary in Social Studies

A critical vocabulary skill for secondary learners is the ability to ascribe characteristics to technical vocabulary. Understanding the nuances of meaning behind terminology, for instance, the similarities and differences between the Bay of Pigs invasion and the Cuban Missile Crisis, is essential to the mastery of any content area. This ability to assign characteristics is also an important element in reading comprehension and builds connections between known and unknown concepts (Gipe, 1978–1979).

Semantic Feature Analysis. A popular instructional strategy for categorizing terms by characteristics is semantic feature analysis (Anders & Bos, 1986). This procedure, also known as SFA, assists students in assigning characteristics, or features, in a grid pattern. Vocabulary terms comprise the rows, and the features make up the columns. Students place a "+" in each cell to indicate a relationship between the term and the feature, and a "−" when it is not a characteristic. Typically, students complete the grid in conjunction with a piece of assigned text. During a U.S. history class, students analyzed terms related to post–World War II U.S. foreign policy. The teacher created the grid in Figure 3.4 for students as they worked through a chapter in their textbook.

Many teachers attribute the power of SFA to its visual arrangement, particularly because it mimics the way the brain organizes information (Pittleman, Heimlich, Berglund, & French, 1991). Marco, a student in this classroom, seemed to confirm this observation when he said, "*Now* I get it! You can really see how these policies didn't all really help each other. No wonder it was so messed up."

Semantic feature analysis is an excellent example of a vocabulary strategy that taps into a student's visual learning modality. The use of multiple modalities of learning has been shown to support new learning (Armstrong, 2009). These modalities, or forms of expression, are frequently categorized as visual, auditory, and kinesthetic (movement). Whereas conventional wisdom cautions against attempting to categorize students according to a particular learning style, educators widely recognize the value of integrating these forms of expression into instruction. Certainly visual supports are widely used. As well, the auditory modality is

Figure 3.4 Semantic feature analysis example.

VOCABULARY WORD / FEATURE	PEACEKEEPING EFFORT	BUILT ALLIANCES WITH EUROPE	EFFECTED BY DOMESTIC POLICY	ESCALATED COLD WAR
Joined United Nations (1945)	+	+	+	−
Berlin Blockade (1948)	−	+	+	+
Declaration of Human Rights (1948)	+	+	+	−
Signed NATO (1949) and SEATO (1954) treaties	+	+	+	+
Mutually ensured destruction policy (1960)	+	+	+	−
U.S. tests hydrogen bomb (1952)	−	−	+	+
Joined World Bank (1947)	+	+	+	−
Bay of Pigs invasion (1961)	−	−	+	+
Cuban Missile Crisis (1962)	−	+	+	+

represented in the chapter on questioning. However, learning through and with movement is often seen as more problematic, especially at the secondary level (Gage, 1995). It can be a challenge for the teacher to manage this type of expression in a busy classroom.

Kinesthetics in Role-Play. An example of kinesthetic expression in vocabulary instruction is role-playing. This practice of "acting out" vocabulary extends from Total Physical Response, a method of language instruction used with students who are English language learners (Asher, 1969) and those who are deaf (Marlatt, 1995). When students are invited to "act out" vocabulary, they engage in physical movement and gestures to portray a word. It is likely that these movements assist the performer in remembering the word because he or she is required to think critically about the features of the word.

The incorporation of role-playing in social studies content has also been documented (Hillis & von Eschenbach, 1996). Marisol Acuna used vocabulary role-play in her social studies class during a unit on health care decisions. The focus of the day's lesson was on the dangers associated with tobacco products. She identified relevant vocabulary and then invited students to study the words in an unconventional way—through drama. Students worked in small groups to research specialized vocabulary words and phrases like *advertisement, big tobacco company,* and *exposure.* After discussion and clarification about word meanings, each group then crafted a script using the identified vocabulary words. A requirement of the skit was that it must accurately convey the significance of the word or phrase.

Corita, Scott, and Kyle selected *tobacco subsidies* as one of the terms to demonstrate during vocabulary role-play. Scott, as the tobacco farmer, tells his wife (Corita) that he'd like to replace his tobacco fields with spinach in order to contribute to the health of the nation. The two farmers then turn to Kyle, the farm management agent, to explain their decision. "We want to plant a new crop," explains Corita. Kyle, as the agent, replies, "You can plant what you want, but you'll lose your *tobacco subsidy* from the government." "You mean I won't get a check for each acre of tobacco I harvest? How can I afford to keep my farm?" says Scott. Ms. Acuna later uses the students' definitions from their skits to illustrate examples in their vocabulary journals.

Vocabulary in Mathematics

It has been a long-held tradition in secondary schooling that explicit vocabulary instruction is an essential prereading activity to support students' subsequent comprehension (Moore, Readence, & Rickelman, 1989). However, many teachers have experienced the dilemma of preteaching the vocabulary to such an extent that the student has little opportunity to apply it, relying instead on rote memorization at the expense of deeper understanding (Johnson & Pearson, 1984). Therefore, a "chicken-and-egg" conundrum results—what comes first, the vocabulary or the connected text?

Vocabulary in Context. Many content area teachers seek to resolve this argument by teaching both the vocabulary *and* the context for its use simultaneously. These teachers find success in timing the instruction of technical vocabulary using a sequence of "introduce, define, discuss, and apply." In this way, students are alerted to the necessity of a new word, provided a definition, given an opportunity to further refine their understanding through peer discussion, then invited to experience the word within connected text. This sequence is particularly valuable when teaching technical vocabulary.

Vacca and Vacca (1999) believe that "vocabulary is as unique to a content area as fingerprints are to a human being" (p. 314). Indeed, few content areas are more defined by their vocabulary than the field of mathematics. Complicating matters further is the importance of what the National Council for Teachers of Mathematics (2000) calls the "factual, procedural, and conceptual understandings that are inexorably woven together in the study of mathematics." This means that in mathematics students must learn the definition of a term, the algorithms associated with the term, as well as the underlying principles that will allow them to apply a flexible understanding to solve unfamiliar problems.

Vocabulary Development Specific to a Content Area. Constantina Burow, a geometry teacher, uses an innovative approach to building flexible technical vocabulary for her students. Through the use of mathematics journals, she encourages students to define and apply their knowledge of the language of geometry. She follows a sequence of instruction that begins with introducing and defining mathematical terms. Discussing real-world examples and applying the vocabulary occurs at length in whole-class and small-group activities. Students apply the new algorithms through guided practice, and then extend their understanding by applying these concepts to novel problems. Sounds familiar, right? This sequence is not uncommon in mathematics classes throughout U.S. high schools. However, Ms. Burow's use of mathematics journals allows students to consolidate these instructional activities. Early in the semester, students are taught a two-page frame to use in their mathematics journals (see Figure 3.5). At the top of the left page, students assemble photos from magazines that mimic the geometric shape in question. On the lower half of the page, students write a summary in their own words. Diagrams, formulas, and theorems appear on the facing page.

By using this format, students are able to skim and scan a great deal of information as they read from the textbook and other source materials. These mathematics journals serve as more than a notebook. Whereas another section is reserved for class notes, these pages are reserved for students' individual expressions of the meaning of geometric terms. Miguel, a student in Ms. Burow's class, had diagrams of quadrilaterals (squares, rectangles, and parallelograms) on a page, along with their accompanying formulas and theorems. On the left, he had clipped an ad for a square Tommy Hilfiger™ watch as an example of a quadrilateral. The photograph represented another meaning as well for Miguel, who pointed out that the Hilfiger logo on the watch face was composed of rectangles, another form of parallelogram. Below the photo he wrote, "Finding the area of a quadrilateral you need to multiply the base of the figure times the true height of the figure (true height makes a 90° angle with base). To find the perimeter you add up all the sides." Sample pages from Miguel's and Guadalupe's journals, focused on pyramids, can be found in Figures 3.6 and 3.7.

Ms. Burow has found that the use of a consistent frame for defining and extending geometry vocabulary has served as an excellent reference for students as well. When reading their textbook and other mathematics materials, students can use their own journals to remind them about the meaning of unfamiliar words, thus reinforcing their growing acquisition of mathematical vocabulary.

VOCABULARY

Figure 3.5   Sample page from mathematics journal.

Real Life: This is where I see _____ In the world . . .	Diagrams:
	Formulas:
Summary (words only)	Theorems:

Vocabulary in Science

The ability to manipulate words can be an important device in acquiring vocabulary. Unfortunately, committing words to paper often seems permanent and intractable to many students, as if the act of writing down terms means they must remain fixed and static. Word sorts can provide students with a way to arrange and rearrange words that mimic the critical thinking processes they use in applying known words to comprehending new text. Much like a key in search of a lock, readers try a variety of related words until they discover the one meaning that supports their ability to understand a passage.

Science Word Sorts. Sorting words involves the manipulation of a set of words, usually written on individual slips of paper, into a series of categories or related concepts. More than 25 years ago, Gillet and Temple (1978) described a process for helping students study the relationships between words. Word sorts typically consist of 10 to 20 terms and can be closed or open. Closed sorting activities are performed using categories provided by the teacher. For example, the words *chromosome, chromium,* and *chromosphere* belong in the categories, respectively, of

|Figure 3.6   Sample page from mathematics journal.

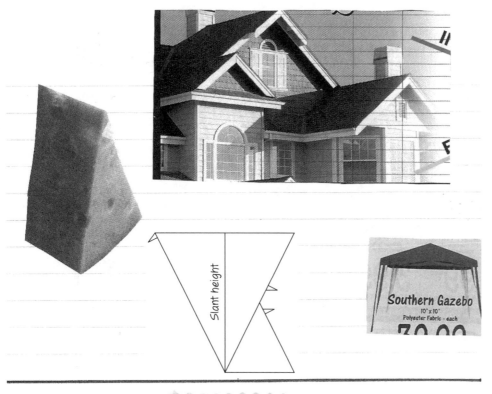

Southern Gazebo
10' x 10'
Polyester Fabric - each

Slant height

SUMMARY

- *The slant height of the pyramid is also the true height of a triangle.*
- *The bases of a pyramid can be a rectangle, square, triangle and pentagon.*
- *To find the volume of a pyramid multiply the area of a base and the true height.*
- *To find the surface areas of a pyramid add the base and the sides.*
- *In a pyramid you will only find one base.*

biology, chemistry, and *astronomy,* which were furnished by the teacher to help students organize their understanding. An open sort is similar, but students create a set of categories to reflect their understanding of the relationships between and among a set of words. Both of these examples represent conceptual

Figure 3.7 Sample page from mathematics journal.

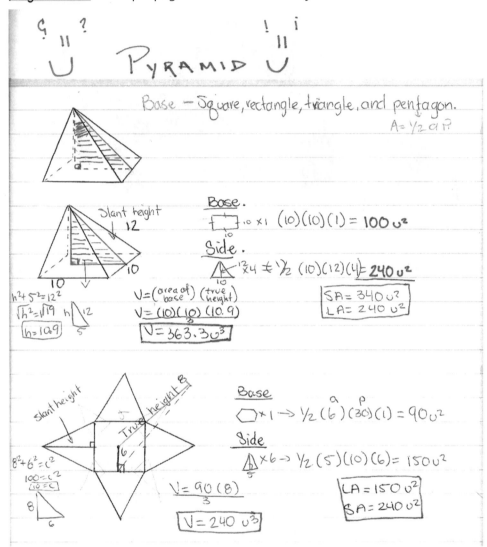

word sorts, because students are using their semantic knowledge of terms. Other word sorts may focus word patterns (e.g., *-at* and *-ag* words), or derivations (words with the Latin root *nomen* or *nominis*).

Science teacher Larry Caudillo uses word sorts to assist his biology students in preparing concept maps. During a review lesson on the molecules of life, Mr. Caudillo presented his students with the words *saccharides, DNA, glycerol, amino acid, fatty acids, carboxyl, RNA,* and *R-group* in an open sort. The class was instructed to work in small clusters to create categories and group accordingly. Group members engaged in a lively conversation about the meanings and relationships between and among the words in the set. After much debate, each group arrived at an arrangement. Using blank cards, Nalia, Maria, Terrence, and Carl created four categories and arranged their cards like those in Figure 3.8.

This correct arrangement reflected the students' knowledge of the four macromolecules that comprise all life-forms. He further challenged them to supply a rationale for their decisions, and was particularly pleased to see them return to their textbook and class notes to justify their answers.

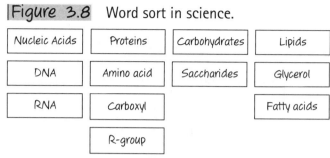

Figure 3.8   Word sort in science.

Nucleic Acids	Proteins	Carbohydrates	Lipids
DNA	Amino acid	Saccharides	Glycerol
RNA	Carboxyl		Fatty acids
	R-group		

Vocabulary in Electives

An important element in mastering new vocabulary words is repetition and rehearsal with purpose (Baker, Simmons, & Kame'enui, 1995). There is little evidence to show that students master vocabulary with traditional methods of rote memorization through oral and written drills (Anderson & Nagy, 1992; Gu & Johnson, 1996). Rather, it is repetition embedded in a meaningful context that supports vocabulary acquisition. This concept of meaningful repetition has its roots in Reader's Theatre, a technique for promoting reading fluency through public performance (Martinez, Roser, & Strecker, 1998–1999).

Meaningful Repetition.   Music teacher Debbie Nevin understands the importance of performance as a learning tool. Students in her band classes must become comfortable with public performance if they are to be successful in her course. She also recognizes that it is vital for her students, especially her English language learners, to get adequate time conversing with adults and other fluent language models (National Center on Education and the Economy, 2001). One technique she uses to accomplish this is Quiz Me vocabulary cards (see Figure 3.9). Students in Ms. Nevin's classes create vocabulary cards that are constructed from 1" × 3" cardstock. As vocabulary is introduced, a word is written on the card, along with the definition. On the back of each card is space for five signatures. A hole is punched in the corner and the cards are strung on a binder ring. Students are required to collect five signatures from adults on campus for each word. They are instructed to approach an adult, explain the assignment, and then request their assistance. The adult quizzes the student on each word, then signs the back of each correct response. In addition to creating a purposeful repetition and rehearsal, Ms. Nevin has also discovered a way for her

Figure 3.9   Quiz Me cards.

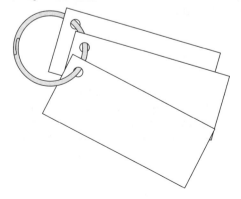

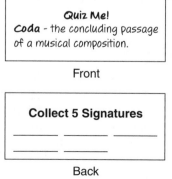

Quiz Me!
Coda - the concluding passage of a musical composition.

Front

Collect 5 Signatures
_____ _____ _____
_____ _____

Back

| Figure 3.10 | Vocabulary cards in clothing design class.

Template

Vocabulary word	Definition in student's own words
Graphic or picture	Sentence using word

Example

Bias	To cut on an angle to the straight grain
	A bias cut uses more fabric.

students to interact with teachers and other adults around campus.

Visual Representations to Understand Word Meanings. Vocabulary cards are used in a different "fashion" in Karen Tennen's clothing design class. Like other content areas, consumer science has its own unique set of vocabulary. Ms. Tennen remarks that "students need to read a guide sheet in order to construct a garment . . . and there are many terms the students need to understand before they can lay out their pattern." When introducing the basics of pattern layout, Ms. Tennen taught specialized vocabulary words that would assist students in accurately cutting out their fabric pieces. They were given a set of 4" × 6" index cards and instructed to divide each into quadrants (see Figure 3.10). Terms such as *bias, bound edge, face, nap,* and *notch* were each written in the top left quadrant, and the definition, after class instruction, was recorded in the student's own words in the upper right quadrant of the card. A sentence using the term is written in the lower right quadrant, and a diagram or graphic symbol representing the term is drawn in the lower left quadrant.

Constructing vocabulary cards serves several uses in this class. First, when placed on a binder ring the cards become an easily accessible reference for the student, preventing costly errors to expensive fabric. The time involved in creating each card also provides an opportunity for students to concentrate on the meaning, its use, and representation of the term, thereby increasing the likelihood that the term will become a part of their permanent vocabulary. Finally, the inclusion of a graphic piece in each card is particularly appropriate for Ms. Tennen's class, because many of these concepts are represented on the tissue pattern as a symbol, rather than a word. For instance, when a pattern needs to be cut on a bias, or angle to the fabric, it is denoted by an arrow (→) indicating the direction. A notch is often represented by ▲. These symbols are universally recognized as indicators of specific sewing concepts, and it is essential that students in this class are comfortable with the lexicon, both in word and symbol, of the field.

Conclusion

The number of words students need in their academic vocabulary skyrockets during their secondary schooling years. Isolated instruction of individual words is an ineffective use of instructional time, and is proven to be inadequate to keep pace with the content area needs. Instead, effective teachers rely on a battery of approaches to foster learning of general, specialized, and technical vocabulary.

Common vocabulary can be successfully taught through word walls constructed from any one of a number of sources for word lists. These visual glossaries can assist students in both usage and spelling. Interesting and innovative resource materials, such as rhyming dictionaries, thesauri, slang dictionaries, and Web sites can expand students' knowledge and usage of words.

A particular challenge for English language learners is the array of multiple meaning words. Often Anglo-Saxon in origin, these small words can offer a broad number of meanings across varied grammatical structures. Explicit instruction in multiple meaning words can boost comprehension.

Specialized and technical vocabulary in the content area is also vital for learning. Vocabulary role-play and word sorts can introduce novel ways for students to experience a deeper understanding of a word and its relationship to other words. Teachers have also found success with structuring activities to invite students to write about words. Examples of these strategies include vocabulary journals and cards.

Remember that each of the vocabulary development strategies in this chapter can be used across the curriculum, and not only in the content areas discussed here. For instance, word walls are used extensively in mathematics and science, and vocabulary cards are regularly featured in English classes.

VOCABULARY

Chapter 4

Well Read: Promoting Comprehension Through Read Alouds and Shared Readings

*T*he 11th-grade U.S. history classroom is shrouded in darkness, lit only by the *soft glow of two colonial-style lanterns. Students have been studying the American Revolution and its effect around the world. They lean in closer as the teacher begins a dramatic reading of* The Midnight Ride of Paul Revere *(Longfellow & Bing, 1860/2001). "Listen, my children, and you shall hear . . ." (p. 3). Richly detailed illustrations by Christopher Bing appear on the projector as the reading continues. The two lanterns are lifted high as the poem describes patriot Robert Newman's ascent to the belfry of the Old North Church to signal Paul Revere of the British approach across the Charles River. "For, borne on the nightwind of the Past, through all our history, to the last, in the hour of darkness and peril and need, the people will waken to listen and hear . . . ." As the poem concludes, 15-year-old Terrell exclaims, "That's the way all poems should be!"*

Interest in the practice of read alouds and shared readings in secondary content area classrooms has increased in the last decade. At one time, public performance of text in high school classrooms was limited to oratory exercises of excerpts from the English canon. It was rare to find narrative or expository text used in content area classrooms, and, in fact, there was some resistance to instruction of any reading strategies in content area classrooms (Price, 1978; Rieck, 1977; Smith & Otto, 1969). However, deeper understandings of the connections between reading and learning have caused content area teachers to reexamine literacy practices in their classrooms.

Struggling Readers

NEED ACCESS TO A WIDE RANGE OF TEXTS

Read alouds and shared readings provide all readers, including struggling readers, access to content information. In addition to this type of instruction, students must read widely if they are to build their vocabulary and background knowledge (Ivey & Broaddus, 2001). During this independent reading time, teachers can facilitate the participation of struggling adolescent readers by selecting high-interest, easily accessible books on the topic under investigation. For example, during a unit of study on the central nervous system, students can and should read from a variety of sources. A struggling reader might read *The Brain* (Simon, 2006), which will build background knowledge and the students' understanding of the science standards.

Two literacy practices borrowed from developmental reading theory and customized for secondary classrooms are read alouds and shared reading. A *read aloud* is a text or passage selected by the teacher to read publicly to a large or small group of students. A primary purpose for the read-aloud selection is to focus on the content of the text. A *shared reading* is a text or passage that is jointly shared by teacher and student, but is read aloud by the teacher. In shared readings, the students can also see the text, and it is usually chosen both for its content and to draw attention to a particular text feature or comprehension strategy. In both read alouds and shared reading, the reading is done by the teacher, not the students.

Read Alouds

The practice of reading aloud in public dates to the dawn of written language. Throughout history, town criers shared local news, religious orders proclaimed scriptures, and lectors read classical works and newspapers to Cuban cigar factory workers, paid for by the laborers themselves (Manguel, 1997). Even in widely literate societies, the act of being read to continues to enthrall. The advent of iPods has led to even greater demands for audio books, as an adult audience rediscovers the pleasure of being read to by expert readers.

Although read alouds have been shown to be effective for young children's literacy development, they can also be used to motivate older, reluctant readers (Erickson, 1996). In a study of 1,700 adolescents, Herrold, Stanchfield, and Serabian (1989) found positive changes in attitude toward reading among students who were read to by their teacher on a daily basis. Likewise, a survey of 1,765 adolescents conducted more than a decade later reported that 62% of the participants identified teacher read-alouds as a favorite literacy activity (Ivey & Broaddus, 2001). Students themselves have reported that a preferred instructional practice is having teachers read aloud portions of text to introduce new readings and promote interest (Worthy, 2002). It appears that adolescents appreciate the read-aloud event as an opportunity to share the teacher's enthusiasm and interest in the topic.

Another advantage to the use of read alouds is that the level of text complexity can be raised. When text is read aloud by the teacher, students with reading difficulties can access books that might otherwise be too difficult for them to read independently. This is essential in content area classrooms. Text complexity rises rapidly during the secondary school years and students who have reading difficulties often find themselves unable to comprehend the information independently in content area books. A vicious cycle then begins when these students fail to assimilate the information, further impacting their ability to use it as background information for new content. Thus, the gap continues to widen as students with reading difficulties fall further behind their classmates. It comes as no surprise that student interest and attitudes toward reading also decline precipitously after sixth grade, coinciding with the increased reading demand in their content area classes.

Read alouds alone cannot compensate for these gaps, but they can introduce important texts that some students might not otherwise be able to read and comprehend independently. Students without reading difficulties will also benefit. A recent empirical analysis of secondary textbooks revealed that many students reading at grade level were unsure about their comprehension of the readings (Wang, 1996). Read alouds are a viable strategy for clarifying difficult text.

Read alouds have been successfully used to promote engagement and foster critical thinking skills in content area instruction. A discourse analysis of a seventh-grade social studies classroom revealed the level of sophistication reached through a detailed examination of the picture book *Discovering the Inca Ice Maiden* (Reinhard, 1998). The teacher used the content of the text and the illustrations to cultivate deep comprehension (Albright, 2002). The students in this study questioned assumptions about gender roles, made connections to the background knowledge they possessed, and generated questions about the text.

Although the evidence for using read alouds in secondary education is compelling, teachers may be confused about how to use them, and how to select effective materials. Albright and Ariail (2005) surveyed middle school teachers about their read-aloud practices. They were encouraged to learn that 86% of the study's participants read aloud to their students. The most common purpose cited was to model good reading behaviors such as pronunciation and inflection. Teachers frequently cited access and comprehension as other popular reasons. However, their text selections were somewhat constrained. The majority read aloud from the textbook, or read narrative chapter books to their students. Informational texts, newspapers, magazines, picture books, and poetry were rarely used (Albright & Ariail, 2005). This is unfortunate, because read alouds provide an opportunity to expose students to content that is multidimensional. This may reflect a widespread belief among secondary content teachers that the textbook is the sole source of written information in the classroom.

The successful use of read alouds in secondary content area classrooms has been well documented. They have been shown to be effective in foreign language instruction (Richardson, 1997–1998), social studies (Irvin, Lunstrum, Lynch-Brown, & Shepard, 1995), and mathematics (Richardson & Gross, 1997). However, text selection can be daunting for teachers unfamiliar with the range of possibilities associated with their discipline. It is important to note that read alouds in content area need not be confined to narrative text, or unrelated to the topic of study. In other words, we wouldn't advise the algebra teacher to read from *Canterbury Tales* (Chaucer, 1400/1985). However, that same algebra teacher might be interested in a read aloud from *The Number Devil* (Enzensberger, 1998) detailing the intricacies of irrational numbers, referred to by the title character as "unreasonable numbers." Several excellent teacher resources on text selection are available, including *The Read Aloud Handbook* (Trelease, 2006), a compilation of short stories, poems, and newspaper articles suitable for a number of classroom applications; and *Read It Aloud!* (Richardson, 2000) which is organized by secondary content areas, including mathematics, geography, music, physical education, and social studies.

READING

THE BENEFITS FOR ENGLISH LANGUAGE LEARNERS

English language learners benefit from exposure to read alouds as well. Adolescents acquiring a new language are subjected to a bewildering array of social, pragmatic, and academic language patterns (Nieto, 1992). Read alouds create opportunities for the teacher to use multiple pathways to promote understanding of the content of the text, including intonation, facial expressions, and gestures (Cummins, 1980).

Read alouds also support language acquisition for English language learners because they provide fluent language role models (Amer, 1997). The text choice for the read aloud is also crucial for English language learners. Selection of books that use engaging illustrations or photographs adds another dimension to assist students in creating new schema (Early & Tang, 1991).

Planning for Read Alouds in Secondary Classrooms

There are several elements to consider in planning and delivering read alouds to secondary students. These items also serve as indicators of effective instructional practice for administrative observations (Fisher, Flood, Lapp, & Frey, 2004).

1. *Select readings appropriate to content, students' emotional and social development, and interests.* Read alouds can be especially useful for activating prior knowledge and connecting to student experiences.

2. *Practice the selection.* You wouldn't go on stage without rehearsing, would you? Think of the read aloud as a performance. Rehearsal allows you to make decisions about inflection, rate, and pitch.

3. *Model fluent oral reading.* A read aloud serves as a place for students to hear fluent oral reading. Reading acquisition for students with reading difficulties and some English language learners can be inhibited by their own disfluent reading.

4. *Engage students and hook them into listening to the text.* Creating anticipation for the reading, as the teacher did in the *Midnight Ride of Paul Revere* scenario, can activate student interest and increase meaning. When appropriate, pair read alouds with other supporting materials such as props, diagrams, manipulatives, or illustrations.

5. *Stop periodically to ask questions.* Talk within the text enhances student understanding. Plan questions for critical thinking in advance and write them on a sticky note as a reminder. Don't rely only on "constrained questions" (Beck & McKeown, 2001) that can be answered in a few words. For example, "What do you believe was the author's purpose for writing this?" allows for a more detailed response than "Where did this take place?" Create inferential questions that invite connections beyond the text as well.

6. *Engage students in book discussions.* This is related to the questioning that is done during the reading. Choose read alouds that foster further discussion once the reading is complete. Perhaps you may ask students to consider why you chose this particular reading, and how it relates to the current topic of study.

7. *Make explicit connections to students' independent reading and writing.* A read aloud should relate directly to the content. It should also connect to other literacy experiences. For instance, the end of a read-aloud event might signal an ideal time to invite students to write a response. Questions raised through the discussion following the reading might prompt further research and outside reading by students.

Shared Reading

In addition to read alouds, teachers also extend literacy experiences through shared reading. Shared reading is the practice of reading collaboratively with students. Unlike read alouds, where only the teacher can see the text, an important feature of a shared reading experience is that students can follow along silently as the teacher reads aloud. Another difference is that in shared reading there is a lesson specifically related to a comprehension strategy, text feature, or reading behavior. As with read alouds, the practice of shared reading has its roots in emergent literacy practices for young children (Holdaway, 1982).

Shared reading serves as an instructional bridge between the teacher-directed read aloud and student-directed independent reading. Although read alouds are teacher controlled and independent reading is student controlled, these literacy activities provide little opportunity for teacher and students to alternatively take and relinquish the lead. Pearson and Gallagher (1983) proposed a model for comprehension instruction called the gradual release of responsibility. They suggest that using guided practice as a method for instruction allows students to attempt new strategies for eventual use in their own reading. Thus, through instructional practices like shared reading, teachers move from modeling in read alouds to applying strategies in independent reading.

Shared reading is grounded in the sociocultural theory of Vygotsky's zones of proximal development (1978). This allows for scaffolding of information to extend learning through guided instruction. Vygotsky theorized that when students receive support just beyond what they can accomplish independently, they learn new skills and concepts. He defined the zone as

> the distance between the actual developmental level as determined by independent problem solving and the level of potential development as determined through problem solving under adult guidance or in collaboration with peers. (p. 86)

The scaffolded instruction in shared reading extends students' learning because the learner receives immediate feedback and further prompts to arrive at solutions (Tharp & Gallimore, 1989). Students may not be able to initiate a new strategy alone, but they can easily apply one with guidance, further advancing their zone of proximal development.

Thus, shared reading events allow teachers to address comprehension strategies through modeling (Fisher, Frey, & Lapp, 2008). For instance, teachers who work with English language learners and students with reading difficulties recognize the power of a daily fluent reading model (Early, 1990). This allows teachers to model prosody (the use of rate, pitch, inflection, and tone) to demonstrate how markers such as punctuation influence meaning (Pynte & Prieur, 1996). Whereas read alouds also present opportunities for modeling prosody, they lack the visual prompts that signal fluent readers. Because students can see the text in shared reading, they can associate the punctuation, layout, spacing, phrase boundaries, and other text cues used by the teacher to make decisions about how the piece should be read and interpreted. Perhaps the most powerful endorsement of this effect comes from students.

Implementing Shared Reading

As with all instruction, practical application is as important as the theoretical underpinning. One of the first decisions teachers make in shared reading is how students will interact with the reading. Teachers employ several methods to share the text with students, such as using an interactive white board to display enlarged print on a screen.

This is particularly convenient with use of textbook passages, graphs, or charts. This technique also allows the teacher to highlight words or phrases using virtual markers. At other times, photocopies of a passage can be distributed to each student to encourage students to make notations directly on the paper. Although marking passages in a school textbook is usually discouraged for obvious reasons, this method provides students with guided practice for interacting with text. When teachers construct participatory approaches to text, they assist their students in moving away from ineffective beliefs about reading as a passive experience (Wade & Moje, 2000).

Selecting Texts for Shared Reading

Text choice is equally important in shared reading, and it differs on several levels from text choice for read alouds. Recall that a primary purpose for read alouds is to build prior knowledge, often through ancillary text that might otherwise be above the students' independent reading level. In shared reading, teachers focus on a comprehension strategy or a text feature that enables the learner to understand the content of the text. Therefore, the text selected should be at the independent or instructional level of the students. It should also offer the teacher an opportunity to discuss the identified strategy. Examples of comprehension strategies suitable for shared reading instruction include:

- inferencing,
- summarizing,
- self-questioning and self-monitoring,
- text structures (e.g., cause/effect, sequence, problem/solution),
- text features (e.g., headings and subheadings, captions, directions), and
- interpreting visual representations (charts, graphs, diagrams).

Notice that these comprehension strategies are not the exclusive domain of any one content area; rather, they transcend reading for meaning in any discipline, with any text. A more complete guide to comprehension strategies for use during shared reading can be found in Figure 4.1.

Want to discuss inferencing? Then choose a text that implies attitudes or opinions without stating them outright. Text features and interpretation of visual representations are easily modeled using the course textbook. Self-questioning and self-monitoring (that small insistent voice inside every fluent reader's head that

Figure 4.1 Reading comprehension glossary of terms.

Cause and effect—text structure used to explain the reasons and results of an event or phenomenon. Signal words for cause include *because, when, if, cause,* and *reason.* Words like *then, so, which, effect,* and *result* signal an effect.

Compare and contrast—text structure used to explain how two people, events, or phenomenon are alike and different. Some comparison signal words are *same, at the same time, like,* and *still.* Contrast signal words include *some, others, different, however, rather, yet, but,* and *or.*

Connecting—linking information in the text to personal experiences, prior knowledge, or other texts. This is commonly taught using three categories:

- Text to self—personal connections
- Text to text—connections to other books, films, and so on
- Text to world—connections to events in the past or present

Determining importance—a comprehension strategy used by readers to differentiate between essential information and interesting (but less important) details.

Evaluating—the reader makes judgments about the information being read, including its credibility, usefulness to the reader's purpose, and quality.

Inferencing—the ability to "read between the lines," to extract information not directly stated in the text. Inferencing is linked to a student's knowledge of vocabulary, content, context, recognition of clues in the text, and experiences.

Monitoring and clarifying—an ongoing process used by the reader to ensure that what is being read is also being understood. When the reader recognizes that something is unclear, he or she uses a variety of clarifying strategies, including rereading, asking questions, and seeking information from another source.

Predicting—the reader uses his or her understanding of language, content, and context to anticipate what will be read next. Prediction occurs continually during reading, but it is most commonly taught as a prereading strategy.

Problem/solution—text structure used to explain a challenge and the measures taken to address the challenge. Signal words for a problem include *trouble, challenge, puzzle, difficulty, problem, question,* or *doubt.* Authors use signal words for a solution like *answer, discovery, improve, solution, overcome, resolve, response,* or *reply.*

Question-answer relationship (QAR)—Question-answer relationships were developed to help readers understand where information can be located. There are four types of questions in two categories.

1. *In the Text*—these answers are "book" questions because they are drawn directly from the text. These are sometimes referred to as *text-explicit* questions:
   - *Right there*—the answer is located in a single sentence in the text.
   - *Think and search*—the answer is in the text but is spread across several sentences or paragraphs.
2. *In Your Head*—these answers are "brain" questions because the reader must generate some or all of the answer. These are sometimes called *text-implicit* questions:
   - Author and you—the reader combines information from the text with other experiences and prior knowledge to answer the question.
   - On your own—the answer is not in the text and is based on your experiences and prior knowledge.

(continued)

|Figure 4.1   *Continued.*

> **Questioning**—a strategy used by readers to question the text and themselves. These self-generated questions keep the reader interested and are used to seek information. Specific types of questioning includes QAR, QtA, and ReQuest. **Questioning the author (QtA)**—an instructional activity that invites readers to formulate questions for the author of the text. The intent of this strategy is to foster critical literacy by personalizing the reading experience as they consider where the information in the textbook came from and what the author's intent, voice, and perspectives might be.
>
> **Synthesizing**—the reader combines new information with prior knowledge to create original ideas.
>
> **Summarizing**—the ability to condense a longer piece of text into a shorter statement. Summarizing occurs throughout a reading, not just at the end.
>
> **Temporal sequence**—a text structure used to describe a series of events using a chronology. Signal words and phrases include *first, second, last, finally, next, then, since, soon, previously, before, after, meanwhile, at the same time*, and *at last.* Days of the week, dates, and times are also used to show a temporal sequence.
>
> **Visualizing**—a comprehension strategy used by the reader to create mental images of what is being read.

Source: Language Arts Workshop: Purposeful Reading and Writing Instruction by N. Frey and D. Fisher, 2006, Upper Saddle River, NJ: Merrill/Prentice Hall. Used with permission.

keeps asking "Does this make sense?") can be demonstrated through the teacher's own questions as a reading is shared. If the word "ancillary" in the previous paragraph was a little vague to you (and you noticed) then you are self-monitoring.

Here are guidelines for successfully implementing a shared reading so that students will learn both the content of the text and strategies for reading with meaning.

1. *Choose text that is appropriate for the purpose.* In the case of shared readings, not only should the text be associated with the content of the class, but it should also provide clear illustrations of the strategy or reading behavior being modeled. For example, a passage about how the biceps muscle of the arm contracts to move a lever (the radius) on a fulcrum (the elbow) is an excellent example of cause-and-effect text, especially if it contains signal words like *accordingly, therefore, as a result,* or *because.*

2. *Make the purpose of the reading explicit.* If you are modeling a particular strategy, tell your students what it is before you read. Remind them each time you model the strategy.

3. *Decide how the text will be accessible to all students.* If you are projecting the reading, make sure the font is large enough for those in the back row to read. If they are reading from paper, make sure there are enough copies.

4. *Scaffold, scaffold, scaffold.* This is the foundation of shared reading. Don't assume that they "got it"—teach the strategy or reading behavior explicitly and provide multiple examples. Then have them do it with you during the course of the reading. This leads to the last element of a shared reading . . . .

5. *Make sure students are aware of what they are supposed to do with the new knowledge.* A frustration of teachers is that students ask questions like "Is this going to be on the test?" when the teacher really wanted them to see the

usefulness and practicality of what they had been taught. Our experience has been that when students ask questions like this, it is because we have not made it clear what they should do with the new information. After you have modeled a strategy, and given them guided practice in using the strategy, you must connect it to their independent reading. When students can apply the strategy independently, the instructional cycle of shared reading is complete.

Many teachers use shared readings to demonstrate a *think-aloud* technique for explicit modeling (Davey, 1983). A think aloud is a metacognitive process that allows students to hear what goes on "inside the head" of a fluent reader. When using a think aloud, the teacher interjects questions and statements from his or her mind as the text is read aloud. Think alouds are worded in the first person, so that the teacher can discuss what he or she is thinking about at that time. For example, if the purpose of the shared reading is to model how a reader handles the vocabulary of a reading in 2-D art, the teacher might pause at the word *chiaroscuro* and state, "That's a word I've heard before, but I can't remember what it means. It sounds Italian. I'm going to look in the glossary to remind myself of the definition." This think aloud demonstrates to art students a useful strategy for handling a difficult word in the textbook. Figure 4.2 provides more tips for successful think alouds.

We've discussed read alouds and shared reading at length, and have examined both the research and the practical considerations for implementing both in the classroom. Now let's look inside classrooms to see how teachers apply these instructional strategies in the content area.

Strategies at Work

Read Alouds and Shared Reading in English

Read alouds can be effectively used throughout the period to introduce a new topic at the beginning of class, to emphasize a discussion point by returning to quote a text passage, or to end the period with well-crafted prose. Many teachers see this time as an opportunity to hone their students' critical thinking skills. Read alouds and shared readings are used regularly throughout units of instruction to engage and model comprehension. This gives the teacher opportunities to demonstrate how these comprehension tools are used throughout a reading.

DR-TA in English. The complex processes of reading require strategies to be practiced before, during, and after reading. The *Directed Reading-Thinking Activity (DR-TA)* is an excellent instructional tool for modeling these reading processes during shared reading using either expository or narrative text. DR-TA allows the readers to increase their metacognitive skills so that they become aware of their own thinking processes and develop the ability to regulate, evaluate, and monitor them. These strategies can be learned if they are explicitly explained, modeled, and regularly included in literacy instruction (Helfeldt & Henk, 1990). This is accomplished through a cycle of questioning that helps readers become aware of the strategies they can activate to support their comprehension.

Figure 4.2   Tips for effective think alouds.

Choose a short piece of text.

Think alouds are often the most effective when they are focused and well paced. A brief think aloud delivered using a passage of one to four paragraphs will have more impact because student interest is maintained. As well, it prevents the temptation to model too many strategies.

Let the text tell you what to do.

Don't plan to think aloud using cold text, because your teaching points will be unfocused. Read the text several times and make notes about the comprehension strategies you are using to understand. These will provide you with ideas for the content of your think aloud. Annotate the text so you will have something to refer to as you read.

Keep your think alouds authentic.

It can be a little disconcerting to say aloud what's going on in your head. Most teachers adopt a conversational tone that mirrors the informal language people use when they are thinking. An overly academic tone will sound contrived. It's better to say, "Hey—when I read this part about the penguins, right away I saw a penguin in my mind," rather than, "I am metacognitively aware and activated my visualizing strategy to formulate an image of a penguin as I read that paragraph."

Think like a scientist, mathematician, historian, artist, literary critic . . . .

Your shared reading texts are chosen because they have content value. Thinking aloud doesn't mean that everyone suddenly has to be a reading or English teacher. Make your think alouds authentic by telling students how you process text through the lens of *your* content expertise. This elevates the think aloud because you are showing them how your understanding of content text is influenced by what you know about the content.

Tell them what you did.

Using an authentic voice doesn't mean you can't name the strategy. Tell your students what strategy you used to help you comprehend. This allows them to begin to form schemas about reading comprehension. Underline or highlight words or phrases that helped you understand and encourage students to do likewise, if possible.

Resist the urge to "overthink."

The meaning of the passage should not be sacrificed for the sake of the think aloud. Don't insert so many think alouds into the reading that the intended message is lost. Fewer well-crafted think alouds will have far more impact than a stream-of-consciousness rap that leaves the students bewildered by what just happened.

Stauffer (1969) describes DR-TA in three basic steps: predicting, reading, and proving. Students are instructed to continually ask themselves three questions:

- What do I think about this?
- Why do I think so?
- How can I prove it?

At each segment of the text, the readers predict aloud, read to confirm, stop, and engage in the self-questioning. The DR-TA assists students in recognizing that the text is split into sections that build upon each other (Richardson & Morgan, 1994). Because the text is divided into smaller portions, students can focus on the process of responding to higher-order questions. Students make predictions about specific sections of the text and then read the next segment to confirm or alter their predictions.

The segmentation of the text is a critical part of teacher preparation for a DR-TA. This chunking of text information is a distinctive element of critical thinking instruction because it allows the reader to concentrate on both larger concepts and smaller supporting details. To prepare a content area reading for your students, read the text closely to determine where the natural stopping points are located. These may occur at the end of a paragraph, or before a major heading. We've included a teacher preparation checklist to assist you in preparing a DR-TA lesson (Figure 4.3).

A typical sequence of instruction for a DR-TA looks like this:

1. *Activate background knowledge.* The teacher elicits purposeful predictions to explore the students' prior knowledge relative to the reading assignment by asking questions about the title, headings, and any charts or pictures featured in the reading. Prediction or speculation aids students in setting a purpose for reading and increases their attention to text objectives and their motivation to read (Nichols, 1983). These prereading questions also serve to activate and build background knowledge (Nessel, 1988). The new text is discussed with regard to the previous assignments so that the students can make relevant connections. Students may be invited to write their predictions, which are reviewed and shared after the reading.

2. *Develop vocabulary.* It is essential that vocabulary is introduced prior to reading. Students need multiple opportunities to read and use new words so that they can learn how they relate conceptually to one another. By introducing vocabulary at the beginning of a DR-TA, you are signaling readers to their importance to the piece of text being examined.

3. *Identify significant patterns of text organization.* Some patterns are cause/effect, description, problem/solution, temporal sequence, and compare/contrast. Students can scan text quickly to determine what general text structures they should anticipate. Examples of various text structures can be found in Figure 4.4.

4. *Ask springboard questions.* Ask questions that align with the purpose for reading and focus the students' thinking before reading. Prepare questions that target some of the main ideas of the reading, and use their predictive questions as well. Craft questions that are not readily answered in a few words, but rather are higher level in nature. Students will revisit these questions as they read, supporting their search for possible answers. We have found it helpful to post these springboard questions on the board so that students can refer to them during the reading.

5. *Read the selection.* Identify the stopping points in the passage for students to use during the DR-TA. Remind them that they will read the text and monitor their own comprehension using the three central DR-TA questions: What do I think about this? Why do I think so? How I can prove it? These questions scaffold students' self-regulation of metacognitive strategies while reading. While the students are reading, circulate and assist students in making notes that answer these questions.

6. *Review, reinforce, and evaluate.* After the reading is completed, have students move into small discussion groups and share their predictions. In particular, they should focus on the revisions they made to their predictions, and

Figure 4.3   Directed reading-thinking activity planning guide.

DR-TA Planning Guide
Teacher: _____   Date: _____ Name of text: _____
Lesson focus: *What will students know and be able to do?*
Introduce the text: *How will I establish the purpose of the reading?*
Vocabulary: *What is the relevant vocabulary?* *How will I teach it?*
Engagement: *What is my springboard question?*
Survey the text: *What are the text features I will emphasize?*
Read the text: *Where will I chunk the text?*
Cycle of questioning: *What do you think? Why do you think that? How can you prove it?*
Check for understanding: *What questions will I ask?*

what parts of the reading led them to those revisions. Lead the whole class in a discussion of the springboard questions and ask students to support their responses using the text. Additional questions are likely to evolve, and should be connected to further reading or projects related to the content.

Figure 4.4   Common expository text structures.

Common Expository Text Structures

The most common types of informational or expository text structures include:

- Exemplification (concept/definition)
- Compare/contrast
- Cause/effect
- Problem/solution
- Sequential or temporal

Exemplification text describes people, places, or phenomena. Nearly all informational texts have passages that are descriptive in nature. Signal words for exemplification text structures include descriptive adjectives, adverbs, and phrases. For instance, the life of a soldier in the Civil War wasn't merely difficult:

> Confederate as well as Union soldiers endured <u>unimaginable</u> conditions. <u>Basic</u> necessities such as shoes, blankets, and equipment were in <u>desperately short supply</u>. Famished Confederate soldiers separated from their units were often <u>forced to steal or beg food</u> from <u>equally hungry Southern sympathizers</u>. Advances in weaponry inflicted <u>horrific</u> injuries on the battlefield, and both sides suffered <u>terrible</u> casualties as men died due to <u>lack of adequate medical care</u>.

Compare/contrast text structures also rely on descriptive text, but instead explain how two or more people, places, or phenomena are similar or different. As with exemplification, most textbooks contain some compare/contrast passages as well. Signal words such as *although, both, yet, while, however, same/different, like/ unlike,* and other words that show opposites are likely to appear.

> Black as well as white men fought for the Union cause. <u>However</u>, black soldiers were paid less than were whites. <u>Unlike</u> whites, these free black men were permitted to work only as laborers.

Cause/effect text structures, which show the causal relationships between phenomena, can be deceptively similar to compare/contrast, but their signal words give them away. Words such as *since, because, as a result,* and *if . . . then* statements are frequently seen in these passages.

> <u>Because</u> nearly all the battles of the Civil War were fought in Confederate territory, Southern states suffered great losses in its infrastructure.

Another text structure is *problem/solution*. Seen frequently in mathematics textbooks, they contain signal words such as *question, answer, thus, accordingly,* and *decide*. A challenge of problem/solution text is that it is subtler than some of the others and may develop over the course of several sentences or paragraphs.

> In the summer after the war's end, a series of black codes were passed by Southern states. These codes were meant to preserve a form of enslavement so that the traditional Southern way of life would not change. Radical Republicans saw these black codes as <u>problematic</u> because they took away freedoms that had been fought for in the war. <u>Accordingly</u>, they worked together to pass the Civil Rights Act. They <u>decided</u> to propose an amendment to the Constitution to make sure the law could not be overturned. <u>Thus</u>, the Fourteenth Amendment was passed into law.

More easy to detect are *sequential* or *temporal* (time-based) structures. These passages use chronology or a sequence of events to inform the reader. Common signal words related to sequential or temporal text jump out for most readers and include words such as *first, next, last, before, afterward, another,* and *finally.*

> Many enslaved people in the South were forced to pick cotton. This was difficult work, and people suffered greatly. <u>First</u>, an enslaved person had to bend down to grasp the plant. <u>Next</u> the fluffy cotton had to be pulled by hand from the sticky boll that held the fibers. <u>After</u> the heavy sack was full, it had to be dragged to the scales to be weighed. <u>Finally</u>, after 16 hours of toil in the fields, the workers were allowed a small bit of food and rest before beginning again at dawn.

READING

Lee Mongrue knows that read alouds and shared readings offer him powerful tools for creating interest and modeling reading comprehension strategies. He began a unit using a read-aloud technique to introduce his ninth-grade English class to *I Know Why the Caged Bird Sings* (Angelou, 1969). "Our next unit of study will focus on the essential question, 'Why is change necessary, and how does it affect people?' You'll be reading several titles in our literature circles, but our central text will be Angelou's book." Mr. Mongrue uses a central text with the entire class in each unit of study, reading it through a combination of read alouds and shared readings. He also divides his class into smaller groups, called literature circles. Each group is assigned a different text that is related to the essential question. By doing this, he can differentiate the reading levels of his class because he knows that all of his students are not able to read the same book at the same time.

The teacher begins by projecting an image of the front cover of the book to his students. He asks them to talk to a partner to describe what they see. His students describe the arresting image of the author, seemingly gazing directly at the viewer. Many students use words such as *proud* and *confident* to describe the award-winning author. "Wow, that's perfect. *I Know Why the Caged Bird Sings* is her autobiography of her early life. But this woman underwent many changes in her life. You'll hear of her childhood longing to wake up as a white girl. Keep that in mind as I read aloud the prelude." Mr. Mongrue reads the first four pages of the book, the author's recount of a painful Easter Sunday memory of self-loathing and shame as she unsuccessfully attempted to flee the church to use the bathroom. He read the last lines of the prelude quietly. "If growing up is painful for a Southern Black girl, being aware of her displacement is the rust on the razor that threatens the throat. It is an unnecessary insult" (p. 4). He glances at the sticky note he had prepared to remind himself of his teaching points. Using stickies in books allows teachers to plan questions in advance, as well as ensure a natural stopping point. "That's a metaphor. What does she mean when she refers to 'the rust on the razor'?" For the next 10 minutes, students discussed the literal and figurative meaning of the metaphor, with the teacher leading them back to the essential question. "This girl seems so far removed from the woman on the front cover. As we read this each day, let's consider the issue of change in her life, and in our own lives."

He then began a DR-TA to model reading comprehension strategies he knew his students would need to use in their literature circles. He began by returning to his essential question, which he is using as a springboard for discussion. "Can you think of a time when your life changed, and it was not of your own choosing?" he asks.

Corrine immediately put her hand in the air. "I had to change schools in sixth grade when my family moved to another apartment," she remarked. "It was hard."

Gregorio offered, "My parents split up." Many other students nod.

"Man, we all had to come to ninth grade!" Kevin smiles.

"You're so right," Mr. Mongrue says. "Many of you have been through lots of changes, and they weren't of your choice. Can you remember how you felt at the time? You don't have to say it out loud; just think for a moment about that time." After a minute or so of silence, the teacher asks his students to recall those emotions as he begins a shared reading of the first chapter of the central text for this unit.

Mr. Mongrue introduces a few vocabulary words needed for the reading, including *segregated*, *affluent*, and *prophesied*, then places a copy of the first page on the overhead. "You'll remember that when we do a DR-TA, it's to focus on how we monitor our understanding as we read. That means pausing from time to time to think about what we know, and making predictions about what the author will tell us next. I've drawn a line at various points so we can stop to talk about what we know and what we expect. These are the kinds of thinking strategies you should be using when you read independently."

For the next 20 minutes, Mr. Mongrue conducts a shared reading, pausing at predetermined times to engage in a cycle of questioning with his students. He begins by asking them what they know so far in the reading. This allows students to summarize their understanding about Angelou's early memories of being sent to Stamp, Arkansas, to live with her grandmother. He asks them to cite evidence in the text to support their answers, which proves to be of great assistance to the struggling readers in the class. Mr. Mongrue then invites them to make predictions based on their knowledge thus far. Some of them predict that things will turn out badly, because she was placed on a train at the age of 3 with a ticket and a name tag pinned to her coat.

Mr. Mongrue knows that with each round of questions, he is encouraging students to make predictions, analyze information, and monitor their understanding. When they reach the end of this short chapter, he tells them, "Remember, this is what you need to do when you are reading your lit circle books independently. Are you ready to get your books now?" With that, the teacher distributes copies of *Looking for Alaska* (Green, 2005), *Shattering Glass* (Giles, 2002), *Godless* (Hautman, 2004), *Al Capone Does My Shirts* (Choldenko, 2004), *The Breadwinner* (Ellis, 2000), and *Who Am I Without Him?* (Flake, 2004). These books offer a range of text difficulty, which will meet the diverse needs of learners in his class. In addition, he has chosen these books because they are told from the perspective of a younger person going through a painful life change. Mr. Mongrue later remarked, "I really like using read alouds so that they can hear the words of a skilled writer. I use the DR-TAs because I want to get them in the habit of monitoring their understanding as they read. I've found that interspersing the DR-TAs with their independent reading has made their literature circle conversations much richer. I have to chuckle when I hear a 14-year-old say, 'How can you prove that?' It's like I'm hearing myself!"

Shared Reading in Mathematics

A critical aspect of reading is *fluency*, the ability to decode and understand words, sentences, and paragraphs in a way that is smooth and accurate. Fluency is closely related to the concept of prosody discussed earlier in this chapter. Whereas the rate of reading alone is not the only indicator of a good reader, consider the labored reading of a struggling student (Rasinski, Padak, McKeon, Wilfong, Friedauer, & Heim, 2005). When reading is choppy and disfluent, it becomes difficult to attend to the message behind the words. Meaning for the reader (and listener) is lost in a string of pauses, false starts, and hesitations.

Rereading. An effective instructional strategy for building fluency is repeated readings (Mastropieri, Leinart, & Scruggs, 1999). Repeated readings are just that— the repeated reading of the same text passage. There is a great deal of evidence to suggest that repeated readings lead to a practice effect. If you are skeptical, try it yourself. Select a passage from this chapter and read it aloud for 1 minute—be sure to time yourself. When the timer rings, count the number of words you read and record it. Now read the same passage again, beginning at the same starting point, and count the number of words you read during this second 1-minute interval.

Repeat this cycle one more time and then compare your results. If you are like most readers, you read more words at cycle 3 than you did at cycle 1. Many of you may have read more during each cycle.

If you completed the above exercise, then you have also identified a difficulty with repeated readings. Many students, and especially adolescents, are not terribly motivated to reread. In fact, we often hear them say something like "I read this before! Why do I have to read it again?" Indeed, less able readers often believe that any text needs to be read only once, with no new information to be gained from subsequent readings (Alvermann, 1988). However, fluent adolescent readers recognize that rereading is an important tool for comprehending text, especially dense content area readings (Faust & Glenzer, 2000).

Reader's Theatre. A popular method for engaging in repeated readings to build fluency and comprehension is Reader's Theatre (Rasinski & Padak, 2005). Reader's Theatre is the public performance of a scripted text, but unlike traditional theatre, the lines are not memorized, and props, movement, and other acting devices are not used. Instead, students read the text using prosodic elements while their classmates follow along silently using their own copies.

The success of Reader's Theatre for promoting repeated reading and conversations about meaning seems to be related to the performance itself. Think about what motivates you—if you know that you will be presenting an oral reading for your peers, you are probably going to rehearse, reread, and discuss the methods of performance with your fellow actors. That is precisely what happened in Aaron Sage's 10th-grade algebra class.

Reader's Theatre in Mathematics. Toward the end of the semester, Mr. Sage needed to prepare students for the end-of-course examination. He used a number of different review techniques, including structured study groups and student presentations.

However, he also recognized that it was important to interject some novelty and inventiveness in the review. To do so, Mr. Sage used the book *Math Talk* (Pappas, 1991), an innovative collection of poems of mathematical concepts, written to be read by two voices (or two sets of voices). Mr. Sage began by showing the students a large strip of paper connected to form a continuous band, with a single twist in the loop. With great flourish, he cut the strip down the center, producing not two thinner strips as many had predicted, but rather one larger loop. He then read aloud the poem "Mobius Strip" with another teacher and explained the mathematics behind the phenomenon.

Next, he divided the class into five groups of students. Each group was assigned a poem to perform. In addition to performing the poem, they were also to explain the mathematical concepts represented by their poem. The poems he chose for this lesson addressed concepts studied during the semester, including square roots, radicals, integers, variables, and imaginary numbers. He included an advance organizer for each group that summarized the main concepts of their assigned poem.

Students rehearsed for 30 minutes or so, and Mr. Sage noted that they repeatedly returned to the text, their notes, the advance organizer, and the algebra textbook in order to support their understanding. After sufficient rehearsal, each group performed their poem, which was displayed on an overhead for all to see. They ended their performance with a review of the selected mathematical concept.

Mr. Sage later remarked, "There's no way I would have gotten any of them to read about square roots for half an hour straight, let alone talk about it with their classmates. I think this activity really gave them a different way to find out what they know."

The use of read alouds and Reader's Theatre was not simply something that Mr. Sage's students experienced at the end of the school year in preparation for their exams. Mr. Sage and his colleagues in the math department regularly read aloud. For example, Mr. Sage starts his school year with a read aloud of *A Gebra Named Al* (Isdell, 1993), a novel in which students are transported to an imaginary land where orders of operations are real places and fruits that resemble Bohr models grow on chemistrees. In addition to a number of newspaper and magazine articles in which mathematics is featured, Mr. Sage's students explored exponential growth with *One Grain of Rice* (Demi, 1997), struggles with math in *Math Curse* (Scieszka, 1995), math riddles in *The Grapes of Math* (Tang, 2001), math in the world via *Fractals, Googols, and Other Mathematical Tales* (Pappas, 1993), and were introduced to their future geometry class with *Sir Cumference and the First Round Table* (Neuschwander, 1997).

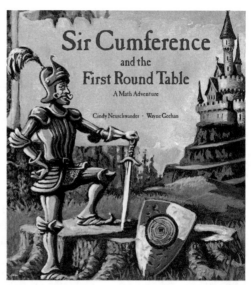

Shared Reading and Think Alouds in Social Studies

U.S. history teacher Tom Fehrenbacher uses shared readings to introduce important topics that students will read more about during their reciprocal teaching group sessions. Mr. Fehrenbacher started the conversation with his students with these questions posted on the board: "Do police stop some people more often than others? Does a person's racial identity, clothes, gender, or age make him or her more likely to be questioned by the police?"

After a partner discussion in which students shared their thinking with one another, Mr. Fehrenbacher asked for comments from the whole class.

"Of course they do. You can get in trouble just for 'driving while black.'" Melissa responds. The class laughs.

"So, you believe that African Americans get stopped by the police more often than others do." Mr. Fehrenbacher rephrases Melissa's remark, while posing another. "Is that the only group?"

"No. So do Mexican kids."

"Asians, too."

"So we can say that different ethnic and racial groups can be profiled. Is that right? Do clothes make a difference? Does the person's age or gender matter?" Mr. Fehrenbacher continues.

"Sure. If you're young they're going to pick on you."

"Yah. Just cuz you're young, everyone is always thinking you're trouble." Others in the room join in agreement. Mr. Fehrenbacher brings the class back to a focus. "Is that all?"

"Well, they might pick on guys more."

"Anything else?"

The class pauses and Mr. Fehrenbacher asks,

"How about the way you are dressed? Can that make a difference? If you are wearing baggy clothes, got a couple of tattoos, decked out in jewelry, would that attract the police's attention?" Accountable talk around the students' writing continues in the classroom. As it does, Mr. Fehrenbacher moves the lesson closer to the selected text—an editorial taken from the local newspaper titled "A Case of Racial Profiling."

"Today we are going to look at the case of a hiphop star who got some serious questioning from our local police. To do this we are going to use reciprocal teaching. I'll start by reading the first paragraph and discussing with you the four reciprocal teaching questions posted on the board. Then, I'd like to get some volunteers to come forward to do the next paragraph as a fish bowl for the class. After that, I'd like the entire class to get into groups to try it on their own."

As Mr. Fehrenbacher reads the first paragraph, the students follow handouts of the text. After finishing the passage, Mr. Fehrenbacher refers to his first reciprocal teaching question. "What's that about?" Students provide their views as Mr. Fehrenbacher guides and confirms. When the shared reading portion is done, four volunteers come to the front of the room. They repeat and model the process before the rest of the class. Soon everyone is placed into group and leaders are appointed. With everyone reminded of the task ahead, Mr. Fehrenbacher's classroom goes to work.

At the end of the reading. Mr. Fehrenbacher's students write "zinger questions." These questions are based on the reading and are thrown at another group during the whole-class discussion. Groups receive points if they can stump another group or the teacher with a question on the reading. Of course Mr. Fehrenbacher has guidelines for the zinger questions that ensure the questions are fair, thought-provoking, and are based on the reading. He also requires that the groups write their question and the answer in advance.

Recommendations for using reciprocal teaching in the secondary classroom based on the experiences in Mr. Fehrenbacher's class and those of other teachers can be found in Figure 4.5.

Shared Reading in Science

Many content area textbooks contain a great deal of technical information that is presented in tables, photographs, diagrams, and graphs. This is especially true of science textbooks, where students frequently misinterpret complicated diagrams, thus leading them to incorrect conclusions (Wheeler & Hill, 1990). However, because of the complex concepts inherent in science, much of the information needs to be presented in the form of a diagram.

Could you imagine learning the elements without a periodic table? Science teachers recognize the role of literacy for science students, especially as it applies to interpreting diagrams and drawings (Grant & Fisher, 2010). In many secondary science classrooms, teachers explicitly instruct on graph and diagram interpretation. Antoinette Linton, a 10th-grade biology teacher, also cites testing concerns. "These are just the kinds of things that are on the Golden State Exams (a subject area test for merit scholarships). I've got to make sure they can read and interpret these properly. That's how you think like a researcher."

During a unit on genetics, Ms. Linton reviewed diagrams and tables for displaying scientific information. The students were expected to write a research paper on the ethics of genetic engineering as a final project. Included in the project

|Figure 4.5 Recommendations for using reciprocal teaching.

1. Begin reciprocal teaching with a shared reading. This ensures that students understand the purpose for the reading and know that the teacher cares about the material to be covered.

2. Establish clear group work expectations. Reciprocal teaching is best accomplished in classrooms that regularly practice effective group work. Students should be used to working with a group leader and participating in different roles within their group. Classroom management procedures need to be in place to move students effectively into their groups. In addition, teachers should provide ongoing instruction for working groups and check for understanding throughout the task through report outs or written work.

3. Provide a model for the type of group work that is to be done. Regular use of a "fish bowl" in which the whole class (and the teacher) observes the group will help ensure that group work is effective and efficient. Fish bowls also allow the teacher to gauge if the text is too difficult or not interesting. If this is the case, the teacher may have to provide additional scaffolding of the text to ensure comprehension.

4. Consistently implement the reciprocal teaching cycle. The following steps encapsulate the basic concepts of reciprocal teaching into a simplified process that students can easily accomplish.

   - Read.
   - What's that about? (Question)
   - What don't you understand? (Clarify)
   - What is our summary bullet? (Summarize)
   - What's going to happen next? (Predict)
   - Read.

5. Use "zinger questions" to keep students motivated in their reading. An expectation is that groups write both the question and the answer in advance, before posing it to another group.

READING

were the results from a number of labs, including karyotyping, probability, and bird adaptations. Because of the technical nature of these labs, the results needed to be displayed as graphs, diagrams, and tables, with support and explanation in the text. She used a chapter on Mendel's law of heredity from another textbook because the visuals offered good examples for her shared reading lesson. She reminded her students that the purpose of displaying data is to compare or to show relationships. She then put a variety of tables from the chapter on the overhead and discussed the characteristics of good visuals, especially the importance of labels and captions. She displayed a series of diagrams from the chapter, including a flowchart illustrating the genetic changes in four generations of beans. With a copy of the diagrams and charts in front of them, they interpreted the displayed data. In cases where the tables or diagrams were ambiguous, they made changes to improve the ease of readability.

Ms. Linton later noted that the shared reading about displaying data was particularly useful in the students' final projects. "After all," she said "what good is knowing all the information if you can't use it?"

In her science class, Donna Jeffers uses shared readings to introduce scientific vocabulary and academic language to her students. As she completes her shared readings using a data projector, Ms. Jeffers embeds definitions and her thinking of the words the author uses. For example, as she was reading about the law of universal gravitation, she underlined key terms and explained them. Part of her shared reading sounded like this (from Glencoe Science, 2007):

What the text said	What Ms. Jeffers added
In the 17th century, Isaac Newton was thinking about gravity.	Ah yes, gravity. We've all heard about it, right? Gravity is a force that we've studied before. Let's remind our partners what we know about gravity. [Students talk in pairs.] I heard lots of you talking about gravity being an attractive force. Does that mean it looks good?
He wondered if the motion of falling objects and the motion of the Moon around Earth are caused by the same type of force.	Motion. Force. Let's see, I know that motion is movement and a force is something that can change or produce motion. So, Newton wondered if the way things fall, like this pen to the ground [drops her pen], is similar to the relationship between the Moon and Earth.

Ms. Jeffers knows that, over time, her frontloading of vocabulary and the partner discussions she facilitates will ensure that her students become better readers of scientific information and that they will have a deeper understanding of the content.

Read Alouds and Shared Reading in Electives

Sheryl Segal teaches an elective class titled "Tutoring and Mentoring." This class offers a unique opportunity for students to improve their literacy skills by helping others. In addition to supporting their own academic growth, students in the course earn internship hours. Ms. Segal "sells" the course to prospective participants by telling them "you'll learn something about yourself, too." Each morning, her students go to nearby elementary schools to teach younger students.

A Rationale for Cross-Age Tutoring. Cross-age peer tutoring involves an older student, under a teacher's guidance, who helps younger students learn or practice a skill or concept (Giesecke, 1993; Heron, Villareal, Yao, Christianson, & Heron, 2006). Though features vary from program to program, all cross-age tutoring programs provide individualized and personal attention, high levels of interaction, and immediate feedback. The effects of cross-age peer tutoring on the older student are particularly intriguing. A study of 21 adolescents participating in a cross-age peer tutoring program found significant growth in the tutors' reading scores on standardized measures (Jacobson, Thrope, Fisher, Lapp, Frey, & Flood, 2001). According to Gaustad (1993) and Cobb (1998), cross-age tutoring is beneficial because the process allows tutors expanded opportunities to review material, reiterate the purpose of the assignment, and expand their communication skills. A meta-analysis of 65 studies on cross-age tutoring revealed that the practice of students helping one another enhanced classroom instruction and led to higher academic achievement (Cohen, Kulik, & Kulik, 1982). Through purposeful engagement, cross-age tutoring provides the older learners with an authentic reason for practicing in order to improve their reading performance (Haluska & Gillen, 1995; Juel, 1991). Tutoring has been shown to be effective within classrooms as well. Referred to as peer tutoring, classmates are paired to support each other's learning and problem solving. In addition, cross-age or peer tutoring has been found to promote positive reading attitudes and habits (Caserta-Henry, 1996; Newell, 1996). Cohen (1986) suggests that the act of planning instruction for another aids the student in understanding the text.

Student-Conducted Read Alouds and Shared Readings. An understanding of the reading process is essential in Ms. Segal's tutoring and mentoring class. Students begin the year with study on the characteristics of effective teachers and development of a personal goals statement. They receive instruction on read alouds and shared reading techniques, principles of reading, and child development. Because they work with emergent and early readers, they pay particular attention to directionality, accessing prior information, rereading for fluency, making predictions, and phonics.

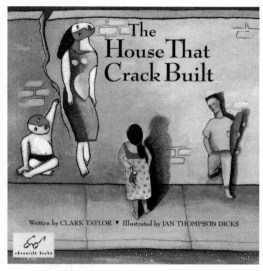

Source: From The House That Crack Built © 1992 by Clark Taylor; Illustrations © 1992 by Jan Thompson Dicks. Used with permission from Chronicle Books LLC, San Francisco.

In addition to working with the younger students, Ms. Segal also emphasizes their own literacy development, particularly through writing. Tutors are expected to maintain reflective journals, develop lessons, and communicate with the elementary teacher. They also propose and write a research paper on a topic related to their experience. Students wrote papers such as "Reading Strategies at the Elementary Level," "Motivation for Mentoring," and "The Impact of Inspirational and Motivating Teachers."

Possibly the favorite project of the class is the picture book they create for their tutee. The tutors develop a story, edit, illustrate, and publish a picture book that they give to their elementary student to keep. The process of bringing a picture book to publication is an involved one, and students conduct research on what makes a picture book appropriate and effective for read alouds and shared reading. Their own experiences with interacting with a large volume of picture books over the course of the year also contributes to their understanding of good children's literature. Layout, print size, and complexity of language must all be considered. Illustrations should support and advance the story. And of course, these books are designed with a particular student in mind. Background knowledge and interests play an important role in shaping the text. Picture books produced have included stories on friendship, how to operate the Wii, and skateboarding. An especially creative young man known widely for his interest in graffiti crafted a story about a boy who learned to write through tagging! (Don't worry—the book's message also emphasized the importance of tagging only where it is invited.)

In addition to teaching middle and high school students to conduct read alouds and shared reading in a cross-age tutoring class, there are numerous examples of electives teachers who regularly conduct shared readings and read alouds with their students.

- Danny Timothy, a physical education teacher, read *Wilma Unlimited* (Krull, 2000) to his students. This motivational piece explores the life of Wilma Rudolph who became the fastest female runner.

READING

- Art teacher Valerie Madrigal shared the book *When Pigasso Met Mootise* (Laden, 1998), a humorous look at the lives of Picasso and Matisse. She also read *Lives of the Artists: Masterpieces, Messes (and What the Neighbors Thought)* (Krull, 1995), which provides humorous biographies of a number of artists, and *My Name Is Georgia* (Winter, 1998), which focuses on the life of Georgia O'Keeffe.

- Health education teacher Jeffery Johnson read *The House That Crack Built* (Taylor, 1992) to introduce the impact that drug abuse has on a community.

- Family and consumer sciences teacher Pam Dahlin regularly reads recipes aloud and then shares her thinking about the vocabulary used (e.g., *zest*), the possible complications (e.g., forgetting to fold in the eggs so the cake won't rise), and potential alternatives to reduce the fat or calories.

Conclusion

Read alouds and shared reading are two instructional practices borrowed from elementary reading practice and customized for secondary content area use. A read aloud is a text or passage selected by the teacher to read publicly to a small or large group of students. A primary purpose for the read-aloud selection is to focus on the content of the text. A shared reading is a text or passage that is jointly shared by teacher and student. In shared readings, the students can also see the text, and it is usually chosen both for its content and as a way to draw attention to a particular text feature or comprehension strategy. Regardless, both are an opportunity to model comprehension through think alouds.

When considering read alouds and shared readings for your own practice, always keep in mind the focus of your course. Although we believe strongly that students should see their teachers regularly engaged in the act of reading for pleasure, we do not suggest that large portions of instructional time should be spent on using readings that are unrelated to your instructional purposes.

The teachers in this chapter made a strong case for their purposes in selecting a particular piece, and clearly saw these experiences as an important way to advance student learning. Having said that, do not underestimate the influence of a teacher who shares a newspaper story that concerned them, an e-mail that made them laugh, or a cartoon that made them think. When students see their teachers reading a variety of genres, they begin to see possibilities in their own literate lives.

Chapter 5
Why Ask? Questioning Strategies in the Classroom

*D*oreen Tabaris has been teaching her family and consumer sciences class about food-related illnesses. Students have learned about salmonella, botulism, and food safety practices for the home and commercial operations. Today she is introducing food-related illnesses that are behavioral in origin— anorexia and bulimia. After opening her class with a series of questions designed to activate background knowledge, she discusses attributes about these two disorders and illustrates the similarities and differences. Next, she asks a series of questions to check for understanding.

"We've talked for a bit about these two disorders. What are some of the similarities between the two?" she asks.

"It happens a lot to teenagers," says Laura.

"Correct, although not only to teenagers. Adults are vulnerable, too. What other ways?" she asks the class.

"People who are anorexic or bulimic might stop hanging around with friends," offers Roberta.

"Yes, that's a good warning sign for either eating disorder. Others?"

"It's a girl thing," replies Antonio.

Ms. Tabaris notes that the answer is incorrect, but also knows that this is a common misconception, as the incidence of both disorders is rising among males. She wants her students to process this with one another, rather than give them the answer. "Everyone turn to your table group to identify a reason why that answer cannot be correct," she says.

Signaled by their teacher that this is an error, students begin reviewing what they know. After a few minutes, she collects information from the groups.

"Illnesses can happen to men and women," suggests one group.

"Boys in sports like wrestling have to pay attention to their weight. That might cause some of them to become bulimic," offers another group.

The groups offer several possible answers to refute the statement. By taking a few minutes to let students analyze what they know, she has deepened their understanding well beyond what a simple correction from her would have done.

Why is Ms. Tabaris teaching this way? What theory or research supports her instruction? How does this activity contribute to her students' literacy? How does she know whether her students are learning? The answer lies in the queries themselves: Ms. Tabaris is using questioning as a means for instruction. If questions are not asked, then expected application to meaningful context will be limited (Routman, 2000).

Traditionally, teachers use questioning more than any other method for developing comprehension. Questions help the teacher assess whether students understand the text (Durkin, 1978–1979). However, in organizing daily lessons, teachers are inclined to plan thinking activities where the learners' potential to question the text is diminished because the teacher dominates the questioning (Busching & Slesinger 1995). Conversely, less time is dedicated to student questioning. In addition, questioning loses its effectiveness when teachers require students to swallow and regurgitate facts before they have had an opportunity to chew and digest information. Another drawback of teachers' routine questioning habits is that their questions too often focus on literal comprehension rather than critical thinking, even in content areas like mathematics (Wimer, Ridenour, & Thomas, 2001), and especially when working with students perceived as struggling readers (Allington, 1983; Durkin, 1978–1979; Gambrell, 1983; Tienken, Goldberg, & DiRocco, 2009).

An important series of studies on the questioning habits of teachers was conducted by Cazden (1986, 1988). Like others before her, she found that classroom instruction is dominated by a particular cycle of questioning known as IRE: initiate, respond, and evaluate (Dillon, 1988; Mehan, 1979). The IRE pattern of questioning is familiar to all—the

Struggling Readers

HAVE QUESTIONS ABOUT THE WORLD AROUND THEM

Not being able to read or write very well does not mean that students aren't interested in the world around them. Struggling readers often have a number of questions about the physical, biological, and social world. These questions can lead to Internet searches, reading, writing, and thinking. Inquiry-based approaches to literacy learning are replacing old models of teacher-directed learning in advanced coursework, but this is a far less common experience for students who struggle to read. Organize instruction around an essential question and then provide students with the digital means to answer their questions. For example, a world history unit on modern conflict was organized using this essential question: "Is war inevitable?" Students in this class worked in pairs to conduct research on current events in Iraq, Darfur, Lebanon, and Moldova. Although many of the students read below grade level, they proved to be adept at locating and synthesizing information gleaned from Internet sources.

teacher initiates a question, students respond, and then the teacher evaluates the quality and accuracy of the responses. Here's an example of IRE:

Teacher: Why was the battle of Gettysburg important? (Initiate)

Student: The Union army defeated the Confederate army. (Respond)

Teacher: Good. (Evaluate) Why else was it important? (Initiate)

Here's the difficulty with that question—the student could have also answered that it was the northernmost battle of the Civil War, or that 54,000 people died, or that Abraham Lincoln delivered a famous speech at a memorial service on the site. Instead, the question is low level and consists of a teacher-directed query that excludes any discussion or debate among students. A classroom where IRE is the dominant form of discourse quickly becomes a passive learning environment dependent on the teacher for any kind of discussion. The danger, of course, in the overuse of an IRE pattern of questioning is that the teacher alone becomes the mediator of who will speak and who will not (Mehan, 1979). The students learn that the only questions worth considering are those formulated by the teacher. Ironically, the teachers in Cazden's study (1988) reported that they wanted a student-centered, constructivist classroom, yet clung to IRE as their dominant instructional method for inquiry. If you doubt the pervasiveness of this questioning pattern, then eavesdrop on kindergartners "playing school." Invariably, the 5-year-old "teacher" will engage in this questioning pattern with his or her "students."

Creating Quality Questions

Unfortunately many students have little practice in answering implicit questions and may be ill-equipped to formulate and respond to questions requiring critical thinking. In secondary schools it is imperative to create a classroom culture of inquiry. However, these same adolescents are likely to require teacher modeling to engage in inquiry. One way teachers can accomplish this is through effective

THE BENEFITS FOR ENGLISH LANGUAGE LEARNERS

Far too often, English language learners allow their peers who are more fluent with the language to answer teacher questions. In many classrooms, especially those in which IRE is the predominate model of classroom discussion, English learners sit quietly and "behave" so that they are not called on (Curtin, 2005; Vandergrift, 2006). Unfortunately, this does not facilitate their language development. ELLs need to be asked questions, just like every other student in the class. Having said that, it is important to consider the types of questions ELLs at each stage of language proficiency should be asked. Further, effective teachers of ELLs understand the role of latency, or wait time, in their questioning (Rothenberg & Fisher, 2007). As Brice and Roseberry-McKibben (1999) note, wait time allows these students time to organize their thinking, transfer their thinking into English, and formulate a response. When teachers use well-constructed questions and wait time as part of their classroom procedures, ELLs develop their skills in listening, speaking, and thinking in English.

QUESTIONING

|Figure 5.1| Questions based on rhetorical styles.

Questions About Logic (Logos)
- Locate major claims and assertions and ask, "Do you agree with the author's claim that . . .?"
- Look at support for major claims and ask, "Is there any claim that appears to be weak or unsupported? Which one and why?"
- Can you think of counterarguments that the author doesn't consider?
- Do you think the author has left something out on purpose? Why?

Questions About the Writer (Ethos)
- Does this author have the appropriate background to speak with authority on this subject?
- Is this author knowledgeable?
- What does the author's style and language tell your students about him or her?
- Does this author seem trustworthy? Why or why not?
- Does this author seem deceptive? Why or why not?
- Does this author appear to be serious?

Questions About Emotions (Pathos)
- Does this piece affect your students emotionally? What parts?
- Do your students think the author is trying to manipulate their emotions? In what ways? At what point?
- Do their emotions conflict with their logical interpretation of the arguments?
- Does the author use humor or irony? How does this affect your students' acceptance of his or her ideas?

Source: California State University, Task Force on Expository Reading and Writing. Used with permission.

questioning strategies. The goal of these restructured questions should be to monitor and guide the ways that students construct and examine meaning in reading, writing, talking, listening, and reflecting.

As students learn to construct and examine meaning, they hone their rhetorical skills. In general, rhetoric concerns the ability to speak and write effectively. Over 2,000 years ago, the Greek philosopher Aristotle described rhetoric as "the ability, in each particular case, to see the available means of persuasion." Aristotle identified three types of persuasion or appeals: ethos, logos, and pathos. Ethos focuses on appeal of the speaker or writer; the character or reputation of the person. Logos is an appeal based on logic or reason. And pathos concerns the use of emotion as an argument. Aristotle's rhetoric has lasted the test of time as it represents complex thinking. To think critically, students must understand, and be able to evaluate, the arguments being used. Questioning is one of the ways we help students develop their rhetorical thinking. Sample questions based on each type of persuasive argument can be found in Figure 5.1. These questions help students develop their understanding of arguments made by speakers and writers. They also help students incorporate persuasive arguments into their own speaking and writing.

The self-monitoring of understanding that comes from self-questioning is underutilized by poor readers. In turn, these struggling readers learn to dislike reading because it is unsatisfying and the concepts of textbook language are unfamiliar. Their comprehension skills then fail to advance because they do not read, reinforcing a cycle of failure (Stanovich, 1986). However, a basic expectation of content area learning is that students learn a variety of strategies and engage in a variety of activities in order to convert new information into learned information. We know that in content area learning, the students develop meaningful understanding gradually, and not in a single brief and isolated experience. Therefore, instruction must routinely incorporate questioning techniques that encourage active participation and high response opportunities for students. Questioning is central to the two tools in every teacher's arsenal—scaffolding and coaching (Fisher & Frey, 2010; Roehler & Duffy, 1991).

When teachers use these strategies to ask probing questions, students grow in their thinking processes. At the same time, teachers should share with their students the reasons for their questions. Additional research suggests that instructional questioning strategies that focus on inferences and main ideas equip the students to respond with improved recall and understanding (Raphael, 1984). This is achieved through higher-order questioning.

"Higher-Order" Questions

If you have read the previous pages, you have probably inferred that some questions are better than others. You have seen phrases like "low-level" and "higher-order" questions. But what distinguishes types of questions? How do you determine what sorts of questions are appropriate? A review of the work of Benjamin Bloom is helpful to understand questioning.

In 1956, Benjamin Bloom, an educational psychologist at the University of Chicago, published a series of handbooks on the domains of learning— psychomotor, affective, and cognitive. The handbook devoted to the cognitive domain outlined a classification system that described six levels of competence. This classification system, referred to commonly as Bloom's taxonomy, has become a cornerstone in the description of questions used in the classroom and on tests (Bloom, 1956). Bloom described these competencies; we've included a sample question to illustrate each one:

Level 1—*Knowledge:* States facts, terms, and definitions.
   Sample question: What is the capital of California?

Level 2—*Comprehension:* Change the information to compare to another form.
   Sample question: Explain why Sacramento was selected as the state capital.

Level 3—*Application:* Solve a new problem using information.
   Sample question: What city in California would you choose as the state capital today?

Level 4—*Analysis:* Identifies components and infers causes or motives.
   Sample question: Why do you believe that the legislature chose to move the state capital from San Jose to Sacramento?

Level 5—*Synthesis:* Create a new product using information in a novel way.
   Sample question: Design a state capital for California that will be useful throughout the 21st century.

Level 6—*Evaluation:* Make judgments and defend opinions.
   Sample question: Assess the suitability of the present state capital and make recommendations for future development.

The questions got more difficult, didn't they? This is where the terminology of higher- and lower-order questions originates.

Knowledge and comprehension questions are sometimes referred to as literal questions because they require the student to draw upon memorization or location of facts. In other words, the answers to these types of questions are usually located verbatim in a text. They are also the easiest questions to compose and test. Guszak (1967) estimated that 70% of the questions asked in a typical classroom are knowledge or comprehension questions. That means that only 30% of the queries required students to apply knowledge in unique ways, or to construct understanding by assembling disparate information. It is the imbalance between literal and nonliteral questions that is problematic, not the questions themselves. Brophy and Good (1986) noted that students who have experience with lower-order questions do well on tests of basic skills because these tests mirror this type of question.

Tests do not consist only of basic skills; they also demand that students can draw inferences, justify answers, and defend opinions. These same higher-order skills are also widely recognized as critical for adult success (Pithers & Soden, 2000). Therefore, classrooms should include ample experiences in responding to questions that require students to analyze information, identify problems, develop original solutions, and formulate opinions. These are also the more difficult questions for teachers to develop.

Questioning Techniques

Effective Questioning Techniques

Asking a good question is a matter of thinking about the level of cognitive engagement; however, a well-crafted question will go to waste without a clear understanding of the techniques involved in asking, prompting, and probing. A useful technique for quality questioning is called the QUILT framework (Walsh & Sattes, 2005). This method, which represents Question and Understand to Improve Learning and Thinking, invites teachers to consider what happens both before and after the question is asked. In particular, attention should be given to providing adequate wait time once the question has been asked so that students can process the information. Once the student has answered, it is essential to provide feedback about the accuracy of the answer, and to build and expand correct responses to promote deeper understanding. Ms. Tabaris's questioning approach at the beginning of the chapter is a good example of this. It is also useful to involve other students in reacting to the answer to foster more discourse in the class, as when Ms. Tabaris invited students to come up with a reason why the answer given by Antonio was not correct. Finally, Walsh and Sattes remind us that reflecting on our questioning techniques and noticing our distribution of questions is also vital to ensure we're involving all of our students. A table of the QUILT framework appears in Figure 5.2.

Peter Johnston invites us to think about our questioning techniques as a way of inviting (or discouraging) our students to engage. He reminds us that the language we use in the classroom is "constitutive . . . it actually creates realities and invites identities" (Johnston, 2004, p. 9). Therefore, the way we word our questions and our responses can shape students' beliefs about themselves and their place in the world. The questions we ask may include those that foster:

- *Noticing and naming:* "Are there patterns or things that surprise you?" (p. 17)
- *Identity:* "What have you learned most recently as a (reader, writer, etc.)?" (p. 26)

Figure 5.2 QUILT framework.

Stage 1: Prepare the Question
- Identify instructional purpose
- Determine content focus
- Select cognitive level
- Consider wording and syntax

Stage 2: Present the Question
- Indicate response format
- Ask the question
- Select respondent

Stage 3: Prompt Student Responses
- Pause after asking question
- Assist nonrespondent
- Pause following student response

Stage 4: Process Student Responses
- Provide appropriate feedback
- Expand and use correct responses
- Elicit student reactions and questions

Stage 5: Reflect on Questioning Practice
- Analyze questions
- Map respondent selection
- Evaluate student response patterns
- Examine teacher and student reactions

Source: Quality Questioning: Research-Based Practice to Engage Every Learner, by J. A. Walsh and B. D. Sattes, 2005, Thousand Oaks, CA: Corwin Press. Used with permission.

- *Agency:* "How did you figure that out?" (p. 31)
- *Flexibility and transfer:* "How else . . .?" (p. 45)
- *Knowing:* "Let's see if I got this right" (then summarizes students' extended comments) (p. 54)

Notice that these are not only initial questions, they are also effective follow-up probes to elicit student responses. Unlike the IRE discourse so commonly used, these serve as examples of genuine inquiry on the part of the teacher, and not just another round of "guess what's in the teacher's brain."

Strategies at Work

Questioning the Author (QtA)

Questioning the Author (QtA) is a text-based strategy that invites the reader to interact with the information and build meaning from the content by analyzing the author's purpose (Beck, McKeown, Hamilton, & Kucan, 1997). These questions, referred to as queries by Beck et al., are meant to serve as discussion prompts that invite students to develop ideas rather than restate information directly from the text. Queries require the students to take responsibility for thinking and for constructing understanding. As students wrestle with ideas and concepts while

Table 5.1 Questioning the Author Prompts

Goal	Query
Initiate discussion	What is the author trying to say? What is the author's message? What is the author talking about?
Focus on author's message Link information	That's what the author says, but what does it mean? How does that connect with what the author already told us? What information has the author added here that connects or fits in with _____?
Identify difficulties with the way the author has presented information or ideas	Does that make sense? Is that said in a clear way? Did the author explain that clearly? Why or why not? What do we need to figure out or find out?
Encourage students to refer to the text because they have misinterpreted, or to help them recognize that they have made an inference	Did the author tell us that? Did the author give us the answer to that?

Source: "Questioning the Author: A Yearlong Classroom Implementation to Engage Students With Text," by I. L. Beck, M. G. McKeown, R. L. Hamilton, L. Kucan, and J. Worthy, 1996, *Elementary School Journal, 96*, pp. 385–414. Used with permission of the University of Chicago Press.

reading, their inquiry moves into deeper levels of meaning in narrative and expository texts by becoming involved with issues raised. The students realize that the author is challenging them to build their ideas and concepts. As a result, collaborative discussion follows the open-ended and author-oriented queries. Table 5.1 contains a table of QtA queries designed by these researchers.

The goals of QtA are always the same: to construct meaning of text, to help the student go beyond the words on the page, and to relate outside experiences from other texts. The way to achieve these goals is discussion enriched by the student's world and his or her own personal history. QtA involves the teacher as well as the whole class as they collaboratively build understanding during the reading. During this process the teacher participates in the discussion as a facilitator, guide, initiator, and responder. The role of the teacher is not to dominate the conversation, but to lead the students into dialogue with open-ended questions. The teacher strives to elicit the readers' thinking while keeping them focused in their discussion (McKeown & Beck, 1999). The students' answers are not evaluated in this procedure because QtA is designed to engage the readers with the text, not to rate the accuracy of their responses. Melanie Scott used QtA queries in her English class as she introduced the poem "Annabel Lee" by Edgar Allen Poe (1849/1966).

Questioning the Author in English

Poe is a new author for the students, who do not yet have prior knowledge of his life or works. The students will work with ideas they have generated during this shared reading to gain meaning of his poetic narration. After reading aloud the first stanza, Ms. Scott draws their attention to Poe's message and listens to their responses.

"What is Poe talking about in this poem? Is he the speaker in 'Annabel Lee'? Let's look for clues in the poem about this. What is Poe's message?"

Voices echo, "Death. Love. Sorrow. Marriage."

With a smile and a nod, Ms. Scott alerts the class to listen to the rhyme, rhythm, and sounds of the words as she continues to read aloud. During her reading, Ms. Scott pauses and asks, "Do you feel that Poe really loves Annabel Lee?"

The class shouts, "Yes!" One student confirms, "Of course he does."

Ms. Scott keeps probing. "How do you know that he loves her?"

Eric immediately replies, "Because he talks about angels in heaven were jealous of Poe's and Annabel's love. But, I don't get it when he talks about him being a child, and her, a child."

Josh adds, "Yeah, on Valentine's Day I see little angels with hearts, bows, and arrows on cards. Are Poe and Annabel Lee sweethearts? Are they grown-ups or are they kids?" Carolina calls out, "I think that maybe they were teenage lovers and the angels are symbols of their love."

As the students generate thoughts and questions, Ms. Scott is doing less and the students are doing more. She guides them through the next stanza, then stops and asks, "Have you ever loved someone? Think about how you felt at that time. How did you feel when that person left?" The class remains silent. Waiting, she encourages the students to think about Eric's and Carolina's ideas. "What is the 'reason' that Poe refers to in the following lines? What is Poe really saying in these lines?"

> And this was the reason that, long ago,
> In this kingdom by the sea,
> A wind blew out of a cloud, chilling
> My beautiful Annabel Lee . . .

"He blames the angels for Annabel Lee's death because maybe she got very sick and died. Poe can't really explain how she got sick, so he tells us the wind came from the angels, and it made her sick," offers Tanisha.

Shaking his head, Thomas interjects, "How can the wind come from the angels and how can the wind make Annabel Lee sick?"

Instead of answering Thomas, Ms. Scott responds with a question to dig deeper. The teacher inquires, "Is the information about Annabel Lee's death as important as the previous information about their love?"

Murmurs fill the room and some student voices are heard above the rest.

"Maybe it isn't important for us to know how she died, because Poe would have told us," says Roberto.

"Or he really didn't know," Joelle interjects.

"I think it's important that Poe and Annabel Lee loved each other and when she died, he still thought that they were married," offers Ting.

Engaging the students in the final segment of text, Ms. Scott reads aloud the last stanza. She then asks, "If you could, would you bring Annabel Lee back to Poe? Why do you think this way?"

Tanisha replies, "Definitely, I would bring her back to life because Poe's in a lot of pain. He's sleeping by her side in the tomb!"

Eric retorts, "I wouldn't. Once you die, it's never the same when you come back. People change all the time."

To prevent this comment from leading the students away from the poem's content, Ms. Scott reveals an important fact from Poe's life that they had not known.

"Mr. Poe died two days after he wrote this poem. If you could speak to Mr. Poe right now, what would you say to him? Take 10 minutes to write your response and then you'll share them with the class."

With the stated prompt, Ms. Scott sparks the students' thinking about Poe as both author and speaker and provides an opportunity for the students to write their thoughts. Using their written responses, the students then interact with each other and their teacher using class discussion practices including *marking, turning back, revoicing,* and *recapping.* Marking is repeating students' comments in a manner that draws attention to certain ideas. Turning back occurs when the teacher turns the responsibility of the conversation back to the students. Revoicing involves restating student words to add clarity; it is the "in other words" approach. Recapping the discussion reviews key points and provides closure. These discussion techniques are taught at the beginning of the year. At this point in the course, students are able to use these skills during class discussions.

Concentrating on the quality and depth of meaning that students are constructing during the reading and discussion of "Annabel Lee," Ms. Scott keeps the focus on the topic while guiding the discussion and helping clarify confusion. Her in-depth questioning allows the students to transform the author's ideas into their ideas and to challenge the author's words in order to make connections to the text based on their constructive thinking and curiosity.

ReQuest

ReQuest (Manzo, 1969) is another useful questioning technique designed to assist students in formulating questions and answers based on a text passage student partners read a passage together, then write two to three questions and answers to quiz one another. This procedure builds prior knowledge and vocabulary through discussions. Designed first for one-to-one instruction, ReQuest has been used as a group activity as well.

The ReQuest process is a simple one to implement in the secondary classroom. The teacher chooses a passage of text, then designates short segments within the passage. When ReQuest is introduced, it is advisable to conduct the first round so that the teacher is the one to answer questions generated by the students. The teacher/respondent keeps the book closed during the questioning, and students may be requested to rephrase questions if necessary. Manzo cautions that the teacher must answer to the best of his or her ability. The student/questioners have their books open and check the teacher's answers against the text. Once this phase is complete, the roles are reversed. After reading the next segment of text, the teacher, with book open, becomes the questioner while the students answer. As before, those who are answering the questions can ask to have the question restated or clarified. Once students are familiar with ReQuest, the sequence can be used in small groups to support their understanding of the text. ReQuest can also be tailored to suit the specific needs of students. For instance, questions can include those related to specific vocabulary featured in the reading. Respondents can also be asked to validate their answers with evidence from the text. Task cards for a student-led small-group ReQuest procedure appear in Figure 5.3. Let's watch Rita Peña's class of English language learners use ReQuest.

Figure 5.3   ReQuest task cards.

Questioner Task Card

1. Read the first passage silently. Pay attention to the information it contains.

2. Think of questions to ask. Try to use your own words, not exact phrases from the passage.

3. Keep your book open while you ask your question. Listen to the answer, then check to see if it is accurate. If it is not, ask another question to help the person arrive at the correct answer.

4. When finished, change roles. Repeat 2–3 times.

Respondent Task Card

1. Read the first passage silently. Pay attention to the information it contains.

2. Think of questions you might be asked. Check the passage you just read for possible answers.

3. Close your book and answer each question you are asked. You can ask the questioner to rephrase or clarify a question you do not understand.

4. When finished, change roles. Repeat 2–3 times.

ReQuest in Social Studies

Today the students are engaged in learning how to compose questions and apply questioning strategies that help in comprehending a passage from their textbook titled *The Rise of Chinese Civilization*. They have had previous experience with ReQuest, and the emphasis of this lesson is on using multiple sources for locating information to answer questions. Because her students are English language learners, she is always interested in refining their oral language skills. Ms. Peña reminds the class of the words used in formulating questions, especially *who, what, when, where, why,* and *how.* "I'm going to show you how I make questions that I ask the author, my peers, the teacher, and myself," she says as she draws a circle on the board and divides it into quarters with the respective labels: author, peers, teacher, self. The teacher then explains that she will use headings and captions in the text to formulate her questions.

Rather than reading silently, Ms. Peña invites her students to participate in a shared reading, "China—The Land and the People." After reading three sentences, Ms. Peña pauses and invites a student to ask a question of the class. Henok asks the class, "Why is it that the Chinese are calling themselves the 'Central Country'?"

Margarita replies, "Because it is the cultural center of the world."

Ms. Peña reads the second paragraph and invites another student to pose a question. Flordia says, "Why would China want to change its name to the People's Republic of China?"

When no one has an answer, Ms. Peña points to the quarter circle marked "questions for the teacher."

Students then ask her about the history of the name change and the reasons. After explaining the political changes that swept China over the last century, they return to the text.

QUESTIONING

In paragraph three, the students are introduced to countries bordering China. Tran asks, "How did China get along with its neighbors who were hunters and herders?"

Anna responds, "I don't understand the question."

Ms. Peña asks Anna, "What do you need to do to understand the question? Would you like me to write it on the board so you can see it?" When Anna responds affirmatively, the teacher posts the question on the board and clarifies the *who*, *what*, and *how* information. Her explanation focuses on vocabulary and context clues found within the text. Confidently Gabriela answers, "They shared things like food, ideas, talk, and money."

Ms. Peña repeats, "What did you need to do to understand the question?"

Gabriela replies, "Reread the text for who, what, and how."

The teacher instructs the class to read the next paragraph silently and write questions for their peers on index cards. They read about the Hwang Ho River and its flood plains and record questions on their index cards. When they finish reading, she returns to the question circle on the board and directs the students to the quarter that reads "questions for peers." She then says, "Reread your questions and ask the person sitting next to you to answer some of them."

A buzz immediately begins. One student is overheard saying, "I found out the Hwang Ho River is also called the Yellow River. It has two names." Other pairs compare information, clarify understanding, and even return to the text.

In this classroom, ReQuest has become a valuable means for English language learners to formulate questions and locate accurate answers. Perhaps more importantly, these students benefit from opportunities to use language in a precise fashion. These questioning events allow them to refine and restate their questions so that they will yield the information they are seeking, which supports the development of their metacognitive strategies (Ciardiello, 1998).

Question–Answer Relationship (QAR)

The question–answer relationship (QAR) strategy describes four types of questions: *Right There, Think and Search, Author and You*, and *On Your Own* (Raphael, 1982, 1984, 1986). It is based on the three categories of question classification described by Pearson and Johnson (1978): *text explicit* (the answer is directly quoted in the text); *text implicit* (the answer must be implied from several passages in the book); and *script implicit* (requires both the text and prior knowledge and experiences).

QAR requires teachers to model the different levels of questions that are associated with a text. QAR should not be confused with Bloom's taxonomy of questions (Bloom, 1956) because QAR "does not classify questions in isolation but rather by considering the reader's background knowledge and the text" (McIntosh & Draper, 1996, p. 154). In addition to serving as a tool for teachers to develop questions, it is also a framework for students to apply in answering questions. QAR is a student-centered approach to questioning because it "clarifies how students can approach the task of reading texts and answering questions" (Raphael, 1986, p. 517). A classroom poster on question–answer relationships appears in Figure 5.4.

It is advisable to pair both Right There and Think and Search questions to encourage the learner to self-assess for uncertainties. This inquiry interaction promotes more personal involvement than using questions with separate phrases of isolated facts (Busching & Slesinger, 1995). In contrast, Author and You and On Your Own questions invite the reader to integrate personal experiences and prior

Figure 5.4 Question-answer relationship chart.

In the text...	In the text...
RIGHT THERE	THINK AND SEARCH
When was the Declaration signed?	*What are some of Thomas Jefferson's notable accomplishments?*
The Declaration of Independence was adopted on <u>July 4, 1776</u>.	<u>The Declaration of Independence</u> was adopted on July 4, 1776. John Hancock signed first, and <u>Thomas Jefferson, the author,</u> signed as a delegate of Virginia. He later became <u>the third president</u> of the United States.
Answers to Right There questions are in the text. The words in the question usually match a sentence in the text.	Answers to Think and Search questions are in the text. The answer is compiled through segments of several sentences.
In your head...	In your head...
AUTHOR AND YOU	ON YOUR OWN
What influence did participation in the development of the Declaration have on the signers?	*If you were a delegate of the Second Continental Congress, would you sign?*
Answers to Author and You questions are not in the text. You need to consider both what the author has told you and what you already know about the topic.	Answers to On Your Own questions are not in the text. You need to consider your personal experiences to answer.

QUESTIONING

knowledge into their responses. These inferential and evaluative questions require the reader to make connections between text, self, and world (Keene & Zimmermann, 1997). During this time, the reader must deduce, infer, connect, and evaluate (Leu & Kinzer, 1995; Raphael, 1982, 1986).

The instructional power of QAR lies in the explicit instruction of identifying what type of question is being asked, and therefore what resources are required to answer the question. Raphael (1984) notes that less effective readers are often puzzled by where to locate answers to questions based on a reading. Some students rely only on the text, sometimes fruitlessly searching for an answer that is just not there. Conversely, other students rarely return to the text for any answers, believing that they can only depend on information they can recall from memory. By teaching the relationship between questions and answers, students can apply the framework to answer more efficiently and accurately. This ensures they become better readers and thinkers, and along the way they perform better on tests and assessments (Raphael & Au, 2005). Figure 5.5 contains a summary of the QAR strategy.

The QAR framework can typically be taught in one lesson. We advise the teacher to model this strategy in a shared reading using a small segment of text. Then ask a question about what was read. The teacher reflects aloud on the selection and answers the question. It is critical to identify the level of the question

Figure 5.5 Question–answer relationship comparison chart.

QAR STRATEGY	CATEGORY	DESCRIPTION
Right There	Text explicit	The question is asked using words from the text and the answer is directly stated in the reading.
Think and Search	Text implicit	The questions are derived from the text and require the reader to look for the answer in several places and to combine the information.
Author and You	Script and text implicit	The question has the language of the text but in order to answer it, the reader must use what he/she understands about the topic. The answer cannot be found directly in the text, but the text can provide some information for formulating an answer. The information is implied and the reader infers what the author meant by examining clues in the text.
On Your Own	Script implicit	The question elicits an answer that comes from the reader's own prior knowledge and experiences. The text may or may not be needed to answer the question.

and the source of the answer. When students learn to classify questions and locate answers, they learn to recognize that the reading process is influenced by both the reader and the text. Eventually, students are ready to formulate original questions in response to text. To see students in action, let's visit Robert North's science class.

QAR in Science

The chemistry students follow Mr. North's voice and pointer as it moves from line to line on the text displayed on a document camera. He is engaging his students in a shared reading that describes and explains the nature of solvents, solutes, and solutions. Directing his attention to the students, he informs them that in order to learn the information, they will use the QAR strategy. Mr. North has modeled QAR and taught it to his students. Today, the students are using QAR in a whole-class activity. They will be answering questions and generating new questions for their classmates to answer.

Mr. North reads, "It is important to realize that agitation affects the rate in which a solute dissolves." He stops and asks, "What affects the rate that a solvent dissolves?"

The class unanimously answers, "Agitation."

He quizzes, "What kind of question did I ask?"

Together they respond, "Right there."

Mr. North continues reading. "Agitation cannot influence the amount of the solute to be dissolved in a solution. In the solution, the dissolving medium is the solvent." He deliberately repeats the last statement and students raise their hands as if on cue.

Serina is acknowledged and she asks, "What is the solvent?"

Mr. North nods and checks the class, "Are you ready? What kind of question is Serina asking?"

After answering "Right there!" they add, "The dissolving medium is the solvent."

Before he reads the remaining text, Mr. North skims the second paragraph. He notes the term *thermodynamics*. "Someone make my day and tell me what that word means. We've met the word before."

When no one responds he continues, "Let's divide the word into two. *Thermo* means what? *Dynamics* means what?"

Rosario replies, "Thermo means temperature."

April adds, "I think dynamics means change." As the students answer, Mr. North writes their definitions on the board.

By clarifying vocabulary without using a dictionary, Mr. North taps into his students' prior knowledge and reminds them how to discover meaning by looking for context clues. "That's an On Your Own question, folks."

Mr. North returns to the passage of the text that explains the nature of a saturated solution. He poses the question, "What is sodium chloride?"

Phan calls out, "Salt."

Mr. North asks with a knock on the desk, "What kind of salt?"

Brian adds, "Table salt."

Mr. North then queries, "If I dissolved a box of salt in a beaker of water, can I dissolve two more boxes in the same beaker? Any educated guesses?"

Serina asks, "How big is the box and how big is the beaker?"

Jorge chimes in, "Serina's right, Mr. North, because the answer to your question depends on the amount of solute and solvent. We need to know more information. It's an Author and You question." At this point, the students must rely on their own understanding about solutions, as well as information in the text.

Mr. North encourages the students' responses with a compliment and another probing question. "What if we agitated the solution, would that influence the amount of salt that goes into the solution?" This is a Think and Search question because the answer can be constructed by linking information from several parts of the text.

Phan replies, "No. The agitation would increase the rate at which it dissolves, but not the amount that dissolves."

"Mr. Phan Nguyen, you made my day!"

Ahmed asks, "Mr. North, you were talking about thermodynamics. So what's the temperature of the solution going to be?"

"Very good question, Ahmed. How would the temperature influence your answer to my question? That's an On Your Own question, and a great segue." Mr. North continues, "Today you covered all the points of our shared reading. Different variables like temperature, volume of solution, and quantity of solutes are crucial in answering our scientific questions. Tomorrow during lab, we will do experiments that change the respective variables. And we'll answer Mr. Ahmed's question at that time."

Mr. North's chemistry class knows that QAR is a useful strategy for locating answers and his budding chemists recognize explicit and implicit text language. Mr. North's learners also realize that their experiences and knowledge contribute to their questions and answers. As a result of these teaching and learning practices, he is strategically developing and improving these students' literacy abilities in order to enhance their understanding of the content.

Using Questioning for Study (SQ3R, SQ4R, and SQRQCQ)

Effective questioning is essential for reading and class discussion. The ultimate purpose of teacher questioning is to teach students to formulate their own questions as they read, for this is a tool that will support their comprehension of text. It is also at the heart of three study strategies, SQ3R (*survey, question, read, recite, review*), SQ4R (*survey, question, read, reflect, recite, review*), and a customized framework for mathematics called SQRQCQ (*survey, question, read, question, compute, question*).

SQ3R is a systematic way of studying text to support the student's reading by previewing, skimming, and setting purpose questions before actual reading. This study system, originated by Robinson (1946), includes a series of steps that are offshoots of teacher modeled reading lessons, including DR-TA. While students read to learn, they use the following steps of SQ3R:

S	Survey	Skim text for headings and charts
Q	Question	Turn headings into questions
R	Read	Read to answer questions
R	Recite	Answer questions and make notes
R	Review	Reread for details and unanswered questions

- *Survey* the text to acquire its essence from headings, charts, bold print terms.
- *Question* the material. Turn each section heading into a question or set of questions.
- *Read* with the purpose of answering the questions.
- *Recite* the answers to the questions after reading and without looking back in the text, then making notes on learned concepts.
- *Review* what has been read and try to answer from the text all the self-questions to evaluate responses and summarize important information.

The sequence used in SQ3R is intended to echo the behavior of effective readers. As students *survey* the material before reading, they predict what the material will be about, what prior knowledge will be relevant, and which strategies will be useful in approaching the new text. They formulate *questions* in anticipation of the content they are about to encounter. The students' prior knowledge and use of *reading* strategies assist them in constructing meaning of the content area text. However, their comprehension does not necessarily lead to learning that is meaningful and useful. Learning takes place when the new information becomes an interactive part of existing knowledge. Therefore, they *recite* answers to their own questions and make notes for later use. They then *review* the text, rereading for details and to clarify questions that remain unanswered (Armbruster et al., 1991).

The metacognitive sequence used by SQ3R is a clear model of the reading behaviors of effective readers, yet it seems to be underused in many secondary classrooms. Vacca and Vacca (1999) suggest that this may be due to the way SQ3R is taught. Because there is a prescribed set of steps to be followed, there is a temptation to teach the strategy through rote memorization only, with little time spent on the purpose for each step. When students perceive strategies like these to be an instructional exercise with no real purpose beyond the lesson, they are unlikely to generalize them to other settings. Even more importantly, they will not adopt the approach into their metacognitive repertoire, thus defeating the purpose of teaching the strategy in the first place. Although it will take longer, we strongly urge teachers to invite students to discover *why* the steps are useful.

SQ3R has inspired several adaptations for guiding students to study and learn from text. These include SQ4R (*survey, question, read, reflect, recite, review*), and like its predecessor it is implemented across the content areas. SQ4R (Thomas & Robinson, 1972) adds a reflective step after the initial reading to make connections to what is already known. In addition to these learning strategies, there is the SQRQCQ (*survey, question, read, question, compute, question*), which assists mathematics learners to interpret and use the needed textual information in solving word problems (Fay, 1965).

SQRQCQ is an effective framework for solving mathematical word problems because its steps form a systematic approach to determining the information provided in the question, and the mathematical operations necessary to arrive at the correct answer. Like SQ3R, it has a series of steps to be followed:

S	Survey	Skim to get the main idea of the problem
Q	Question	Ask the question that is stated in the problem
R	Reread	Identify the information and details provided
Q	Question	Ask what operation needs to be performed
C	Compute	Solve the problem
Q	Question	Does the answer make sense?

- *Survey* the question to get the essence of the problem. This first reading is for general understanding.
- *Question* what the problem is asking. Restate the question using your own words, being careful not to lose the technical terminology in the problem.
- *Reread* the problem to locate details and eliminate unnecessary information, if applicable.
- *Question* the problem again. What operations are necessary to solve the problem?
- *Compute* the answer.
- *Question* again. Does the answer make sense? Does it answer the question posed in the problem?

It is not uncommon for students to be intimidated by word problems. Frameworks like SQRQCQ can increase student confidence because they learn a systematic approach to solving problems. It also encourages elimination of extraneous information meant to distract the student.

David Skillman implements questioning techniques like SQRQCQ to meet the diverse levels of the English language learners in his geometry class. He adapts questions that require knowledge of facts and mathematical processes before introducing higher-level questions related to concepts and principles. His students use the series of questions to reach a correct answer. Let's join him and his class as they tackle a geometry word problem.

SQRQCQ in Mathematics

Students in Mr. Skillman's Geometry class successfully met the previous day's challenge of cutting and assembling a geometric puzzle to visually prove the Pythagorean theorem, but struggled with applying the principle in word problems. The class agreed that the fifth problem on their assignment was particularly vexing. Mr. Skillman first engaged in reflective questioning on his own:

- Are the students unable to work with the given information (vocabulary)?
- Are the students unable to apply the Pythagorean theorem?

Based on the feedback from the students, he decides that there is reason to believe that both vocabulary and application may lie at the heart of the problem, so he leads them through an SQRQCQ sequence. He reminds them of this familiar strategy for solving word problems and provides guided instruction to find the solution to this one—determining the hypotenuse formed by a fallen tree.

Mr. Skillman reads aloud the problem to get the general idea and he instructs his English language learners to survey the illustration of the fallen tree and its metric measurements. He asks, "What is the problem?"

Alberto responds, "We don't know how many meters of tree are left."

Looking for details and being sure not to mention too much detail, Mr. Skillman scans the problem. He says as he draws a vertical line on the board, "There's a great big tree. How tall is the tree?"

The class replies, "36 meters."

"How many feet roughly is a 36-meter tree? Does anybody know? How many feet are approximately in 1 meter?"

Jessica answers, "About 3."

Mr. Skillman picks up a yardstick and shows its length to support the visual relationship between meters and feet. "What is 3 times 36?" Mr. Skillman is asking these questions to involve the students in examining and applying visual information to mathematical concepts. Students are busy calculating and they arrive at an answer of 108 feet. Now they have a visual understanding of the tree's height.

Mr. Skillman has them restate the question posed by the problem and invites them to write it down. "What happened to this poor tree?" he says, then answers himself, "It broke off, crack, bang!" He then rereads the problem to identify further details. He adds the new details to his drawing of the fallen tree. While he labels the given measurements, he asks, "Is 24 meters part of the tree?"

Maria shakes her head, "No. It's part of the ground."

Mr. Skillman expands Maria's answer. "It's the distance from the tree trunk to the top of the tree, as it lies on the ground." Pointing to the board drawing, Mr. Skillman questions again, "How long is this line? I can only use x for its length." He writes $36 - x$ over the fallen section of the tree. He repeats, "The original height of the tree is 36 meters, but the tree broke above the ground at the height of x, so my fallen part is $36 - x$."

He asks, "What process for solving this problem should we use? Do I have enough information to do the Pythagorean theorem?"

The class responds in the affirmative.

Mr. Skillman confirms with a smile, "Yes, I sure do." He writes on the board:

$$a = x, b = 24, c = 36 - x$$

"Using the theorem $a^2 + b^2 = c^2$, I can substitute for all of these values and I need to solve for x." He cautions the class about computing the problem.

"There could be a little trouble in solving this one. When using Pythagorean, what will you have to do with $36 - x$?"

Alfredo answers, "You have to square it."

Mr. Skillman writes the equation on the board and encourages, "It looks to me that you're ready to solve the problem."

While the students enter the information into their calculators, Mr. Skillman interacts one-on-one with the students. When they've finished he asks, "Does your answer make sense? Check it against the facts in the problem and substitute your answers in the problem."

It is worthwhile to note Mr. Skillman's method for reading word problems from the students' perspective. He read quickly with the students; however, in their initial reading students read at a moderate pace (slower for English language learners) so they could get the general ideas of the word problem for later discussion and application. Drawing the figure with its numerical relationships was also helpful for supporting their understanding. Mr. Skillman's methods are typical of the critical thinking skills required for mathematical application.

The students then read to look for details and interrelationships. They again self-questioned by asking, "How do I solve it?" The students continued by asking, "What does x equal and how is the other information shown? What do I know and what don't I know?" They set up their equation by translating the words of the problem into an equation. Only then were they ready to compute the answer. Finally, the students questioned whether their answers made sense and tested their answers through substitution in the equation.

When the teacher repeatedly models a strategy like SQRQCQ to solve a problem students have struggled with, there is an increased likelihood that they will later use it independently. Furthermore, students make connections across content areas when literacy strategies are available to construct meaning from a text.

SQRQCQ is a useful tool to assist students in analyzing a confusing word problem. However, it should not be viewed as the limit of questioning in mathematics. Inquiry is at the heart of mathematics, and effective teachers know that the goal in this content area is to question, not merely calculate. Reciprocal teaching is an effective method for encouraging mathematics students to work together to generate the types of questions needed to solve a complex problem.

Questioning Through Reciprocal Teaching in the Mathematics Classroom

Todd Kupras's students are on their hands and knees. Yardsticks clap down the sides of the algebra classroom. Groups of students huddle together over graph paper strewn across the floor of their trapezoid-shaped classroom. Today, students are assigned the task of measuring the classroom and calculating the cost of new carpet.

"How many of these little graph squares equals a foot?" demands Nakita.

"One square. One foot." David has answered the question before.

"How many feet long did you think this wall was going to be?"

"A lot more than 26 feet," admits David.

Working in groups of three or four Mr. Kupras's students are completing the first of a four-step mathematics inquiry project. At each step, they use reciprocal teaching to help arrive at their solution. You'll recall from chapter 2 that students predict, question, clarify, and summarize during reciprocal teaching. Of course they also refer to mathematics formulas and their textbook. Finishing with their first step of putting the room's layout on paper, the students are ready to start the next.

"So, we are supposed to come up with a possible answer first." Natika is eager to move on with the project.

"Well, the room looks like it's got a lot of square feet," Saram joins the discussion.

"And, what's a lot?"

"I'll say 200," decides Saram.

"You've got to be kidding. This room is bigger than that," Nakita argues.

"Okay, 400."

"Try doubling that. I bet it's 800 square feet," informs David.

The database continues, as each member of the group makes or adjusts his or her estimate. Upon completion, the students continue the process using reciprocal teaching's next question: How do you go about finding an answer to the question?

"How do you find out?" Nakita continues.

"Beats me," Saram replies, waiting for the others to help.

"Are you so sure? What was Mr. Kupras talking about? We gotta find squares and triangles on our grid paper."

"Then what?" Saram continues.

"Are you saying you forgot already? Then we use the area formula to figure out the square foot of the shape," concludes David.

The group continues their discussion using Mr. Kupras's reciprocal teaching questions as their guide. Before moving to the next step of the process, they will arrive at an answer to the room's square footage and clarify that answer by recheck-ing their calculations. In this algebra classroom, Mr. Kupras uses reciprocal teaching to foster questioning to arrive at the problem's solution by gathering information, completing computations, and sharing the entire process through a presentation.

Implementation Tips for the Mathematics Classroom

Based on the experiences in Mr. Kupras's class and those of other mathematics teachers, here are some recommendations for using reciprocal teaching in the sec-ondary mathematics classroom in order to foster student generated questions:

1. Review and discuss with students all mathematical principles, concepts, and formulas to be used in arriving at the solution to the problem.

2. Apply several sequential mathematical operations to solve the problem. The problem should be authentic and of importance to your students.

3. Place students into heterogeneous groups and share the mathematical inquiry process (see Figure 5.6).

4. Manage by walking around the classroom; answer student questions and provide individual and small-group instruction as needed.

5. Provide a forum for groups to share their answers and the ways in which they arrived at their answers. Groups not presenting should take notes and add them to their findings.

Student-Generated Questioning in Electives

Perhaps the ultimate sign that questioning strategies have been integrated into stu-dent learning can be seen in Dinah Nesbit's child development careers class. This course is an elective in the regional occupational program (ROP). Students enrolled in the class are pursuing a certificate in early childhood education for an eventual

Figure 5.6 Mathematical inquiry process: Using reciprocal teaching to arrive at a solution.

Problem framing: Deciding on the steps to be taken
- Prediction: What would be a reasonable answer to the problem?
- Question: What is being asked and how might you go about finding the answer? (Note: If students are to demonstrate the practical ability to solve mathematical problems, the cultivation of such inquiry is essential. However, the development and employment of appropriate steps is required for the successful completion of this activity. Should groups of students not arrive at the correct strategy, assist as necessary.)

Data collection: Gathering information to use
- Prediction: What would be a reasonable answer to this step? What might the collection of data look like after you are done?
- Question: What is being asked in this first step? How do you go about finding the answer at this point?
- Summary: Have you recorded or charted the data?
- Clarification: Are your data correct? How can you check your data? What results do you get when you checked or repeated the process?

Mathematical applications: Applying mathematics to the data
- Prediction: What would be a reasonable answer to the application of this formula?
- Question: What are the steps of the formula or application? How do you go about its application?
- Summary: What answers do your calculations provide?
- Clarification: How do you know your answer is right? What answer do you get upon checking or using another method? (Note: The mathematical applications part of this process may take several consecutive operations. Students may wish to refer to their textbooks, handouts, and other written materials to assist in arriving at the solution. Reciprocal teaching questions may be used more than once during this part of the process.)

Verification of solution: Reflecting on the process
- Prediction: Was your prediction accurate? How close was your approximation to the actual solution?
- Question: How successful were the steps you took to complete the problem? Did you choose the best ones?
- Summary: Is your answer the correct one?
- Clarification: Have you checked your math? Could the problem be answered a different way? If so, can you arrive at the same solution?

Presentation of problem's solution: Sharing with your peers
- Prediction: Before you started any work, what did your group think the answer would be to the problem? Why did you think this answer was a reasonable one?
- Question: What steps did your group take to arrive at the solution to the problem?
- Summary: What answer did you arrive at? How does this answer compare to the predicted answer?
- Clarification: How do you know this answer is the correct one? How did you check your answer? Were you able to find other ways to arrive at the same answer during the process?

---

career in licensed day care and preschool programs. Course work includes planning and delivering instruction that is consistent with principles of child development. Ms. Nesbit's students are preparing to read aloud stories and question their listeners, all kindergartners at a local elementary school.

The ROP classroom is abuzz with activity. Ms. Nesbit has just announced to her class that they will read to their kindergarten charges tomorrow. The students are excited and anxious about their teaching visit. Sensing her students' motivation, Ms. Nesbit uses this opportunity to review questioning strategies that will help their "little buddies" understand the story *The Quest for One Big Thing* (Fancher, 1998). She stresses that asking questions is not the goal; understanding and learning from listening to the story is. Ms. Nesbit advises, "Sometimes it's helpful to have the children repeat a question before they attempt to answer it."

QUESTIONING

She continues, "And if the child answers your questions, what follow-up questions will encourage him to think more deeply?"

Enrique responds, "I would ask, what makes you say that?"

Andre chimes in, "I'd say, how do you know that?"

Ms. Nesbit takes the lead and asks, "What do you do if the children ask you a question? How could their questions help you as the teacher of the story?"

"From their questions we can see if the kids understand the story or if they are mixed up," offers Lila.

"What do you think about posing 'what if' questions?'" asks Ms. Nesbit.

Carlos joins the discussion. "The kids like when I ask 'what if' questions because they can use their imagination and answer the way they like to."

"They think 'what if' questions are fun," Louisa agrees. "I've seen them asking each other that kind of question when they're playing."

"Can anyone give an example of a 'what if' question you could use with this story," asks Ms. Nesbit.

Angel volunteers, "What if you were a circus bug that was helping with the harvest in the story? What would you do?"

"You did that so well, Angel. Let's try posing an open-ended question to solve the harvest problem," challenges Ms. Nesbit.

Angel hesitates and Leslie jumps in and questions, "How would you get the One Big Thing back to the bug colony?"

Ms. Nesbit smiles with satisfaction as she records their questions on the board. She writes a list of the questions the students have identified during the review of QtA and QAR. Then Ms. Nesbit directs the students to write specific questions about the characters, setting, events, and message of the story.

After preparing their questions, the students share their inquiry choices and write them on small sticky notes to serve as reminders when they read the story aloud. Ms. Nesbit points out the importance of questioning as a teaching strategy as well as a strategic approach to learning. "When we elicit ideas through questions as teachers and learners, we gain information and valuable insight into our own thinking processes. When we demonstrate strategic ways of reading, we stimulate thinking for our peers and other learners, namely the kindergartners."

We couldn't help but notice that Ms. Nesbit's focus on questioning strategies has benefited her own students as well. Their awareness and practice of questioning strategies guides their own comprehension. As a result, the process of applying strategies to content area study becomes internalized as students use questioning techniques in the context of a group activity or independent reading.

Conclusion

The range of questioning strategies discussed in this chapter provides teachers and learners with ways to monitor and guide their construction and examination of meaning in reading, writing, talking, listening, and reflecting. These approaches serve as methods for modeling questions, clarifying, expanding, and revising questions. By maintaining a balance between asking and answering questions, the teacher returns responsibility for critical thinking to the students. The use of effective questioning also directs and focuses students' reading, thereby energizing the reading by inviting students to make connections to both personal experience and prior knowledge.

Chapter **6**
Picture This: Graphic Organizers in the Classroom

*D*aniel arrives at Alice Lin's physics classroom a few minutes after the bell rings for dismissal. Twice a week Ms. Lin offers help after school for any of her students. Daniel has come because he is having difficulty understanding the relationship between work and potential and kinetic energy. He did not do well on Ms. Lin's "daily checkup" (her term for a 10-item ungraded self-assessment she gives each day), so Daniel has scheduled time to meet with his teacher for some tutoring. Ms. Lin and Daniel talk for a few minutes and she realizes that although he knows the definitions, he doesn't yet understand the concept. Ms. Lin takes a blank piece of paper from the printer and begins to draw a graphic organizer (see Figure 6.1). As she and Daniel talk, she adds more details. She then asks Daniel to explain it himself, using the impromptu organizer as a guide for his description. Twenty minutes later, Daniel leaves with the graphic organizer in hand, confident that he'll do well on tomorrow's daily checkup.

Graphic organizers are a popular tool for promoting and extending student understanding of concepts and the relationship between them. These visual displays of information, often arranged in bubbles or squares with connecting lines between them to portray conceptual relationships, are commonly found in many secondary classrooms. Howe, Grierson, and Richmond (1997) surveyed teachers to find out what content area reading strategies they perceived as being most useful. Whereas 82% recommended that graphic organizers like concept maps should be used

Figure 6.1   Graphic organizer on energy.

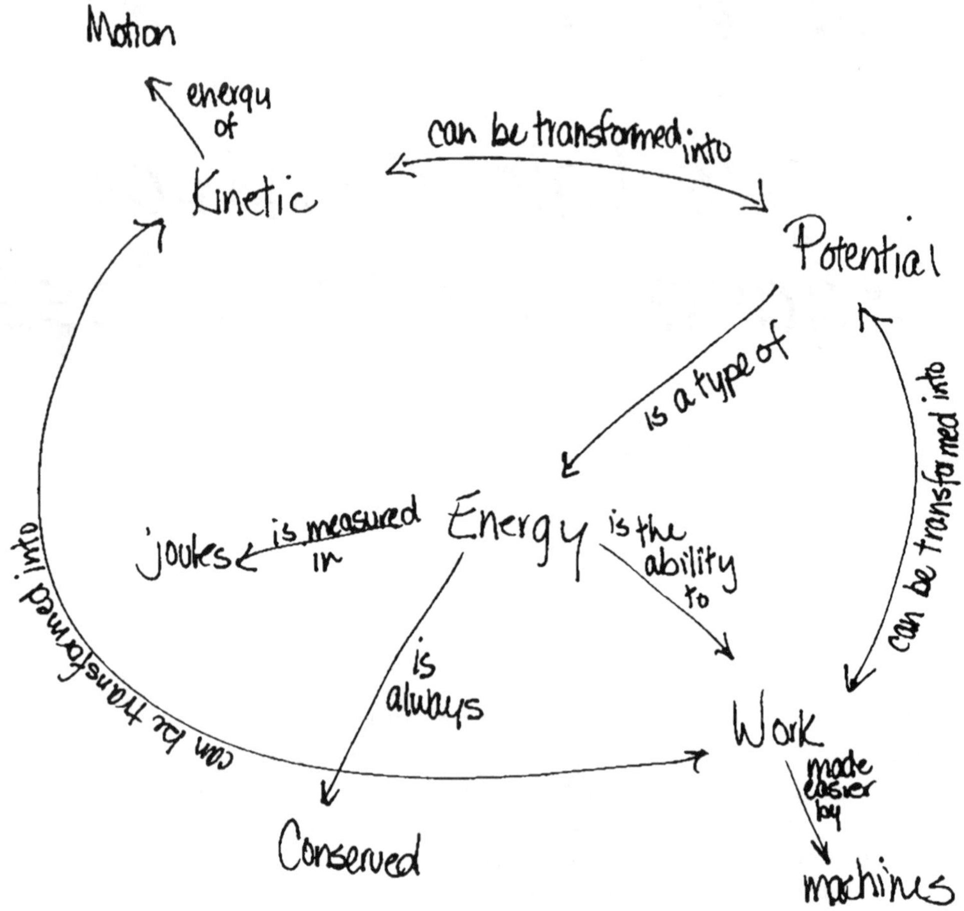

frequently, only 59% admitted that they used them often. This disparity may be due to the perceived difficulty of preparing them in advance.

Teaching and Learning With Graphic Organizers

Robinson (1998) traces the origins of graphic organizers to the advance organizer work of Ausubel (1960). As you may recall from our discussion in chapter 2, advance organizers are brief textual statements that summarize the main points of the upcoming reading, as well as offer explicit connections to larger concepts that may or may not be discussed in the text. They are used as a prereading strategy to assist students in organizing the information through schema building. Advance organizers were immediately a popular instructional tool, and interest soon turned to finding novel ways to use them. Barron (1969) used advance organizers arranged in a nontraditional manner to display vocabulary in ways that represented connections between words, arguably one of the first graphic organizers.

Graphic Organizers Facilitate Comprehension. Comprehension is the ability to derive meaning from text and requires students to mobilize strategies when they do not understand. However, it is more than just understanding—it is being consciously aware of what needs to be done in order to support one's own learning, planning and executing the strategies, then reflecting on their effectiveness. The opportunities presented through graphic organizers activate these comprehension strategies and metacognitive skills. Alvermann and Van Arnam (1984) found that graphic organizers prompted students to reread text passages in order to clarify understanding. Importantly, graphic organizers are effective across disciplines. Zollman (2009) demonstrated the effect of graphic organizers on students' mathematical problem-solving abilities.

Graphic organizers have been shown to be of great assistance to students with learning disabilities. These tools can scaffold information to assist students in constructing written products (James, Abbott, & Greenwood, 2001). They are also effective in promoting recall of information (Dye, 2000). Gajria, Jitendra, and Sood (2007) synthesized numerous studies on instructional practices to support students with learning disabilities in general education classrooms, and recommended graphic organizers as an effective means for modifying difficult textbooks. Their usefulness in the science classroom extends beyond texts—they are also effective for portraying complex science models to students with disabilities (Woodward, 1994).

Struggling Readers

HAVE DIVERSE LEARNING STYLES

Much has been written about learning styles, most notably Gardner's (2006) theory of multiple intelligences. In describing types of intelligences (e.g., linguistic, logical-mathematical, spatial), he and others have been careful to situate this theory within an instructional context. They caution that the goal should not be to identify and then teach to a specific learning style for each student, but to ensure that all are challenged to apply a host of intelligences through the school day. This is proven to be particularly challenging in courses that emphasize a single intelligence over others, such an linguistic intelligence in English. Adolescents who struggle to read may be disadvantaged in part because they have limited opportunity to use a broader repertoire of learning styles, and it appears that there are specific intelligence models related to reading ability (Vanderwood, McGrew, & Flanagan, 2001). Visual displays of information such as graphic organizers provide readers who struggle with a means to view, process, and manipulate information using spatial intelligence. This nonlinguistic form can be especially useful for students who feel disadvantaged by the emphasis on the written and spoken word, as it allows them to demonstrate their understanding and clarify their thinking.

VISUALS

THE BENEFITS FOR ENGLISH LANGUAGE LEARNERS

The reasons graphic organizers are effective in general are the same reasons they're effective with English language learners—they allow for visual representations of complex ideas. As Fisher, Frey, and Williams (2002) noted, graphic organizers help ELLs make connections between what they already know and the content or information at hand. In addition, graphic organizers promote interaction between students (e.g., Egan, 1999), which helps socialize ELLs as well as provide them opportunities to develop their speaking and listening skills. Finally, graphic organizers provide students who are less linguistically proficient an opportunity to engage in rigorous curriculum. Graphic organizers are one way for teachers to ensure that students can show their abilities.

When to Use a Graphic Organizer

The strength of any instructional tool is not only in its use, but in its timing. The science of teaching may be in knowing what to do; the art of teaching lies in knowing when to do it. The same is true for graphic organizers. These visual displays provide students with an opportunity to construct their understanding of a subject in ways that are less linear and therefore better suited for representing complex relationships. Depending on when they are used, graphic organizers can activate prior knowledge, encourage brainstorming, record events in detail, or serve as a review of the topic. In all cases, they are a means of building comprehension.

Instruction in text comprehension often occurs in three phases: before, during, and after reading. Likewise, graphic organizers can support comprehension instruction at each of these key junctures. Take prereading, for instance. Graphic organizers can alert students to important ideas they will encounter during an upcoming reading. Graphic organizers are not confined to prereading experiences. They can also be used during reading. When used in this manner, the graphic organizer resembles a note making tool. The teacher may partially construct a graphic organizer based on previously taught information. However, blanks are strategically used to represent the likely location of a key piece of new vocabulary or concepts. An example of this type of graphic organizer can be viewed in Figure 6.2. As students read and encounter new information, they add them to the graphic organizer. The advantage of this method over traditional note making lies in the portion of the graphic organizer created by the teacher, for it continually draws the student's eye back to material learned prior to the reading.

Figure 6.2   Graphic organizer for use during a reading.

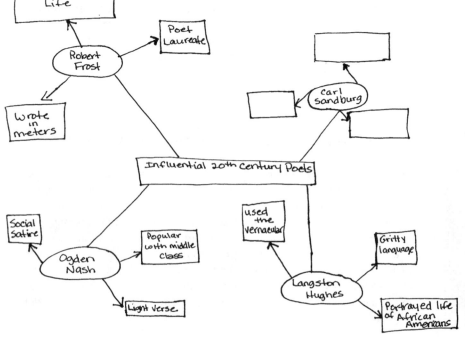

The most popular use for graphic organizers is as a postreading instructional activity. Like those used before and during readings, charts used after a reading are intended to increase comprehension. Many of the examples shown later in the chapter were conceived as a postreading event; indeed several are used as reviews of previously taught information. Vacca and Vacca (1998) point out that strategic readers seek out the structure of the text, looking for the organizational patterns that will give them a framework for ordering new information. When matched carefully with text, graphic organizers can help students clarify the connections and relationships they are finding in the reading. Venn diagrams are an excellent example of a graphic organizer traditionally used after a reading. (We say "traditionally" here, but you will see an art teacher use the same graphic organizer as a prereading tool later in the chapter.) This ubiquitous chart features two overlapping, though not congruent, circles. The portions of the circle that do not overlap are used for contrasting two ideas, phenomenon, or events, while the overlapping portion in the center is reserved for similarities shared by both. Since many high school textbooks contain compare/contrast passages, the Venn diagram is a possible graphic representation of such readings. Keep in mind that the success of a particular graphic organizer in boosting comprehension lies in matching it carefully with the text. It may be this difficulty that prevents so many teachers, like those in the study by Howe et al. (1997), from using graphic organizers more frequently.

Perhaps the biggest mistake made with graphic organizers is that they are viewed as an end product, not a tool to lead to something else. We'll state this as plainly as possible—when the sole purpose of a graphic organizer becomes filling it out correctly, it is nothing more than a worksheet. Too often, students fill it out, turn it in for a grade, and then put it in a folder. They never use it again. Correctly implemented, graphic organizers are an intermediate step to transforming information orally or in written form. Once completed, the graphic organizer should lead to something else: a discussion with a peer, a presentation, an essay, a project display. Students must transform information in their mind or on paper before the information becomes their own.

Types of Graphic Organizers

Graphic organizers are a component of a larger category of instructional aids called adjunct displays (Robinson, 1998). Advance organizers and outlines are two other forms of adjunct displays, because they serve as complementary devices for representing the information contained in a text. Hyerle (1996) reminds us that these devices are important because they allow us to "stor[e] information outside the body . . . [because] human beings are the only form of life that can store, organize, and retrieve data in locations other than our bodies" (p. x). However, graphic organizers have been shown to be more effective for this function than outlines (Kiewra, Kauffman, Robinson, DuBois, & Staley, 1999), perhaps because they allow for nonlinear representations of relationships across concepts.

Graphic organizers come in a variety of forms and go by a number of names, including semantic webs, concept maps, flowcharts, and diagrams. Although there are myriad versions, they all have a few things in common. Each portrays a process or structure in a way that relies on relative position and juxtaposition of words or phrases that are bound by a shape or line. Frequently, they also feature lines to depict associations between and among ideas. Robinson (1998) categorizes graphic organizers into four groups: *concept maps, flow diagrams, tree diagrams,* and *matrices.*

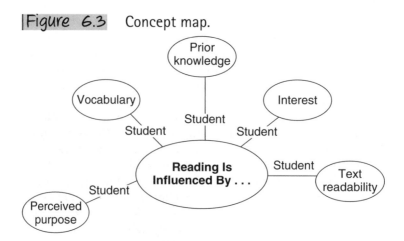

Figure 6.3   Concept map.

Concept Maps. Concept maps are what most people first visualize when they think about graphic organizers. They are shape-bound words or phrases radiating from a central figure that represents the main idea or concept. Lines connect the shapes and may contain words to further explain the relationship. A concept map on the relationship between the reader and the text might look like the one in Figure 6.3.

Concept maps are favored by many educators because they lend themselves to quick and efficient illustrations of complicated ideas. Hyerle (1996) reminds us that students should not simply copy concept maps that have already been created by the teacher, because the power of the concept map lies in the learner's opportunity to "negotiate meaning" (p. 32). Instead, he advises that students be allowed the freedom to construct their own concept maps, even though they may vary from the teacher's schema.

Flow Diagrams. A second type of graphic organizer is the flow diagram. These visual displays are ideal for processes, event sequences, and time lines. Flow diagrams are derived from flowcharts, but they differ in the ways they are constructed. Flowcharts use a standardized vocabulary of shapes to describe an operation or procedure. For instance, oval shapes signal the beginning and ending of the procedure whereas a diamond shape contains questions. Flow diagrams do not adhere to these rules, although they do contain shape-bound text. Arrows show the direction or sequence of the topic illustrated. A flow diagram of a Directed Reading-Thinking Activity (Stauffer, 1969) could look like the one in Figure 6.4. Again, as with concept maps, students should be encouraged to create their own flow diagrams, rather than fill in a predetermined number of boxes.

Tree Diagrams. Tree diagrams are another type of graphic organizer. Like the others, they are suitable for specific purposes. Tree diagrams are most frequently used to categorize and classify information. They are commonly used in mathematics, particularly to represent probability, such as

Figure 6.4   Flow diagram.

```
┌──────────────┐      ┌──────────────┐      ┌──────────────┐
│   Activate   │      │              │      │ Identify text│
│  background  │ ──▶  │   Develop    │ ──▶  │  patterns for│
│  knowledge   │      │  vocabulary  │      │ organization │
└──────────────┘      └──────────────┘      └──────────────┘
                                                    │
                                                    ▼
┌──────────────┐      ┌──────────────┐      ┌──────────────┐
│   Review,    │      │              │      │     Ask      │
│reinforce, and│ ◀──  │   Read the   │ ◀──  │  springboard │
│   evaluate   │      │  selection   │      │  questions   │
└──────────────┘      └──────────────┘      └──────────────┘
```

VISUALS

in repeated tosses of a coin. A tree diagram of the elements of language is found in Figure 6.5.

Tree diagrams can be constructed on the horizontal, as displayed in Figure 6.5, or on the vertical. They typically radiate from a general concept ("language") to a primary level of classification ("receptive" and "expressive"). Supporting categories branch off the primary level of information ("listening," etc.). With each additional level, a greater degree of detail is introduced.

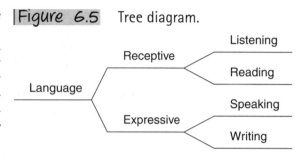

Figure 6.5 Tree diagram.

Matrices. A final commonly used adjunct display is the matrix. A matrix is an arrangement of words or phrases in table format to be read both horizontally and vertically. Like many graphic organizers, matrix designs show relationships, either by comparing and contrasting concepts, or by classifying attributes. Another type of matrix display is a synectic chart (Gordon, 1961). This organizer is meant to foster creative thinking by requiring the learner to link disparate ideas. This type of creative thinking exercise demands that students look for analogies to explain relationships. It begins with a term to be defined and discussed. Students may look up the definition and record it. Then they brainstorm a list of related words that:

- are *similar* to the focus word;
- describe what the word *feels like* (a stretch for many students);
- are *opposite* of the focus word;
- are *similar* to the focus word, but not the same as those listed before; and
- *redefine* the focus word.

This exercise is best done in small groups, where students can discuss each attribute to construct the matrix. Dictionaries and a good thesaurus are helpful tools in completing this type of graphic organizer. If generating words and phrases is too difficult, the teacher can supply a list of words that have been cut apart into small slips of paper to create a word sort. A synectic matrix on language might look like the one found in Figure 6.6.

Teaching Graphic Organizers

Like all good teaching strategies, graphic organizers must be introduced carefully to students (Merkley & Jefferies, 2001). On the surface, they are such a simple tool that there is a temptation to merely distribute them and ask students to fill them in. As we noted before, without proper scaffolding graphic organizers are reduced to

Figure 6.6 Synectics matrix on the concept of language.

Similar	Feels Like	Opposite	Similar	Redefine
talking	recognition	silent	tongue	it separates and unites
communicate	my identity	quiet	poetry	it is art
speech	intelligence	still	prose	it makes me human

VISUALS

the level of a fancy worksheet, completed only to satisfy the teacher. Organizers are visual illustrations; a tool to help students understand, summarize, and synthesize the information from texts or other sources. As students create graphic representations, they manipulate and construct organizational patterns for the informational or narrative text. The students become actively involved in concrete processing of abstract ideas in print form. Here are some considerations to move from teacher-centered to learner-centered instruction for creating and interpreting graphic organizers:

- Set the purpose for the graphic organizer. How will students use the tool to create something new?
- Introduce a specific type of graphic organizer by showing how it represents the structure of a text or concept.
- Model how to use the graphic organizer with a familiar text that the students have read. Emphasize that there is no one "right way" to use a graphic organizer, although there are wise practices (legibility, striking a balance between too little and too much information) that make them more helpful over time.
- Show the class examples of graphic organizers you have created for yourself so that they can see the usefulness of the tool.
- Give students questions to guide them to the important information they should seek in the text.
- When students become more practiced, choose a new text, or new information, and have them apply the same graphic organizer. Create guiding questions with the students; then pair them to complete the process.
- Give students many opportunities to practice using the graphic organizer in pairs, moving toward independent use.
- As students add to their repertoire of graphic organizers, be sure to provide lots of blank copies that are readily accessible. Many teachers keep an open file in the room containing labeled folders of graphic organizers.

With practice and reflection on the process and its benefits, students may begin to alter or design their own graphic organizers. When this happens, celebrate! It's a sign you've done a great job in teaching an important tool for learning.

Using Graphic Organizers for Assessment

Although we have emphasized the practicality of graphic organizers to represent learning as it is being constructed, we don't want to overlook their usefulness as an assessment tool. The goal of assessment, after all, is to provide students with an opportunity to demonstrate what they know. Whereas this is traditionally done with tests that limit students to selecting a correct answer (multiple-choice, true/false, and matching tasks), the true measure of understanding is the ability of the learner to construct an answer. However, extended essays can be time-consuming to grade, particularly if it is a formative (midunit) assessment.

Graphic organizers offer an opportunity for students to construct an answer while allowing the teacher to quickly assess their understanding (Struble, 2007). We witnessed this in a physics classroom when the teacher assigned students to work in small groups to create a concept map representing the states of matter. Several groups created a map that looked like the one in Figure 6.7. All of these manifestations had been discussed during previous classes and dutifully recorded in science notebooks but a few other groups created concept maps that looked like the one found in Figure 6.8. As the physics teacher walked around the classroom, he was able to quickly assess who had read the lab instructions and who had not, because plasma had been featured at length in the text but not in his lecture.

We've reviewed types of graphic organizers and their uses, including construction of understanding transformation of concepts, promotion of creative thinking processes, and assessment. These visual displays foster nonlinear thinking and reveal the relationship of parts to whole. Let's look at how teachers use graphic organizers in their content area classrooms.

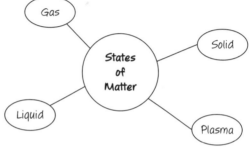

Figure 6.7   States of matter concept map.

Figure 6.8   States of matter concept map.

Strategies at Work
Graphic Organizers in English

With notes in hand or markers in their grip, groups of students gather at tables to design poster-size graphic organizers in the shape of a mountain on large sheets of white butcher paper (see Figure 6.9). At one table, five students take on different tasks to complete the activity on time. At the foot of their story mountain, one group member, Chuong, has drawn a rectangle labeled "Setting" to hold bulleted phrases indicating the place and time of the story *The Circuit: Stories From the Life of a Migrant Child* (Jiménez, 1997). Above "Setting" float cloudlike clusters of information labeled "Title & Author" and "Characters: Protagonist & Antagonist."

Two other members of the group, Lupe and Thao, work as partners. They check notes and confer together as they combine ideas and compose summary sentences that lead to the summit of the mountain. An empty rectangle labeled "Climax" perches on the mountain peak. The two girls first write a sentence in pencil and ask Chuong to check the structure and spelling before they add it to the sequence of events strips that slowly climb the mountain. "Chuong, how is this?" Lupe asks as she reads aloud: "The family packed their belongings in cardboard boxes, loaded Carcanchita, and drove to Fresno to look for work."

Chuong checks the structure and spelling of their sentence, gives them an "OK" and continues sketching the rest of the story mountain components. He slides an arrow down the other side of the story mountain, pointing to another empty rectangle, and writes the word "Resolution" inside.

Two others in the group, Naima and Abdurashid, don't agree on the content of the box labeled "Conflict," so they decide to add a second box with the subtitles "human vs. society" in one, and "human vs. self" in another. "Maybe there are two conflicts in this story," Naima suggests. "One is that the migrant family has to struggle to survive against poverty and always find work from place to place."

|Figure 6.9 Story grammar chart.

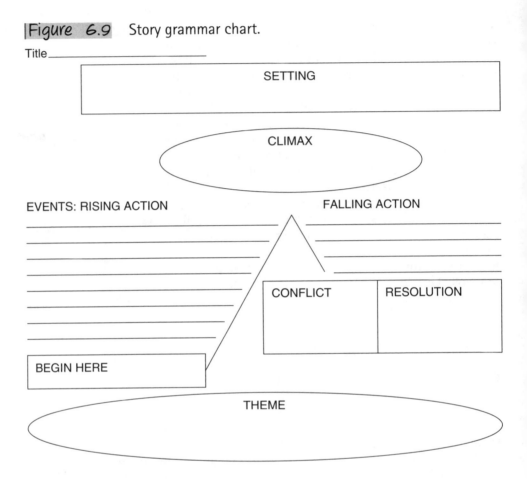

Abdurashid adds, "But the other is that Francisco has to find the courage in himself to go to school and get help so that he can learn to read. Remember when we did the response journal about why he was crying when they had to leave one place? I wrote that it was because he hated to start going to a new school again."

Chuong joins the discussion, wondering aloud if "human vs. nature" is also a conflict since the migrant workers had to work in the hot sun. "From dawn to dusk," he reads from his notes. They give him a look, nod, and add a third "Conflict" box, then move on to consider the empty box labeled "Theme" centered at the base of the mountain.

Abdurashid reminds everyone, "We didn't talk about the theme in class. This time, we're supposed to decide for ourselves."

"So, what do you think it is?" asks Chuong. They all glance over at the bulletin board filled with information about each literary term.

Abdurashid reads the definition, "The theme is the message, buried under the story. We must dig deep to find its meaning." He then asks his group, "So, what did we learn; what message do we get?"

"That family had to stick together to survive. Is that a message about family values?" Naima wonders.

Just then their teacher, Ms. Elwardi, walks by and listens in, so they wait for her response. She nods her head, but then looks puzzled and asks, "Hmm, and the title, *The Circuit*, does that have anything to do with a message?"

They know that is all the information they are going to get from her, so Chuong goes back to his work on "Resolution," Naima writes a statement about family support under "Theme," and Abdurashid checks his notes on the significance of the title, as the teacher sounds the 10-minute warning.

When Monica Perez-Peters teaches tall tales in her ninth-grade English class, she knows that some of her students, who have come from all over the world, may not be familiar with these American folktales. She finds that matrices are effective tools in the study of this genre. As her class reads folktales about Pecos Bill, John Henry, Paul Bunyan, Johnny Appleseed, and Tony Beaver, they use a matrix to demonstrate the characteristics of tall tales that are properties of all literature, and those unique to the genre. As they read, they realize that most of the people in tall tales are working folks whose character traits have been exaggerated and made stronger and larger than life. The design of a matrix lets students create a structure, and insert signal words and target vocabulary in an organized visual form, ready to process into essays and class presentations. Figure 6.10 contains Anthony's representation of the attributes of the tall tales studied.

To accomplish this, Anthony had to read a number of texts. As a student identified as a "struggling reader," Anthony selected a number of picture books and Web sites from the wide variety of sources Ms. Perez-Peters has in her classroom. She makes a significant number of texts available so that her students can find things they can and want to read. In doing so, she knows that her students will read widely on a topic and that the graphic organizer will serve as one way for them to keep track of the information they read. For example, Anthony selected *The Story of Johnny Appleseed* (Aliki, 1963), *Folks Call Me Appleseed John* (Glass, 1995), and *Johnny Appleseed: A Tall Tale Retold* (Kellogg, 1988).

Ms. Perez-Peters scaffolded instruction on the use of a matrix. She first demonstrated its use at the board, with students quickly joining in on the class discussion that allowed the ideas to take shape. She modeled some portions of it, beginning with the major headings. Then small groups worked together to contribute information. Within a few days of introducing this form, her students were developing their own matrices. Ms. Perez-Peters feels confident that her students can transfer this practice to other subject areas because they now use it independently, without direction from their teacher.

Down the hallway in James Kounalis's English class, students are using graphic organizers as a postreading activity. In his class students don't just read short stories, they rebuild them from the foundation up. Students create flow diagrams that mirror the concept of construction. Mr. K., as they refer to their teacher, explains that these flow diagrams reflect the process used by the author. "One doesn't build a building haphazardly, without a plan or structure. To construct the building, frames and scaffolds are necessary. We can't build a story or produce a piece of writing without making use of a plan in an ordered and detailed process."

Students deconstructed Walter Dean Myer's short story "The Fighter" (Myers, 2001) to analyze the writer's craft. Using the elements of story—setting,

Figure 6.10   A matrix of tall tales.

Tall Tale character	Pecos Bill	Johnny Appleseed	Paul Bunyan	Tony Beaver	John Henry
Famous for...		Scattering appleseeds Selling trees to settlers		Cutting down trees with one swing	
Physical characteristics		Wore paper sacks had a pot for his hat		Strong very big	
Region or State		Appalachia Ohio River valley		West Virginia	
occupation		Planter		lumberjack	
Real or Fictional	Real	real (John Chapman)		fictional	
Family?		No		Yes	

character, plot, conflict, climax, resolution, and theme—students worked in groups to record the building blocks of the tale. However, unlike the story mountain used by Ms. Elwardi's students to identify literary devices, these students looked for evidence of the author's use of sequence to reveal each element to the reader. As Mr. K. remarked, "Walter Dean Myers didn't just gather the building blocks; he placed each one carefully into the story. When an author assembles these elements artfully, the story hangs together."

Figure 6.11 Student flow diagram in English class.

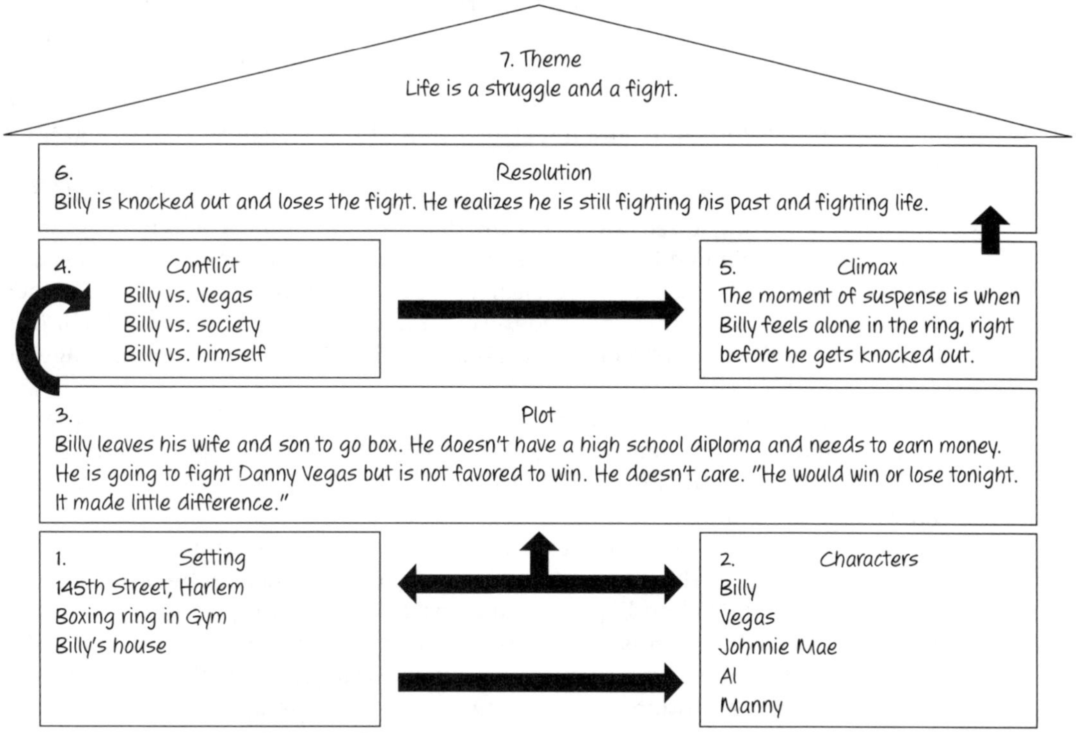

7. Theme
Life is a struggle and a fight.

6.   Resolution
Billy is knocked out and loses the fight. He realizes he is still fighting his past and fighting life.

4.   Conflict
Billy vs. Vegas
Billy vs. society
Billy vs. himself

5.   Climax
The moment of suspense is when Billy feels alone in the ring, right before he gets knocked out.

3.   Plot
Billy leaves his wife and son to go box. He doesn't have a high school diploma and needs to earn money. He is going to fight Danny Vegas but is not favored to win. He doesn't care. "He would win or lose tonight. It made little difference."

1.   Setting
145th Street, Harlem
Boxing ring in Gym
Billy's house

2.   Characters
Billy
Vegas
Johnnie Mae
Al
Manny

Mr. K. observed that while building these maps, students made frequent connections back to the text as they manipulated and analyzed information. Their completed products depicted an understanding of not only what the story was about, but also a recognition of the care the author used to unfold the story. One group's map appears in Figure 6.11. The lively class discussions that followed this activity indicated that students were eager to explain their decisions and answer questions with evidence from the text.

Literary analysis can seem tedious to adolescents who may view a single reading of a story as sufficient. By using opportunities for creative expression, students can explore a text more deeply to examine the writer's craft. Graphic organizers are not the only means to accomplish this goal; however, these tools can prompt higher-order thinking.

Graphic Organizers in Social Studies

With a little "Inspiration" and time in the computer lab, Marisol Acuna's world history class mapped out important concepts as they reviewed information on WWI. Within minutes at the computers, pages of information from both the text and their notes took on a visual form as students organized main ideas and supporting information. As a tool for review, concept mapping gave Ms. Acuna's students the opportunity to recall important concepts pertinent to a historical period, reproduce a structure that reflects the information, and then integrate targeted vocabulary essential to each concept.

VISUALS

Ms. Acuna modeled the use of Inspiration®, a computer program for students and teachers to design graphic organizers and outlines. She chose the Industrial Revolution, a topic covered weeks earlier in class, as the subject for her map. With the aid of her class, she designed a concept map of pertinent information following the directions from a pop-up menu on the screen. Students recalled chunks of information about the unit, and then watched as it was transformed into a graphic organizer.

Ms. Acuna further engaged her students by showing how they could use templates, including a tree diagram, flow diagram, and a cause and effect graphic organizer. She explained that the type of text or information can influence the template they might choose. All were clearly impressed with this feature, and when she clicked on a button that changed the completed concept map into a linear outline, the room filled with "oohs" and "ahhs"! At that point, students were eager to create their own.

Ms. Acuna was also pleasantly surprised to watch her students weave the targeted vocabulary into their maps. As she circled the lab, she spotted words like *reparations, propaganda, ally, warfare, neutral, treaty,* and *policy* either in context or connected to a definition.

No student left the lab without a printout of their concept map and the corresponding linear outlines. Ms. Acuna commented on their value as an assessment tool as well. "When I spotted an error, I was able to question the student about it and clarify any misunderstandings right on the spot." These maps also served as perfect tools to structure expository writing. After the mapping session, Ms. Acuna's students wrote summaries that paraphrased information transferred from their graphic organizers. David's summary created from his graphic organizer appears in Figure 6.12.

Graphic Organizers in Mathematics

"Graphic organizers? My students don't leave mathematics class without them." Carol Chie uses an assortment of graphic organizers in geometry and precalculus, particularly at the beginning and end of units. She explains, "We use graphic organizers to bring in everything students already know, and relate it to current topics. Mathematics is taught unit by unit and very often students don't see any correlation between what we are learning now and what we've learned before. They'll ask, 'When am I going to use this? Why do I have to learn this?'" These questions are often heard in high school mathematics classes. Mathematics is a structure that builds on itself, and if students can build their own structures they will see that these theories interrelate. By using graphic organizers, they are more apt to see connections between what they have learned and what they are currently learning.

Ms. Chie introduces compare/contrast graphic organizers through classroom discussion. Her students identify similarities and differences between mathematical theories and she simply records it, rather than filling it in herself for them to copy. Her role is to ask questions that prompt connections and promote inquiry. As a class, they create a product that is more complete because they are organizing collective knowledge. Ms. Chie sees this practice as vital in precalculus and calculus because these students will soon be working in study groups, common at the university level. Ms. Chie wants students to more than simply use graphic organizers; she wants them to witness the benefits of collaborative study with peers.

VISUALS

Figure 6.12   Summary based on information in graphic organizer.

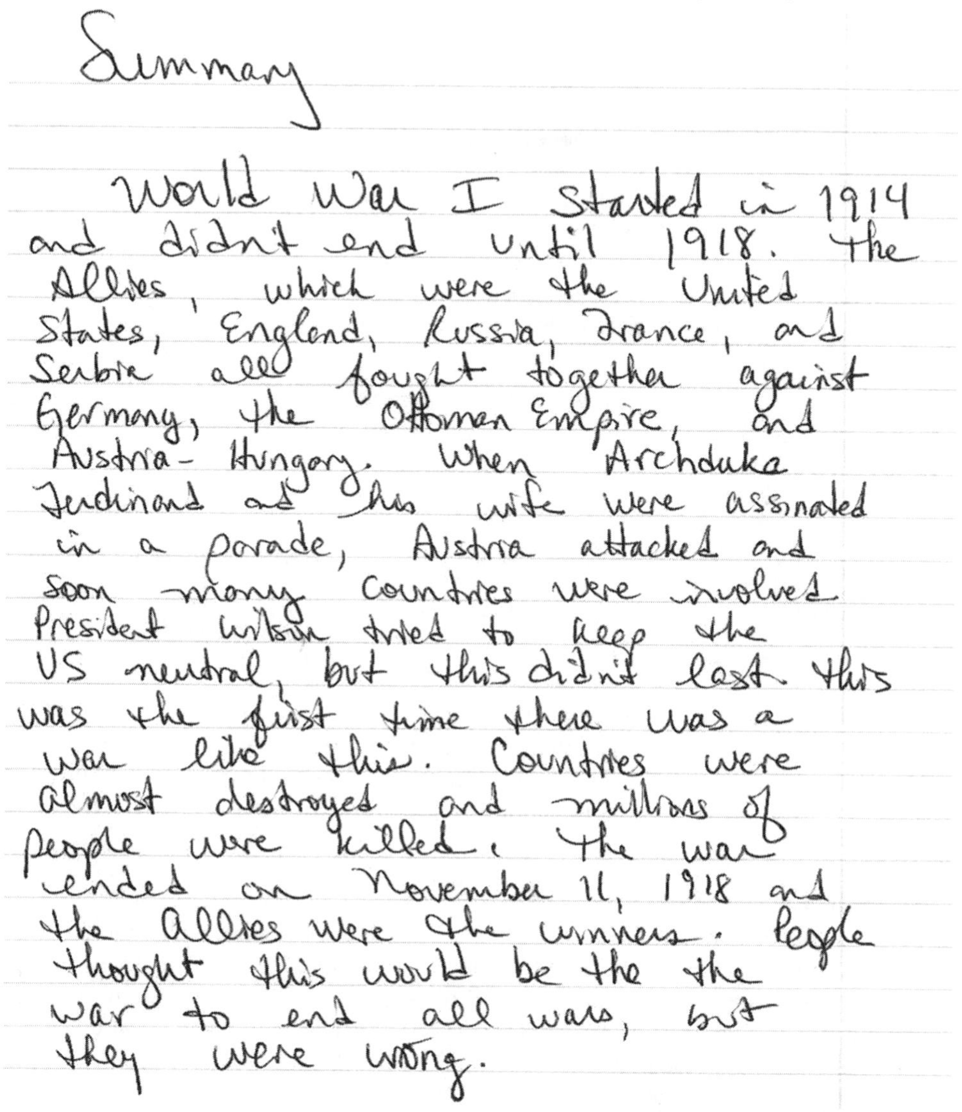

Summary

World War I started in 1914 and didn't end until 1918. The Allies, which were the United States, England, Russia, France, and Serbia all fought together against Germany, the Ottoman Empire, and Austria-Hungary. When Archduke Ferdinand and his wife were assinated in a parade, Austria attacked and soon many countries were involved. President Wilson tried to keep the US neutral, but this didn't last. This was the first time there was a war like this. Countries were almost destroyed and millions of people were killed. The war ended on November 11, 1918 and the Allies were the winners. People thought this would be the the war to end all wars, but they were wrong.

Eventually whole-class practice becomes small-group practice. This transition is vital to Ms. Chie because graphic organizers also serve as an assessment tool. At a glance, she has a clear picture of what each student has grasped. This is important because some similarities and differences are very minute, but critical. For example, in comparing an ellipse and a hyperbola, there is one sign difference between equations. If it's a minus, it creates a hyperbola; if it's a plus, it creates an ellipse. If students are going to have trouble determining whether the equation produces a hyperbola or an ellipse, the graphic organizer pinpoints the misunderstanding. If, on the other hand, the sign is correct, Ms. Chie knows that her students understand that a single sign is the determining factor. One student's organizer appears in Figure 6.13.

VISUALS

Figure 6.13   Compare/Contrast in precalculus.

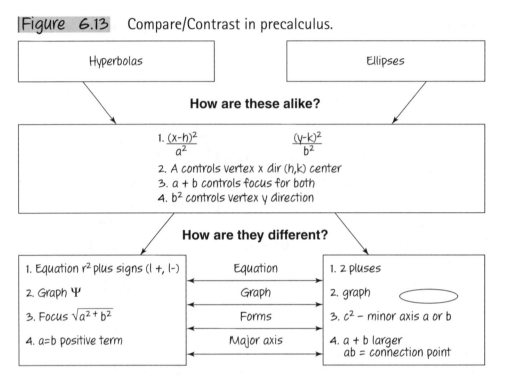

Graphic organizers like the one used in Ms. Chie's class are useful because they challenge students to see both analogous and disparate relationships among mathematical theories. In this way, she extends student understanding beyond memorization of algorithms to a deeper appreciation of how these formulas are woven together.

Graphic Organizers in Science

Science teacher Larry Caudillo uses concept mapping to familiarize his biology students with scientific terminology and to construct schema. He often creates a concept map based on a piece of informational text his students will be reading. In this way, he can introduce a visual display to assist his students in learning new vocabulary. After the first reading of the text and further instruction by the teacher, students revisit the map in order to add new information. Mr. Caudillo then gives them responsibility for creating their own maps. He discovered that his students' concept maps are far more intricate and complex than those he has designed or taken from textbooks.

Mr. Caudillo combines graphic organizers with other instructional strategies to engage his students in higher-order thinking. For example, he used a word sort activity to review before a unit exam in biochemistry. The review focused on macromolecules classified as lipids, proteins, carbohydrates, and nucleic acids. He chose terms as target vocabulary, then printed them on magnetized word cards. In addition, he gave the students blank cards so they could supply other terms they might want to use. When class began, students were asked to list and categorize the words. One group arranged the cards to look like the display in Figure 6.14.

Mr. Caudillo gave further directions. "Each table has 10 minutes to design a concept map of all the target vocabulary you have just sorted. Remember, I expect you to label all the linkages to show the relationships. You'll transfer them to the whiteboard and explain your reasoning. We'll decide which maps are most

|Figure 6.14   Word sort for science class.

complete and accurate." As the groups worked, Mr. Caudillo circulated around the classroom of 40 students to assess their works in progress.

Ten minutes later, a table was selected to display their product on the whiteboard. All eyes followed Ja'leel, who was chosen by his group to serve as reporter. He swiftly shuffled the magnetized word cards into a network depicting the complex relationships, then drew bubbles around words and labeled lines between words to symbolize theoretical connections. While students at each table watched the concept map take shape, many could be seen rereading and revising their own maps. When he was finished, his group's concept map looked like the one found in Figure 6.15.

|Figure 6.15   Student concept map in science.

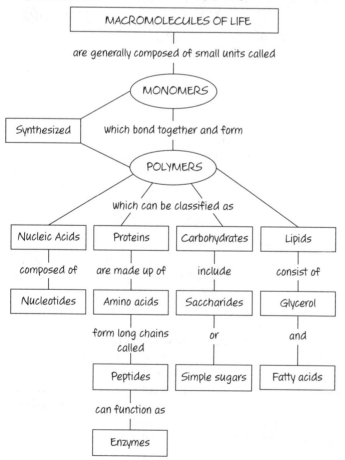

Figure 6.16 Summary based on graphic organizer.

The Macromolecules of Life

The macromolecules of life are the molecules that make up all living things. These are composed of small units called monomers which are synthesized into polymers. The monomers are nucleotides, amino acids, saccharides, and fatty acids and glycerol. They bond together to form the polymers, which are nucleic acids, (DNA and RNA), long peptide chains of proteins, and also carbohydrates that form simple sugars and polysaccharides. The last kind is lipids. They don't become large polymers always, but some are polymerized with glycerol. These long chains of polymers are the macromolecules of life.

But they are not done yet. Mr. Caudillo knows that graphic organizers are tools for students to use to organize their thinking. He doesn't collect these graphic organizers, but instead asks students to individually summarize, in writing, the content. He knows that inviting students to write what they know and have learned is good for the literacy development and science knowledge. Arian's summary of the macromolecules of life can be found in Figure 6.16.

Graphic Organizers in Electives

Jeremy Merrill's students learn principles of art through their own discovery, and graphic organizers are a tool for clarifying this discovery process. For example, when Mr. Merrill's studio art students explored the similarities and differences between geometric and gestural drawings, they used the two interlocking circles of a Venn diagram to define the attributes of each one.

He introduced this activity by asking students to watch as he began to draw two still life forms on the whiteboard. He did not speak again until he had finished the drawings. After adding a large question mark above each drawing, he addressed the class. "You all have copies of a reading at your table. I want you to look for anything that you think might relate to these two sketches. As a group, decide what is similar about these two ways of sketching. Also, discuss what you find is different about them. Your job is to be able to compare and contrast these two forms of sketching."

Mr. Merrill then walked among the tables and listened in as his students read and discussed. They found that the written information matched what they had just seen their teacher render on the board.

After the reading and table discussions, Mr. Merrill asked, "Have you ever heard of a Venn diagram?"

"It looks like two circles that cross over in the middle," students at one table offered. "In the middle part, the two topics are the same, and the outside parts only show what is different." While the students spoke, he drew two large overlapping circles on another whiteboard.

"How should they be labeled?" he asked.

Several students responded, "Geometric and Gestural."

The teacher then distributed chart paper for groups to develop a diagram that reflected both the differences and the similarities between the two drawing techniques. Students could be seen referring back to the text and posing questions of their group members. By putting information into a compare/contrast Venn diagram form, they could now connect what they had seen their teacher demonstrate to what they had then just read.

Within one lesson, Mr. Merrill used three modes of understanding—drawing, reading, and mapping—as he led his students to discover the concepts integral to their next art project. With a clear understanding of the two sketching techniques, students then successfully used both approaches in their drawings of a still life. Just as important, these students moved between written and visual displays of information to construct their own schema of the subject.

Conclusion

Graphic organizers can be used throughout the curriculum to help students understand the relationships between ideas. Because they are tools for categorizing and storing information, visual displays can be useful in helping students understand complex information. In addition, they are particularly well suited for representing nonlinear information by showing the complexity of relationships between and among ideas, phrases, and words.

Graphic organizers are useful before students read, during their assigned reading, and after reading. Although there is no one "ideal" time for using these visual displays, the most common application comes after the reading. However, the versatility of many graphic organizers make them flexible across instructional events. Common graphic organizers include concept maps, flow diagrams, tree diagrams, and matrices. Other choices include Venn diagrams and compare/contrast maps. Graphic organizers are popular with students and teachers, but it is important to match the tool to the text.

As with other instructional routines, it is essential to teach students how to use and construct graphic organizers. Without instruction, they cease to be tools and become fancy worksheets to be filled out for the teacher. Each tool should be introduced and scaffolded, and the growing cadre of organizers should be on hand for students to access when needed. Most importantly, students should be encouraged to construct their own unique organizers. When students are successful in accomplishing this goal, the teacher can be assured that the learners are employing higher-order thinking skills.

VISUALS

Regardless of when they are used, graphic organizers aid in comprehension. They have long been recognized as a metacomprehension tool, and students who successfully use graphic organizers are more likely to grasp the concepts discussed in the text. Graphic organizers should be understood as an intermediate tool for transforming information in the learner's mind or on paper. Further, graphic organizers can be used as an assessment tool providing teachers with an authentic glimpse into a student's thinking. Unlike traditional multiple-choice testing that restricts student responses, student-constructed graphic organizers can provide evidence of sophisticated levels of student knowledge.

VISUALS

Chapter 7

Getting It Down: Making and Taking Notes Across the Curriculum

David Michaels sits behind his potter's wheel and begins a discussion of the various types of ceramics. The students in his art class take out their notebooks and begin taking notes on the information their teacher is sharing. They know that Mr. Michaels will focus his lecture, providing information that they'll need to be successful when they create their pieces of art. Mr. Michaels expects that his students use the correct vocabulary in his ceramics class, from scraffito *to* arabesque. *He knows that he can help his students understand this vocabulary through his focused lectures and their notetaking. He also knows that the notetaking skills his students develop in ceramics can be used throughout their school day and that he is contributing to the overall success, and study habits, of his students. A sample page from a students' ceramics notebook can be found in Figure 7.1. Notice the obvious thinking on the part of the student as well as the careful planning done by the teacher to ensure that information flowed and was connected.*

Why Teach Students How to Take Notes?

During a conversation with a group of teachers, we asked them about the various ways they teach students to store and retrieve information from class lectures and texts. Interestingly, notetaking was a given, something that all students should do. As one of the teachers said, "While people may have different ways of taking notes, I do believe that it's a skill that can be taught. I also believe that students need to be shown how to take notes—good notes—that they can use later." We concur. The

Figure 7.1 Cornell notes from ceramics class.

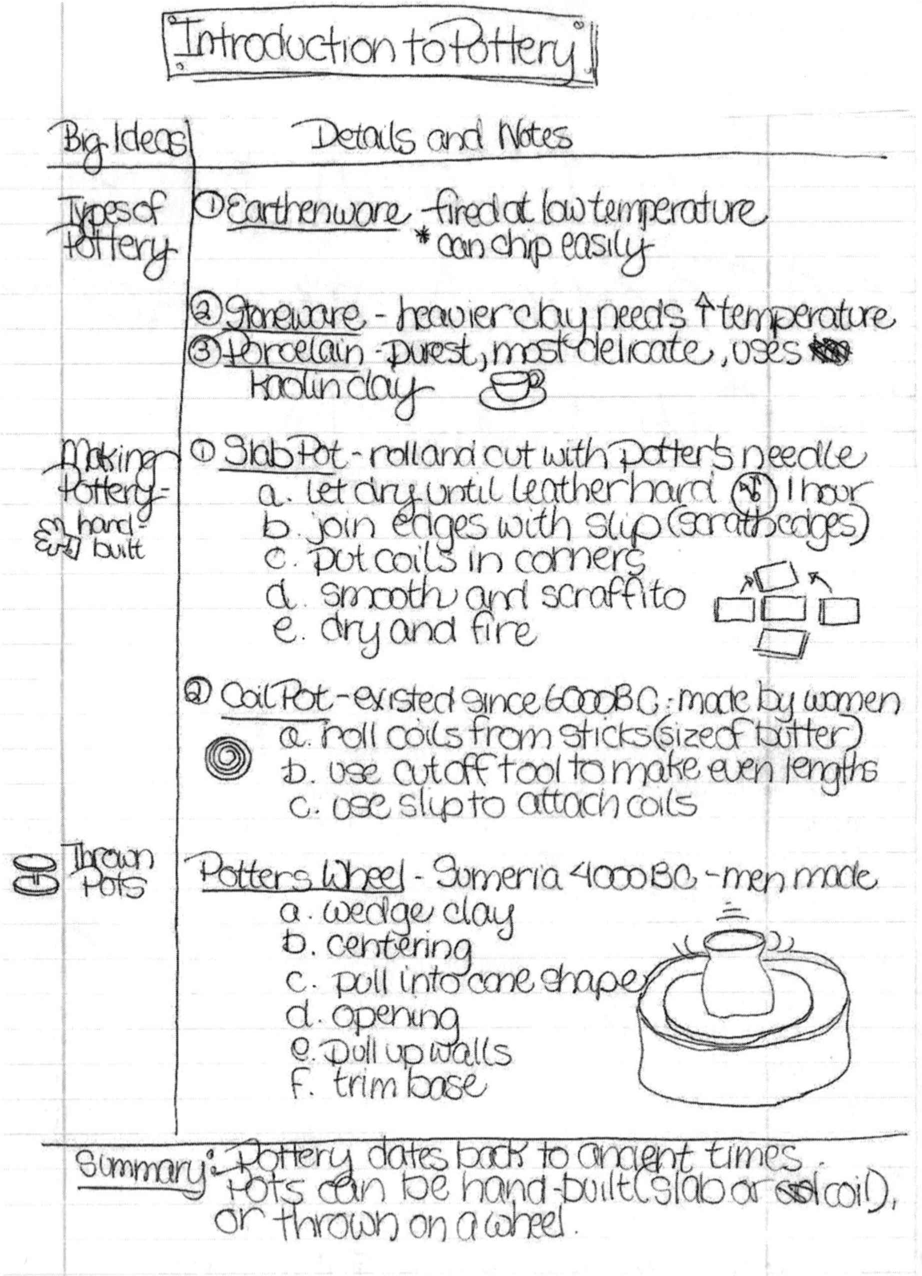

key is to identify for students why their notes can be useful to them later as some students see notetaking as a waste of their time. As Jim Burke (2002) noted:

> Taking notes is an essential skill, one that has many other subskills embedded within it. Taking good notes trains students not only to pay attention but what to pay attention to. It teaches them to evaluate the importance of information and the relationship between different pieces of information as they read textbooks and

THE BENEFITS FOR ENGLISH LANGUAGE LEARNERS

Helping students organize their thinking and understanding is very helpful for English language learners who are likely spending significant amounts of time trying to figure out what is happening in the classroom. Badger, White, Sutherland, and Haggis (2001) report that there is a relationship between notetaking and English language learners' conceptualizations of content. The authors note that using a systematic approach to notetaking in which students understand the purpose of the notes and what to do with the notes is most helpful for them. Further, Gu (2003) found that notetaking helps ELLs learn vocabulary.

articles. It also teaches them to organize that information into some format that serves their purposes. After all, we take different notes if we will use them to write a research paper. (p. 21)

Setting Up Students for Successful Notetaking

Although it is important to teach students how to take and use notes effectively, educators also have a responsibility to organize their lectures in ways that make it possible to create notes. It is instructionally sound to introduce the sequence of topics and concepts for the day's class because it prepares students for learning. This simple preview also gives students a way to organize their notes. Once previewed, students should expect that the sequence will not be drastically altered and that the teacher will present concepts in an organized fashion. Detailed information, including technical vocabulary, names, dates, and formulas, should be presented visually as well as verbally, and well-timed pauses should be used to give students time to record this information. Signal words and phrases like "this is important" or even "be sure to write this down" will alert students to include items in their notes. Ending the class with a review enhances memory and retention and allows students to make corrections to their day's notes.

Distinguishing Notetaking From Note Making. Before we venture any further, a definition or two is in order. We use the term *notetaking* to refer to students' written notes from a lecture or class discussion. We use the term *note making* to refer to the slightly

Struggling Readers

BENEFIT FROM ORGANIZATIONAL SUPPORT

Many adolescent readers who struggle with reading possess inadequate organizational skills to store and retrieve information. This becomes especially problematic when these same students are required to complete homework and other out-of-classroom assignments. At times, they may be in possession of too much information, or the wrong kind of information for the task. Unable to locate and use the information they have (notes, handouts, readings), many give up. Warger (2001) suggests five strategies teachers can use to support their students who struggle with organization:

- Give clear and *appropriate assignments* (record on the board, provide examples, and write directions).
- Make homework *accommodations* (adjust length or complexity).
- *Teach study skills* (label materials, schedule time to work on assignments).
- *Use a homework calendar* (have student graph completion rate).
- *Ensure clear home–school communication* (post assignments on Web, provide families with suggestions on how to assist).

NOTES

different phenomenon of recording notes from printed materials. Whereas many of the procedures are the same, we have to remember that students cannot go back again for more information in notetaking (e.g., the lecture is over); they can in note making (by rereading the text).

In terms of research on notetaking and note making, the evidence is fairly conclusive. Better notetakers generally do better in school and specific types of notetaking produce better results (e.g., Faber, Morris, & Lieberman, 2000; Kiewra, Benton, Kim, Risch, & Christensen, 1995). The reasons for this are interesting. Dating back to the seminal work of DiVesta and Gray (1972), the evidence suggests that notetaking requires both a process and a product function. It seems that both of these are important to produce results—improved comprehension and retention of material.

Process and Product Functions. The process function (recording the notes) and the product function (reviewing notes later) are both required to create valuable notes (e.g., Henk & Stahl, 1985; Katayama & Crooks, 2001). Stahl, King, and Henk (1991) refer to this as the "encoding and external storage functions" (p. 614). The encoding function requires students to pay attention to the lecture while they write. This, in turn, allows students to transform information and deepens their understanding. The external storage function allows students an opportunity to review their notes, and thus the main ideas presented, before using the information on a test, essay, or lab.

In addition to the use of graphic organizers for notetaking, a number of common formats have been suggested. Figure 7.2 contains "12 time-honored criteria for

Figure 7.2 General notetaking procedures.

Date and label notes at the top of the page.

Draw a margin and keep all running lecture notes to one side.

Use other side for organization, summarizing, and labeling.

Indent to show importance of ideas.

Skip lines to indicate change of ideas.

Leave space for elaboration and clarification.

Use numbers, letters, and marks to indicate details.

Be selective.

Abbreviate when possible.

Paraphrase.

Use underlining, circling, and different colors of ink to show importance.

Cover one side of notes to study.

Source: From "Enhancing Students' Notetaking Through Training and Evaluation," by Norman A. Stahl, James R. King, and William A. Henk, May 1991, *Journal of Reading, 34*(8), pp. 614–622. Reprinted with permission of the International Reading Association. All rights reserved.

successful notetaking" (Stahl et al., 1991, p. 615). They have also developed an assessment and evaluation system for teaching students about notetaking called NOTES (Notetaking Observation, Training, and Evaluation Scales). NOTES (found in Figure 7.3) provides teachers with a specific way of giving students feedback on their current performance in notetaking. The assessment page focuses on current habits of notetaking, whereas the evaluation criteria provides a rubric for teachers to use when reviewing a page of notes with a student (see Figure 7.4). Each of these tools is useful for teachers who wish to give their students an important study skill. Beyond this, there are specific approaches to notetaking and note making that will be explored by the teachers highlighted in this chapter.

Strategies at Work

Notetaking in English

Students walk into Mr. Herrera's classroom and are welcomed with a wide, ear-to-ear grin. Within this comfortable atmosphere, his ninth-grade students are taught responsible listening and notetaking practices using a strategy called *dictoglos* (Wajnryb, 1990). The purpose of this strategy is to give students experience hearing and recording English spoken fluently.

To begin the dictoglos activity, Mr. Herrera asks his students to listen to a read aloud. As noted in the chapter on read alouds, he is careful to choose a passage that will immediately engage his students and relate to a unit of study. Today Mr. Herrera has selected the writing of Tupac Shakur (1999) to introduce his poetry unit. Once his students are hooked, Mr. Herrera asks them to listen to the same text, read two more times aloud. During these next two read alouds, they must take notes on what they hear so that they can recreate the text as accurately as possible. Consistent with the dictoglos strategy, he provides his students with a few minutes to write what they remember after each read aloud.

After two attempts at writing exactly what they heard, students pair up and share what they have written and attempt to add more to their notes. Two pairs then join and the four students collaborate to recreate the text verbatim. By this time, students have reviewed their notes, and listened to and read others' notes, as they add and revise their own.

Mr. Herrera finds that by giving his students practice in dictoglos they become better notetakers and skilled listeners. He notes several benefits to teaching notetaking in this way. First, when the students initially hear the text, and even during the second and third reading of the passage, they must listen carefully and maintain an intense focus for the entire reading. This practice teaches students to block out other distractions, a necessary skill for taking notes during a lecture. Most lectures are not repeated and students must record information during their one-time opportunity. Second, students must learn to focus on the most important phrases during their first writing attempt, selecting only the key words that carry the meaning, even if some of the details are not yet scripted. This practice is also essential to good notetaking because one cannot write everything one hears. As students learn how to listen for key phrases, their notes become more valuable to them as study aids. Thus, with periodic practice of dictoglos, ninth-grade English students practice elements of good notetaking—selective listening and scripting of key phrases. They gain skills necessary for success in other content area classrooms by this nonthreatening, engaging, collaborative activity.

Figure 7.3 Assessment for NOTES.

	Never	Sometimes	Always
Prelecture			
1. I read assignments and review notes before my classes.			
2. I come to class with the necessary tools for taking notes (pen and ruled paper).			
3. I sit near the front of the class.			
4. My notes are organized by subjects in a looseleaf notebook.			
5. I have a definite notetaking strategy.			
6. I adapt my notetaking for different classes.			
Lecture			
1. I use my pen in notetaking.			
2. I use only one side of the page in taking notes.			
3. I date each day's notes.			
4. I use my own words in writing notes.			
5. I use abbreviations whenever possible.			
6. My handwriting is legible for study at a later date.			
7. I can identify the main ideas in a lecture.			
8. I can identify details and examples for main ideas.			
9. I indent examples and details under main ideas to show their relationship.			
10. I leave enough space to resolve confusing ideas in the lecture.			
11. I ask questions to clarify confusing points in the lecture.			
12. I record the questions my classmates ask the lecturer.			
13. I am aware of instructor signals for important information.			
14. I can tell the difference between lecture and nonrelated anecdote.			
15. I take notes until my instructor dismisses class.			

NOTES

Figure 7.3   Continued.

	Never	Sometimes	Always
Postlecture			
1. My notes represent the entire lecture.			
2. I review my notes immediately after class to make sure that they contain all the important points of the lecture and are legible.			
3. I underline important words and phrases in my notes.			
4. I reduce my notes to jottings and cues for studying at a later date.			
5. I summarize the concepts and principles from each lecture in a paragraph.			
6. I recite from the jottings and cues in the recall column on a weekly basis.			
7. I use my notes to draw up practice questions in preparation for examinations.			
8. I ask classmates for help in understanding confusing points in the lecture.			
9. I use my notes to find ideas that need further explanation.			
10. I am completely satisfied with my notetaking in my courses.			
11. I can understand my notes when I study them later.			
12. I use the reading assignment to clarify ideas from the lecture.			

Source: From "Enhancing Students' Notetaking Through Training and Evaluation," by Norman A. Stahl, James R. King, and William A. Henk, May 1991, *Journal of Reading*, 34(8), pp. 614–622. Reprinted with permission of the International Reading Association. All rights reserved.

Notetaking in Mathematics

Mr. Williams begins his Algebra II lesson by focusing students on the structured note-taking that they will refer to regularly as they proceed through each lesson. Kiewra and colleagues (1995) refer to this style of notetaking as an *outline* framework. Essentially, Mr. Williams will provide students an outline or format that they can use to take notes. Although outline formats differ, Kiewra et al. (1995) suggest that the outline framework helps students understand the internal connections within the content.

Mr. Williams knows that mathematics is a language in and of itself and that the correct use of terms is vital for comprehension. To establish a target vocabulary, Mr. Williams tells the class, "Please take out three sheets of paper. Everyone will take notes." This is clearly an expectation for all, but any anxiety is quickly allayed with the following statement, "I'll tell you what to write." The gentle directiveness in his style encourages students to negotiate with each other and take risks in this learning community.

Figure 7.4   Notes evaluation criteria.

Value Points and Descriptors of Notetaking Habits			
Format	**3**	**2**	**1**
Use of ink	I use pen consistently.	I use pen and pencil.	I use pencil.
Handwriting	Others can read my notes.	Only I can read my notes.	I can't read my notes.
Notebook	I use a looseleaf binder.	I use a spiral notebook.	I don't use a notebook.
Use of page	I leave enough space for editing.	I leave some space for editing.	My notes cover the page.
Organization	**3**	**2**	**1**
Headings	I use new headings for each idea.	I use headings inconsistently.	I don't use headings for main changes in main ideas.
Subtopics	I group suptopics under headings.	I don't indent subtopics under headings.	My subtopics are not grouped.
Recall column	I use cue words and symbols to make practice questions.	I use cue words in a recall column.	I don't use a recall column.
Abbreviation	I abbreviate whenever possible.	I use some abbreviations.	I don't abbreviate.
Summaries	I summarize lectures in writing.	I write a list of summary lecture topics.	I don't summarize.
Meaning	**3**	**2**	**1**
Main points	I identify main points with symbols and underlining.	I list main points.	I don't list main points.
Supporting details	I show the relationships between main ideas and details.	My notes list details.	I don't list details.
Examples	I list examples under main points.	I list some examples.	I don't record examples.
Restatement	I use my own words.	I use some of my own words.	I use none of my own words.

Students follow his direction and fold each sheet of paper into quadrants and draw vertical and horizontal lines to separate the four areas. He poses the question, "While you are doing that . . . why is it important to take notes in class?"

Anthony responds, "So that you can remember."

"Remember what? And when?" Mr. Williams probes a bit further.

Gabriela offers, "At home, when you are doing homework, you can look at your notes to remind you how to do the problem, and what it looks like."

"You've got it. These notes will guide your work with me, with your partners, and on your own. Now, write this down." He then introduces all of the words necessary for the day's lesson on addition and subtraction of polynomials. He asks students to write one term per quadrant in the top left corner of each box until they run out of words. The list of terms for the day looks like this:

polynomial	equation	like terms
monomial	binomial	trinomial
degree	standard form	coefficient
leading coefficient		

Under each term, Mr. Williams asks students to identify the prefixes and roots in each of the words and to note other words that contain the prefix or root. Once they understand the component parts, he asks them to define the term. Mr. Williams, engaging his students in vocabulary development practice and notetaking, begins with the first word and asks, "What do you know about the prefix 'poly'? What other words do you know that start this way?" As they determine the meaning of each term, he returns to the list on the board and writes the definition that both he and the class have agreed upon. He then says, "Now write this." Slowly, the class is building a word wall, and when this notetaking practice is complete, every student in class will have his or her own glossary of mathematical terms. From that point on, students refer to their notes as Mr. Williams uses the terms. An example of one of the quadrants of the outlined framework can be found in Figure 7.5.

Mr. Williams understands his new class well as he changes pace from structured notetaking to creating equations—out of the bananas, grapes, and plums he has distributed to each table. Students learn the concept of a "term" in mathematics by using the pieces of fruit as manipulatives.

He first creates his own equation by placing four bananas, six grapes, and two plums on the front table and asks the students to write an equation based on the fruit information. As students respond, he urges them to use their notes. "I'm looking for the vocabulary from our list that fits." He sees them glancing from him to their notes, as they negotiate with their table partners an explanation to his question. He has given each group a table tent with "WORKING" written on one side and "READY" written on the other. He reminds them to turn them to "WORKING" or "READY" as appropriate. This lets him know how much time students need to complete the task. He then asks them to write the following equation:

$$4B + 6G + 2P =$$

Next, the students are required to create their own equations, and to explain them, using the target vocabulary at their side. One group of students immediately turned their sign to WORKING and created two bunches: seven plums and six grapes. After a brief discussion, they turned their sign to READY, and Mr. Williams joined their table with his question, "What have you created? Remember, use the notes you have on vocabulary terms."

They glance again at their notes as Ashley begins, "We've created a polynomial that is specifically a binomial. With an equal sign it becomes an equation." They then write the equation on their paper:

$$7P + 6G =$$

| Figure 7.5 | Sample mathematics notes.

Polynomial	Equation
* "poly-" means many * Other words–polyester, polygraph, poly-phonic, polyunsaturated * "-nomial" means terms * Other words–binomial * A polynomial has many terms and has a constant multiplied by one or more variables raised to a nonnegative integral power	
Like Terms	**Monomial**

Mr. Williams asks, "Why can't you go to **13 PG?**"

Eric responds, "You can't because they're not like terms."

This brief moment provided Mr. Williams with a valid assessment of the information he had just introduced and gave students an authentic opportunity to use the target vocabulary from their working notes.

Note Making in Social Studies

"What questions might we ask about the Cold War, just by looking at this page of text?" Ms. Tsai queries her U.S. history class as they participate in a prereading activity to prepare for the next chapter in their text. She knows that creating a skeletal note structure of the text helps her students become effective notetakers and note makers.

Ms. Tsai uses a combination of Directed Notetaking Activity, or DNA (Spires & Stone, 1989) and computer-assisted outlining (Anderson-Inman, 1996) as she engages her students in history lessons. DNA is a process approach to notetaking that includes three instructional principles:

1. a structured format for taking notes commonly referred to as the split-page method;

2. a self-questioning strategy for monitoring levels of involvement before, during, and after notetaking; and

3. direct, explicit teaching of the notetaking process adapted for notetaking instruction from Pearson's model (1985) for teaching reading comprehension. (Spires & Stone, 1989, p. 37)

Consistent with the DNA process approach, Ms. Tsai wants her students to become familiar with the structure of the text, preview the targeted vocabulary, form questions, question themselves and others, and gain background knowledge from all of the charts, maps, illustrations, photographs, and captions.

Stepping into the classroom, one can see how Ms. Tsai incorporates this note making activity with the use of a PowerPoint® presentation, a series of maps pertinent to the geographical areas and time period, and chart paper to list student-generated questions. She orchestrates a class discussion that requires the students to refer to their own notes, follow a multimedia display of text and maps on two separate screens, and contribute to the new set of notes that she transcribes onto an interactive white board. The presentation Ms. Tsai creates with her students' guidance becomes another structure for them to incorporate into their note making as they read the text. As Anderson-Inman (1996) notes, computer-assisted outlining does not confine students to predetermined amounts of space in which to take notes. Further, computer-assisted outlining allows for multiple additions, modifications, and deletions.

With books open, Ms. Tsai and her students skim the chapter, page by page, as they contribute ideas to the class notes displayed on one of two screens set up at opposite ends of the room. An outline of the chapter takes shape as the class decides on bullets for main ideas, from the headings and subheadings of each textbook page and their discussion notes. Ms. Tsai then leaves empty bullets under each main idea, areas requiring support information, to be completed later as students read each section of the chapter.

Engaging Students at Multiple Levels. Students are required to preview any visual aids on each text page, such as graphs, charts, pictures, diagrams, and maps, and add pertinent bulleted information to their skeleton outline. They also list all of the italicized and boldface terms in the vocabulary section of their notebooks. These terms become the target vocabulary, to be incorporated into their notes, with definitions added. As part of her DNA instruction, Ms. Tsai periodically asks students to consider their level of participation in the notetaking activity. She may ask students to think about their level of motivation, their purpose for listening and participating, or if they are separating main ideas from details.

Using Notes in Class. When the skeleton outline is complete, Ms. Tsai uses it in a presentation as she gives the students an overview of the chapter. On subsequent days, she will use the maps on the walls as contextual aids and she will have students begin posing questions based on the main ideas of the bulleted outline. The series of student-generated questions are added to a growing list of questions on a chart in the front of the room.

As her students review their notes regarding the Allies' plan for the postwar world Ms. Tsai repeats the question, "What questions might we ask about the rationale of the Truman Doctrine?" She asks them to consider how geography and politics impacted the Truman Doctrine. She hopes for a deeper level of thinking than that required when students simply memorize facts.

NOTES

"Do you think Truman's economic aid contributed to the containment of communism in Europe after the war? Why?" She smiles as she surveys the scene of students flipping through notes taken over the past week of lectures, class discussions, and textbook facts. A student scribe writes these questions on the large sheet of chart paper attached to the wall. Now the students have access to the map on the overhead projector displayed on the front screen as well as the notes they have constructed from the textbook. Ms. Tsai guides their thinking by the questions being written on the chart paper. The projector screen now displays the main idea of this discussion: **The Truman Doctrine.**

Ms. Tsai hits the return button on her podium and a subtopic bullet appears while the cursor blinks expectantly.

"OK? What do you think? Look over your notes, look at the map, and consider the world of the late 1940s. Europe is crippled; America has emerged from the war as a world leader. What do you suppose were some of President Truman's reasons for asking the U.S. Congress to give economic aid to Turkey and Greece?"

Brian hesitates at first, then reads from his notes, "Truman believed that the U.S. should support those countries that were fighting communism. And since Turkey and Greece were weak after the war, they were ripe for a takeover."

"Hmm, good point," says Ms. Tsai as she types into her interactive whiteboard. The vacant bullet is now filled with a summary of Brian's idea: **Stop the spread of communism.** Her students know she means business when the new notes incorporate Brian's ideas and they copy this point into their notes. A few others begin to search their notes and textbooks for information to share. Ms. Tsai recognizes the familiar reaction of students who know that their ideas are validated. She deliberately uses her students' questions and ideas—either on the chart paper or the interactive white board—to validate their thinking. She believes that the synthesis of students' questions and concerns with historical data is evidence that they are making meaning.

"Yeah, but some Americans believe that we were just messing in other countries' business," Jose interrupts Brian.

"Yeah, like I heard that is what is going on in the Middle East now," Miriam interjects.

Ms. Tsai asks the class if that is a question to include in the growing list of ideas to consider in the future. Most students agree that it should be part of future class discussions. The class scribe adds *9/11* to the chart paper.

Miriam waves her hand and Ms. Tsai nods in her direction and asks, "Did you find other information in your notes to add to the Truman Doctrine?"

Miriam reads from her class notes. "Because America was the only nation with money to help we had to do something to stop the possibility of more war." Ms. Tsai smiles and types the next bullet: **$400 million in economic and military aid.**

"OK. Do you think this idea was only a generous act or could there be other reasons for the doctrine?" The teacher flips on the overhead projector that lights up the room with a map of Europe with the Mediterranean Sea, the Black Sea, and surrounding countries and begins the conversation.

Structured Outline Support Before, During, and After Activities. This repeated practice and use of note making demonstrates to students the ease and efficacy of structuring notes before reading, during independent reading of the text, and in class discussions. Students also learn to monitor their involvement and comprehension so that they can change behaviors if they are not learning. The combination of the Directed Notetaking Activity (DNA) and computer-assisted outlining ensures that students move gradually toward independent skills in note making.

Notetaking in Science

When Ellen Hoenstein teaches life skills (known to many adolescents as Sex Ed), she never has a problem with getting attention. On the contrary, the students are very interested in the topics for discussion; the air is charged with anticipation, anxiety, and nervous giggles. Because many adolescents have not yet developed mature responses to this topic, Ms. Hoenstein uses notetaking to facilitate safe and mature discussions. Throughout the year she travels from room to room and building to building teaching 78 separate classes that encompass over 1,200 students.

Ms. Hoenstein uses a split-page method or Cornell notetaking method (e.g., Pauk, 2000). Students are taught to draw a vertical line down the page with about one third of the paper to the left of the line and two thirds of the paper on the right. In addition, they leave room at the bottom (about 2 inches) to summarize their notes. A sample page is found in Figure 7.6. Ms. Hoenstein asks students to write their notes on the right side of the paper, their reactions and questions on the left side of the paper, and their summary of the information on the bottom of the page.

"Please, write this down, S-T-D, one letter below each other," says Ms. Hoenstein. "As we discuss the topic of sexually transmitted diseases, I will often use these three letters instead of the words they represent." Ms. Hoenstein scans the room and takes in about 30 adolescent and curious faces. A few wide eyes and muffled giggles tell her about the tenor of the class. "Now, write your own definition for each of the words—*sexually transmitted disease*." Based on her classroom experiences and knowledge of effective teaching practices, she gently guides her students into areas of sexuality that require a learning atmosphere that is safe and open.

Following their individual work at creating a definition for STDs, Ms. Hoenstein invites students to share with the class. Jessica tries the first word and says, "sex, you know, sex." LaDonna adds to that, "it means doing it, but you can get a disease by just touching other people." As the conversation continues, the students create a working definition of STD and have a great deal of information in their notes. Next, Ms. Hoenstein turns to the class and says, "Some STDs can be deadly. If or when you become sexually active, you must become aware of how to avoid infection as well as how to seek treatment in case you are infected. You may recall some of the ideas you learned in eighth grade, or from your parents, or even information you picked up from friends. While I write on the board the scientific words that name some of the STDs, you write the names that you know in your notes and we'll compare. Please write these on the left side of a new page of notes and skip about five lines between each one. As we learn the definitions of these diseases and the causes, as well as the treatments, write that information on the right side of your page of notes. You may ask me

Figure 7.6 Sample split-page note format.

Name: _____ Date: _____ Class: _____ Page: _____

questions for clarification or write your questions and reactions on the left side, just below the names of the disease we are discussing."

Notetaking That Encourages Personal Response and Dialogue. Ms. Hoenstein believes that structured notetaking not only gives students a chance to categorize important information, but also provides them with options to deal with awkward and embarrassing feelings. "It opens avenues for students to react to controversial material privately," she suggests. "As we work on these controversial and critical issues, students may have feelings and emotions that are triggered. Writing these notes often opens doors that allow them a nonthreatening tool for deeper personal learning." She also believes that notetaking allows students to react privately to sensitive material before they pose a question or enter into a class discussion.

"It has been my experience that structured notetaking facilitates dialogue which is needed as we learn about human sexual behavior. Because human behavior is affected as much by feelings as by knowledge, this notetaking strategy promotes dialogue which will inevitably include sensitive issues that may provoke intimate feelings."

Notetaking in Electives

When English language learners are introduced to their first research paper, the question "How do I do research?" is as important as "What do I research?" In Marie Butler's culture studies class, no "how" question is left unanswered. In fact, her students master each research skill, step by step, in a scaffolded process that fosters confidence and success for developing writer-researchers.

Notetaking and the Research Process. Ms. Butler begins the process by explaining what research is. The terms *research, sources of information, bibliography, research questions, research grid*, and *paraphrase* are all introduced as key steps in this process. Her students begin to understand that writing a research report will guide them to learn more about something they are interested in. Ms. Butler gives students the chance to choose what they want to investigate about their subject. She provides a written overview of the project:

> The purpose of a **research report** is to collect and present information about your topic in order to share what you have learned. It is an opportunity to explore different **sources of information:** newspapers, magazines, books, encyclopedias, and the Internet.
>
> Research takes time, because you must find the information, then read it and take notes. It is important to keep a record of the sources you plan to use in your report. The final section of the report will be a **bibliography** that lists in a particular format each source you used, which we will practice and learn.
>
> As you locate and search through resources about your topic, you must select only a few (five or six) major ideas to write about. These ideas will become your list of **research questions.** You will collect information to answer each of these questions by using a **research grid** for notetaking.

The first step in the research process is identifying possible research questions. To get students under way, they are required to produce a minimum of five research questions. The following are examples of the questions her students wrote:

1. Research topic: Tenochtitlan
   - Why and where was the location of Tenochtitlan chosen?
   - What was the structure of the city?
   - How was life in Tenochtitlan?
   - What important events took place in Tenochtitlan?
   - Why and when did the city fall?

2. Research topic: Gandhi

- What was Gandhi's childhood like?
- Why was the spinning wheel important to Gandhi?
- What was Gandhi's position or job?
- How many times was Gandhi arrested?
- What did Gandhi do for his people?
- When was Gandhi assassinated and why?
- Why is Gandhi important?

Learning How to Document Information Sources. Students practice the important skill of documenting information in bibliographies before going to the library. First, Ms. Butler and her students identify the various sources available; then she shows them how each type of resource is documented in a bibliography of a research paper. Teachers know that practicing what has just been explained is the key to understanding, and in Ms. Butler's class this next step makes all the difference. Ms. Butler arranges her class in stations, each with multiple copies of one particular resource. Groups of students take turns at each station as they practice recording each resource in the correct fashion, following written instructions and a sample bibliography. When students have completed all of the stations, they have experienced how to document a variety of sources including newspapers, magazines, books, encyclopedias, and Internet information. In this staged classroom activity, students apply newly learned notetaking skills that will help them document their own resources correctly and effectively as they do authentic research.

Using a Matrix Format for Notetaking. Now that students are ready to begin their research, Ms. Butler introduces a *matrix* format for notetaking that will facilitate this process. According to Kiewra and colleagues (1995), a matrix format builds on the outline format. Although both provide students with specific information about internal connections, the matrix format emphasizes the relationships that exist across topics. As they note, "information across topics can be drawn more easily and quickly from a matrix than a linear representation" (p. 174). Not all content lends itself to the matrix format; however, the task Ms. Butler had in mind was perfect for this style of notetaking.

Ms. Butler introduces the "research grid" (see Figure 7.7) and students write their five or six think and search questions in the boxes across the top of the grid. This is posted on the class's wiki so that students can write on it electronically. They enter the sources they found in the left-hand column of the grid so that they will be able to remember where the information came from when they cite it. This is also helpful when they must return to a specific source for additional information.

Students then look through each source and find all of the information they can about each of their questions. They write chunks of information, not complete sentences, in each notetaking box. Students examine each source and find information that answers their question. They continue this form of notetaking until each column is completed with information from all of the sources. Students now have a framework for their research paper.

Next, they must write an introductory paragraph and one or two paragraphs for each of the columns. These paragraphs answer their think and search questions. Students know they can structure their written response by turning each question into a topic sentence for each informational paragraph.

Figure 7.7   Research grid.

Question/Topic				
	Write question/ topic 1 here	Write question/ topic 2 here	Question/topic 3	Question/topic 4
List source 1 from your bibliography here	Write notes about question/topic 1 from source 1 here	Write notes about question/topic 2 from source 1 here		
List source 2 here	Write notes about question/topic 1 from source 2 here	Repeat the process in all the spaces ➙ ↓		
List source 3 here				
List source 4 here				
List source 5 here				

Conclusion

In nearly every high school or college classroom students will be required to take notes from lectures and books. The reasons for this are sound—students who understand notetaking and note making do better on tests and essays. These students also learn more of the content. However, most students do not have sophisticated notetaking strategies. Instead, they rely on haphazard collections of facts and details that are not systematic. This process problem is compounded as many of these same students do not organize and review their notes later. Thus, teachers in secondary schools should provide students with systematic instruction in notetaking and note making. In addition to this type of instruction, we believe that teachers should provide students with feedback on their notes. Specific feedback on notetaking skills, through a process such as NOTES (Stahl et al., 1991), will guide students to independence in this most important study skill.

NOTES

Chapter 8

Powerful Pens: Writing to Learn With Adolescents

*W*alking into Chuck Hayden's geometry class, guests are often surprised to see students writing journal entry responses to a series of questions on the board. Mr. Hayden reminds them, "Don't solve the problem yet! Write down what you are thinking, and I don't mean who you want to ask out on a date. Look at the steps on the board. First, write what you see and recognize in the problem; second, what kind of problem it is; third, what it means you have to do; and fourth and only then, the first step you will take to solve it." As the students write, Mr. Hayden assesses their work, reading and commenting on the written accounts of their thinking processes.

He stops at Kofi's desk, scrolls down the page, and says, "I like the way you thought that through. Now, how will you begin to solve it?"

Kofi explains what he thinks the first step is and waits for Mr. Hayden's response.

"OK, write it down." As his teacher moves on, the young man starts writing.

"So, Jessica, you wrote that it's a parabola. What does that mean?"

The girl smiles, but says nothing.

"Can't explain it? Where will you look to find the explanation?"

Her hesitant response is just above a whisper.

"You're right, the glossary," and he waits for her to locate the word. "Found it? Good, now write down what a parabola is."

When asked why writing is part of his geometry curriculum, Mr. Hayden explains that students have to be specific in a written explanation, much more *so than in speaking. "My students have to think through each step as they explain it in written form and I see what is missing or unclear to them. Then I know how best to guide them through the steps of a problem. It's a process that informs both me and my students."*

Kofi says simply, "It just helps me see what I know."

Defining and Defending Writing to Learn

Before we examine the research related to writing to learn, a few definitions are in order. Writing to learn differs from learning to write in several important ways. Students "learn to write" throughout their lives. When they are in elementary school, children learn to encode words, construct sentences, figure out the mechanics of paragraphs, and develop understandings of grammar. As they get older, students refine and expand on these skills. Teachers who focus on learning to write typically use process writing as an instructional approach (Atwell, 1998; Graves, 1983). Although the processes used by each writer differ and are recursive, Jenkinson (1988) asserts that student writers typically go through some variation of these steps:

1. prewriting activities (jotting down ideas, listing thoughts, brainstorming, gathering information, and so on);
2. writing a draft;
3. peer review of the draft;
4. revising;
5. editing;
6. writing the final draft; and
7. publishing. (p. 714)

Although most common in English classrooms, process writing can be used throughout the curriculum. For example, social studies teachers may wish to engage their students in persuasive essay writing about the causes of WWII or a rationale for democracy. In doing so, teachers provide students feedback and opportunities to revise their writing.

Writing to learn differs from other types of writing because it is not a process piece that will go through multiple refinements toward an intended final product. Instead, it is meant to be a catalyst for further learning—an opportunity for students to recall, clarify, and question what they know and what they still wonder about. Writing to learn "involves getting students to think about and to find the words to explain what

Struggling Readers

HAVE SOMETHING TO SAY

Years ago, while discussing students with autism, Dr. Doug Biklen suggested, "Not being able to speak is different than not having something to say." This same logic can be applied to struggling readers. There are a number of students who have difficulty reading and writing, but who have complex ideas that they want to share. Providing students low-risk opportunities to share their thinking via writing communicates the value of writing as well as the importance of sharing their unique perspectives. Long Beach, California, teacher Erin Gruwell (The Freedom Writers, 2001) introduced her students to the concepts of intolerance and oppression. In response, her students who had been previously labeled "unteachables" (kids who no other teacher wanted to deal with) started keeping diaries of their lives that showed the violence, homelessness, racism, illness, and abuse that surrounded them. When connected with content they were interested in, a good teacher, and opportunities to share their thinking through writing, these students demonstrated that they could have an impact. They also learned that their writing was a powerful force and one that created change.

they are learning, how they understand that learning, and what their own processes of learning involve" (Mitchell, 1996, p. 93). As Jenkinson (1988) explains, "writing should be a process in which writers discover what they know and do not know about their topics, their language, themselves, and their ability to communicate with specific audiences" (p. 714). For example, a social studies teacher may ask students to respond to a writing to learn prompt such as "explain the bombing of Hiroshima to your younger brother or sister." Responding to this prompt requires that the student consider their prior knowledge about the bombing, the cognitive development of their younger siblings, what they have read or listened to about the topic, their own background knowledge, and how to best convey this information in writing. Knipper and Duggan (2006) note that these activities ensure that all students participate. Elbow (1994) suggests that writing to learn, as "low-stakes writing," can help students learn, understand, remember, and figure out what they don't know. In his words, "Even though low stakes writing-to-learn is not always as good as writing, it is particularly effective at promoting learning and involvement in course material, and it is much easier on teachers—especially those who aren't writing teachers" (p. 1). We also know that writing to learn has a small, but positive impact on students' overall academic achievement (Bangert-Drowns, Hurley, & Wilkinson, 2004).

Applying Three Kinds of Knowledge

Writing to learn requires that students use different kinds of knowledge at different times. Cognitive scientists generally think of three kinds of knowledge—declarative, procedural, and conditional (Meichenbaum & Biemiller, 1998; Paris, Cross, & Lipson, 1984; Sternberg & Williams, 2002). These types of knowledge are illustrated in Figure 8.1, using questions an algebra teacher might use.

Declarative Knowledge. Declarative knowledge focuses on things that we "know" such as labels, names, facts, and lists. Although often considered mundane, declarative knowledge is an important part of what we know. It is also the easiest kind of knowledge to impart in lectures and reading assignments. In

Figure 8.1 Types of knowledge.

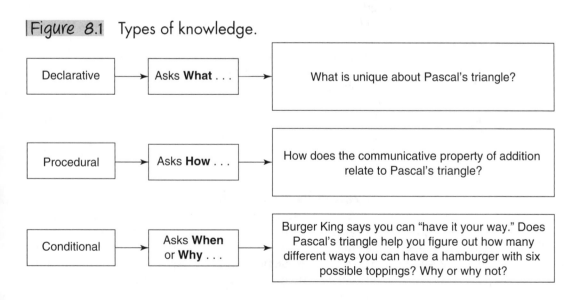

WRITING

THE BENEFITS FOR ENGLISH LANGUAGE LEARNERS

Writing is thinking and thinking is the goal of educators. We want our students thinking and we want to know what they're thinking. Reviewing student writing allows the teacher to check students' understanding of the content and to plan future instruction. When teachers review the writing of their English language learners, they gain an understanding of the language proficiency, language development needs, and content understanding of their students (Zamel, 2000). There is also evidence that writing to learn helps ELLs understand and develop their metacognitive skills (Prescott, 2001). In too many cases, these students are excused from writing tasks due to their language proficiency. As a result, they are not clarifying their thinking or demonstrating what they know and don't know to the teacher.

school, students must have a number of experiences that develop their declarative knowledge. Some writing to learn prompts can be used to demonstrate this type of knowledge. For example, a physical education teacher may ask students to explain the types of muscles in the body.

Procedural Knowledge. In addition to declarative knowledge in which students recall specific information, students must demonstrate their understanding of procedural knowledge. This type of knowledge requires that students know how to do something; they must know how to apply their knowledge. This type of knowledge is more difficult to convey in a traditional lecture or reading—students need experience putting their knowledge into practice. Again, some writing to learn prompts can facilitate and assess this type of knowledge. For example, a chemistry teacher may ask students to describe the steps necessary to complete a science lab. Mr. Hayden asked his students to explain their procedural thinking to solve a mathematics problem in the opening vignette.

Conditional Knowledge. Finally, conditional knowledge is concerned with when or why something is done—the various conditions that influence our decisions to use knowledge. Stated another way, conditional knowledge is about strategies and when to use them. Again, writing to learn can use prompts in which students are provided scenarios and are asked to use their knowledge in novel ways. For example, a biology teacher may ask students to consider the pros and cons of embryonic research.

In other words (and rather simply stated), "what" is declarative knowledge, "how" is procedural knowledge, and "when" or "why" is conditional knowledge. Clearly, students need to develop their knowledge in each of these categories, and teachers can monitor this development with appropriate writing to learn activities.

Strategies to Develop Writing Skills

In many classrooms, there are a number of very poor writers. Although writing to learn prompts and tasks are not focused on perfect writing, there are a number of instructional strategies that teachers can use to facilitate students' skills in composing. As Fisher and Frey (2003) demonstrated, these writing instructional approaches help students develop their skills in sharing their thinking on paper.

Language Experience Approach (LEA). Similar to Purcell-Gates and Waterman's (2000) adult students in El Salvador who were taught using the Language Experience Approach in a Freirean-based class, adolescents are often interested in discussing their life experiences and the experiences they share in class. The procedures for LEA are fairly straightforward. The class, or a group of students, has a discussion with the teacher. The students agree on a message, which can vary in length from a sentence to several paragraphs. The teacher then writes (scribes) the message for the students. In some cases, the students copy the message into their journals. The evidence for LEA suggests that students will improve their writing skills by developing an understanding of the speech-to-print function modeled by the group and the teacher. In addition, LEA helps develop reading skills as students read and reread the messages they have created together (Dixon & Nessel, 1983).

Figure 8.2 Stanzas for an "I Am" poem.

1. I am (special characteristics or nouns about you)
2. I wonder (something you are curious about)
3. I hear (an imaginary sound)
4. I want (an actual desire of yours)
5. I am (repeat first line of poem)
6. I pretend (something you pretend to do)
7. I feel (an imaginary feeling)
8. I touch (an imaginary touch)
9. I worry (something that truly bothers you)
10. I cry (something that makes you very sad)
11. I am (repeat the first line of the poem)
12. I understand (something you know is true)
13. I say (something you believe in)
14. I dream (something you dream about)
15. I try (something you make an effort about)
16. I hope (something you actually hope for)
17. I am (repeat the first line of the poem)

Writing Models. Using existing, often previously published, writing as a model for new writing is another way to facilitate writing development. One common example of a writing model is the popular "I am" poem in which students complete sentence starters that all focus on one main idea (see Figure 8.2). Writing models can also be created by the teacher to provide students with scaffolding for their emerging writing skills. For example, a science teacher may structure a lab report with a number of blank lines to ensure that students have the support they need to write more complex papers. An English teacher may use sentence frames (a form of writing models) to ensure that students' grammar use is correct.

Generative Sentences. This instructional strategy requires that students write a sentence based on a given word in a given position of the sentence. Generative sentences allow the teacher to check students' understanding of common grammar and syntax rules as well as their understanding of the content. Consider the following sentences that students wrote based on the requirement that the word *volcano(es)* be the third word in the sentence:

> I like volcanoes.
>
> When the volcano erupts, lava flows down the mountain.
>
> The Merapi volcano in Indonesia is causing a great deal of disruption.

All of these sentences demonstrate an understanding of grammar and spelling; they also demonstrate the range of understanding of volcanoes in the class. Generative sentence prompts can be created for all types of learning and vary in difficulty from "Write a sentence that starts with the word *democracy*" to "Write a sentence that is at least 10 words long and ends in *constitution*" to "Write a sentence about the Bill of Rights that is at least 8 words long and has the word *representative* in it."

Power Writing. Power writing is a timed fluency activity that requires students to write as many words as they can on a topic in a given amount of time.

WRITING

Importantly, power writing provides students with self-created material to revise, and allows them (and the teacher) to figure out what they know about a given topic. As Fearn and Farnan (2001) suggest, power writing is "a structured free-write where the objective is quantity alone" (p. 501). The introduction of power writing is very simple. The teacher provides students with a topic or choice of topics based on the content of the class. Students are given 1 minute to write everything they can on the topic. At the end of the minute, students count the number of words they wrote on the topic. Typically this is repeated three times per class session, with variations on the topics. Students then record their personal best (highest fluency) on their individual record-keeping chart, often maintained in their notebook or journal. Besides building fluency and providing students with material to revise, power writing requires that students get writing immediately. For example, students in Maria Grant's physics class completed 1-minute power writings on *momentum*, *friction*, and *gravity* in one class period.

Why Is Writing Neglected in Many Content Area Classes?

Unfortunately, many content teachers do not consider writing part of their curriculum. In too many content classrooms, writing is neglected because those teachers believe that writing is best left for the English department (Mitchell, 1996). We believe this is likely a result of overemphasis on process writing and the confusion between learning to write and writing to learn. There exists considerable evidence across disciplines that writing builds and reinforces content learning. For example, McIntosh and Draper (2001) describe the ways in which writing can facilitate learning in mathematics. Beyond mathematics, writing to learn has been employed in English, social studies, science, and family and consumer sciences (Andrews, 1997; Holbrook, 1987; Keys, 1999a, 1999b; Lytton, Marshall-Baker, Benson, & Blieszner, 1996; McDermott, 2010; Mitchell, 1996).

Using Writing Prompts

There are a number of ways that writing to learn can be implemented in content classrooms. Writing to learn is based on writing prompts that the teacher provides students. These prompts can range from very open-ended—"What did you think was confusing about this topic?"—to fairly specific—"Discuss the role of photosynthesis in plant life." The range of prompts can include:

- *Admit slips.* Upon entering the classroom, students write on an assigned topic such as "What did you notice was important in yesterday's discussion?" or "Explain the difference between jazz and rock."
- *Crystal ball.* Students describe what they think class will be about, what will happen next in the novel they are reading, or the next step in a science lab.
- *Found poems.* Students reread an assigned text and find key phrases that "speak" to them, then arrange these into a poem structure without adding any of their own words (Dunning & Stafford, 1992).
- *Awards.* Students recommend someone or something for an award that the teacher has created such as "the best artist of the century, living or dead."
- *Cinquains.* A five-line poem in which the first line is the topic (a noun), the second line is a description of the topic in two words, the third line is three "ing" words, the fourth line is a description of the topic in four words, and the final line is a synonym of the topic word from line one.

- *Yesterday's news.* Students summarize the information presented the day before, either from a film, lecture, discussion, or reading.
- *"What if" scenarios.* Students respond to prompts in which information is changed from what they know and they predict outcomes. For example, students may be asked to respond to "What would be different if the Civil War were fought in 1920?"
- *Take a stand.* Students discuss their opinions about a controversial topic such as "Just because we can, should we clone people?"
- *Letters.* Students write letters to others, including elected officials, family members, friends, people who made a difference, and so on. For example, students may respond to the prompt "write a letter to Dr. Martin Luther King informing him of the current issues regarding racism in our country."
- *Exit slips.* Used as a closure activity at the end of the period, students write on an assigned prompt such as "The three best things I learned today are . . . ."

The critical element that all of these writing to learn events have in common is that students do not correct or rewrite their pieces. Instead, each becomes a starting point for learning.

Perspective Writing Through RAFT. Naturally, there are several hundred ways to structure writing to learn prompts. Those mentioned are just a few. In addition to these general types of prompts, students can be taught perspective writing during writing to learn by using RAFT prompts (Santa & Havens, 1995).

RAFT stands for:

R = Role (who is the writer, what is the role of the writer?)

A = Audience (to whom are you writing?)

F = Format (what format should the writing be in?)

T = Topic (what are you writing about?)

When students are first introduced to RAFT, everyone responds to the same prompt. For example, students may enter a social studies classroom and see the following written on the board:

R = A sailor at Pearl Harbor, December 7, 1941

A = People on the mainland

F = A telegram

T = We've been attacked!

In a geometry classroom, students may be asked to respond to a writing to learn prompt in which they are asked to think about:

R = Isosceles triangle

A = My angles

F = E-mail

T = Our unequal relationship

Once students become familiar with the RAFT format, teachers can assign groups of students different components and then invite group conversations about the topic at hand. For example, in a social studies class, students may enter the room to find information like that in Table 8.1 written on the board.

WRITING

Table 8.1 Sample of RAFT Format

	Last Name A–M	Last Name N–Z
R	King George	Colonists
A	Colonists	King George
F	Informational letter	Protest letter
T	Why the taxes?	Why the taxes?

As you can imagine, this type of writing provides students with an opportunity to use their knowledge and skills in writing and discussion as they share their responses to the RAFT exercise above. As you will see, teachers across the curriculum use writing to learn to facilitate learning within their content area.

In addition to RAFT prompts created from course content, these writing to learn prompts can also be created for the readings students do. RAFT prompts can be written for content area picture books that students independently read during class time. Completing the RAFT prompt helps students clarify their thinking about the book and content and allows the teacher an opportunity to check for understanding. A collection of RAFT prompts for picture books used in a biology class are included in Table 8.2.

Strategies at Work

Writing to Learn in English

"Look beyond the literal meaning of the words in the selection. When you write, go deeper." This is Claudia Penczar's encouragement to her world literature students as they write to learn in their learning logs (e.g., Mitchell, 1996). Although these students read volumes of literature in this course, they may not comprehend some of the inferences as they read through a selection the first time. Writing also makes the writer pay more attention—to what the character is saying, why the character is saying it, and who comprises the audience. These students can easily recall and recite the basic elements of literature, but until they give themselves time to reflect and write, they often do not identify implied meaning. Ms. Penczar schedules regular writing time as she knows that otherwise students may do only superficial reading, instead of thinking in depth about underlying themes and motives. Her learning logs are spiral-bound notebooks that students maintain over the course of the term. She uses various prompts at different times in the school year to focus her students on texts.

Learning Logs. During her unit on short stories, Ms. Penczar's students respond in their learning logs to questions that she periodically posts on the board or shares orally. For example, in the short story *Bad Influence* by Judith Ortiz Cofer (1996), a young girl is sent from her home in Patterson, New Jersey, to spend the summer with her grandparents in Puerto Rico. Much like the main character in

Table 8.2 Picture Book RAFTS for Biology

Water Dance (Locker, 1997)	If the World Were a Village (Smith, 2002)
R = Single drop of water A = The land F = Letter T = My journey	R = Statistician A = Citizens of California F = List T = If California were a village
The Wildlife Detectives (Jackson, 2000)	**A Drop Around the World (McKinney, 1998)**
R = Wildlife detective A = Poacher F = Warrant for arrest T = You're under arrest	R = A drop of water A = The world F = A travel itinerary T = My trip around the world starting and ending in San Diego
How Do Bats See in the Dark? (Berger & Berger, 2000)	**Where Have All the Pandas Gone? (Berger & Berger, 2001)**
R = Nocturnal creature A = Diurnal creature F = Invitation T = You don't know what you're missing!	R = Environmentalist A = The public F = Public service announcement T = Where have all the animals gone?
Galapagos Means Tortoise (Heller, 2000)	**Outside and Inside Birds (Markle, 1994)**
R = Charles Darwin A = Himself F = Journal entries T = Biodiversity of the Galapagos	R = Ornithologist A = Students F = Diagram T = Features of a bird
What Is a Plant? (Kalman, 2000)	**Planet Earth/Inside Out (Gibbons, 1995)**
R = Plant A = Mushroom F = Eviction letter T = You are not a plant!	R = Solar system A = Planet Earth F = Break-up note T = You've changed
The Atlantic Ocean (Petersen, 2001)	**Nature's Green Umbrella (Gibbons, 1994)**
R = Atlantic Ocean A = Pacific Ocean F = Court brief T = Why I should be named the greatest ocean	R = Rainforest A = Planet Earth F = Plea for help T = You must protect me

the story, Ms. Penczar's students initially viewed the grandparents stereotypically. When the class responded to the question "What does Rita know about her grandparents?," their responses were literal—"They're old," "They got married at fifteen," "They loved Rita [their granddaughter]." In contrast, when they later responded in their learning logs to the question "What did Rita learn about her grandparents?" their responses were more reflective, such as the student examples that follow:

> They [the grandparents] are very serious towards their religion and hold a great deal of respect towards each other. . . . Her grandfather is a great spiritualist who's well respected by all. During the summer Rita learned the value of family and friends. [Omar]
>
> Originally, Rita thought her grandfather was a crazy old man. But when the richest woman on the island (who could afford anything she wanted) asked for his help, Rita realized that he was a very wise, spiritual man whom the people of the town respected and went to for help. Her grandmother also received the respect of the town's people. From their example Rita learned about friendship—the fact that you can learn about and become friends with the most unexpected people. [Andrea]
>
> Rita thought her grandfather was loony. Later she learned that he had a special talent, which was that he could communicate with spirits, ask them for help. He could see into a person's heart, thoughts, and dreams. [Eric]

As they read, Ms. Penczar also suggests that they choose three quotes, or "golden lines," from each chapter. They must explain their reasons for the choices, including questions each choice brings to mind. In addition, they must describe how the golden line relates to either a character or the progression of the plot. Ms. Penczar makes good use of her students' writing. As she reviews the learning logs, she is able to use her students' insights to refer back to the important elements of the text. Their responses are also a source for quotes later in the course when students compose a character analysis or thematic essay. The teacher can use student samples from writing to learn events to assess what grammar structures or writing conventions need to be retaught.

Writing to Learn in Mathematics

The opening vignette for this chapter described a writing to learn process used by Mr. Hayden in his geometry class. He begins each class period with this activity, which he calls Name That Math! Students learn that this is part of the classroom routine and know to begin as soon as they arrive. However, Mr. Hayden knows that he needs to explicitly teach the process so that students can do it independently. The first time students see Name That Math! is when Mr. Hayden models his own thought process with a problem he has written on the whiteboard:

"What is the volume of a cylinder with a height of 6 feet and a radius of 2 feet?"

Teaching Students to Ask Themselves Questions. Mr. Hayden wants students to make a habit of asking themselves the following questions when he asks them to play Name That Math:

1. What's the key word in the problem?
2. What's the rule?
3. What's the first step?

Mr. Hayden then reads the word problem on the board as he thinks aloud his response to question 1. "What key word can I identify in the problem that tells me what I need to know?" he asks himself. He tells the students that every word problem or mathematics question has a clue. "Look for that clue and you'll know what you have to do. It might be connected to surface area, or volume, or the Pythagorean theorem, but the first step is to find it." To illustrate this, Mr. Hayden then points to the key word "volume" in the above problem.

Next, Mr. Hayden explains how to think through question 2, "What's the rule?" by telling the students that rules can be formulas, definitions, theorems, or proofs that are connected to that key word. He reminds them that until they know what the rule is, they can't do the first step. Mr. Hayden again models what he wants the students to do. He explains that the rule for the above problem is the formula for volume of a cylinder. He thinks aloud and says, "The formula for volume of a cylinder is $V = Bh$, where B is the base area and h is the height."

Students begin to see that they can attempt the first step of solving the problem only after finding the key word and identifying the rule. Mr. Hayden then tells his students the answer to question 3, "What is the first step?" when he informs them, "You must plug the values into the formula to solve the problem. Now, and only now, can you proceed to solve the problem with math."

Modeling Each Step. Mr. Hayden understands the importance of modeling each step. As he explains, "I modeled for the students throughout the year so that whenever they see a problem they will immediately identify what kind of mathematics problem it is. They must be able to Name That Math. After modeling this thinking process for a week, he lets the students begin the same process on their own. These writing to learn steps clarify the thought process students need to solve mathematics problems. The students write the following on a sheet of paper:

1. The problem from the board is:
2. What am I thinking? (Students must think through Name That Math in the three steps they have seen their teacher model.)
   - What's the key word in the problem?
   - Whats the rule?
   - What's the first step?
3. Solve it with mathematics.
4. Solve it with words.

When students first attempt this writing to learn practice, Mr. Hayden does not tell the students what to write down for step 2, "What am I thinking?" It is their turn to practice what their teacher has modeled; they must write what they are thinking when they see the problem. This written statement allows students to explain the thought process they go through to solve the problem. As students write, Mr. Hayden circulates and quickly reads each response. Depending on what they write, he can see whether or not they have understood the process. For example, Maria used writing to learn to solve a problem as follows:

1. Find the 1/16" scale volume of a square pyramid with a height of 75 feet and a base area of 2,500 feet squared.
2. What am I thinking?

The problem I have chosen is a volume problem. For this I need the volume of a pyramid with a square base. Another part of the problem tells me that I will need to find the similitude of the pyramid to a 1/16th scale. The rules for my problem

WRITING

are the formula for volume of a pyramid and finding the volume of the scale will be the volume of the model divided by the ratio cubed. The formula for volume of a pyramid is as follows: $V = 1/3 \, BH$, where B is base area and H is height. My problem gives me the height and the base area of the pyramid so the hard part of this question is going to be drawing it to scale. The first part of my process will be finding the volume of the model and then I will cube my ratio because this is a volume of the model to find the volume of the actual size.

When students get accustomed to implementing these steps on their own, the teacher can see that they are also independently incorporating the target vocabulary for this content area into their writing. In the student example above, Mr. Hayden saw just such a development. "Another part of the problem tells me that I will need to find the *similitude* of the pyramid, to a 1/16th scale," wrote Maria. *Similitude* is a term that Mr. Hayden taught in class and it has now become part of Maria's thought process. She used the target vocabulary, all the proper formulas, and all the terminology. She also used the sequenced steps the class has been working on all year. Mr. Hayden's modeling and the writing to learn prompts are beginning to pay off.

Step 3, "Solve it with mathematics," and step 4, "Solve it with words," both require that students solve the problem in numbers and then explain each step of the problem in written form.

Mr. Hayden knows the importance of step 4 because it informs him, on the spot, of his students' thinking about mathematics. "It's truly authentic work. It can't be something that has been duplicated. They can't just copy an answer and be done with it," he notes.

Mr. Hayden also sees the improvement in the paragraphs the students are now writing. He reflects, "The first time we did this, I would get one-line statements such as the following. 'First I find the math. It's this. Then I do this.' They were very simplistic, one or two sentences. But, with practice, the responses became full-page written explanations using the proper vocabulary, terminology, and thought processes required. I can see how they thought out the whole thing and they haven't even started working on the problem yet. It's all just thought process."

Mr. Hayden, like many mathematics teachers, acknowledges the problem of decontextualized word problems—in other words, problems that are removed from student experiences. However, standardized tests are dominated by this type of question. Using Name That Math at the beginning of class allows Mr. Hayden to provide the necessary practice while lifting the experience beyond traditional multiple-choice test items. A student example from a trigonometry class can be seen in Figure 8.3.

Writing to Learn in Social Studies

In Angie Swartz's U.S. history classes, students regularly practice writing to learn that is connected to her shared reading activity as well as partner discussions and individual student reflections on current events articles. Ms. Swartz uses questions that students can find in the text, as well as questions that require them to think and search. She also is interested in her students' responses to texts, so she often includes a question that requires students to "think about their thinking" by listing the metacognitive strategies they applied.

Thinking About Thinking to Develop Questions. During a community-wide discussion on the use of drug-sniffing dogs in high schools, several articles appeared in the local newspapers. Ms. Swartz uses these newspaper articles as

Figure 8.3   Sample notes from trigonometry.

Trig Ratios

Warm 4

1. $\begin{array}{r} 24 \\ \times 6 \\ \hline 144 \end{array}$ $144\,in^2$ 2. $\begin{array}{r} 16.38 \\ \times\ 3 \\ \hline 49.14\,cm^3 \end{array}$ 3. Trapezoid

4. $13^2 - 5^2 = x^2$ $x = \sqrt{144}$
$1169 - 25 = 144$ $x = 12\,feet$

The Perimeter of a rectangle is 66. The length is twice the width. What is the length of the diagonal?

$2w = 22$ $P = 66$ $11^2 + 22^2 = x^2$
$6w = 66$ $121 + 484 = 605$
$w = 11$ $x = \sqrt{605} = 24.6$

Name that Math

1. Perimeter, length = twice the width
2. Perimeter formula + Pythagorean theorem
3. Substitute length for 2 width
4. $6w = 66$ $l^2 + w^2 = $ diagonal
   $w = 11$ $484 + 121 = x^2$
   $605 = x^2$
   $x = \sqrt{605} = 24.6$
5. First add all w's and set them equal to sixty-six, solve for w. Substitute 2w for length then use Pythagorean Theorem and solve for the diagonal.

$TanA - 1.6 - 58°$
$TanA - 4.8 - 78°$
$SinA - 0.7 - 44°$
$CosA - 0.7 - 46°$

$\dfrac{Opp}{Adj} = Tan$ $QS = 4.41$ $.4663 = \dfrac{QT}{4}$
$QT = 1.8652$
$Tan25° = .4663$ $m\angle TQS = 65°$ $Qt = 1.87$
$RS = 1.8652$

part of her Newspapers in Education program (see http://www.nieonline.com) and asks students to consider the following questions:

1. What are the problems with using dogs to sniff out drugs in high schools?
2. What does the Supreme Court say about limiting students' rights?
3. What are the benefits of using drug testing and dog sniffing in the high schools?

4. Is the author biased? What is your evidence that she is or is not?

5. Take a stand—what do you think about this issue?

Ms. Swartz gives students time to write down the questions, consider the type of question, and decide what to look for as they read. They do not write yet. Instead, Ms. Swartz reads a newspaper article titled "Taking the Dog's Word Over the Kid's" while students follow along with a copy of their own. The class does not just sit back and listen; students are busy highlighting, underlining, and marking up their copies of the text with marginalia as they keep in mind the focus questions.

Responding to Questions Through Sustained Writing. After her shared reading, Ms. Swartz asks students to respond to the questions during 10 minutes of sustained silent writing. During this focused writing time, students revisit the text, looking again at the notes, highlighting, or underlining they made during their first reading. Their writing has purpose because they know that they will be sharing it with peers in a few minutes. Ms. Swartz circulates throughout the room coaxing any reluctant writers.

Arnold's responses to the questions included:

1. There is confusion such as the one stated in the article where the dog sensed the smell of drugs on a student, but there was no proof that the student was in possession of any.
2. It's OK because they are doing it with the excuse that they want to keep schools safe.
3. Schools are able to identify or have a chance to investigate a potential drug user.
4. Yes, she does not agree with drug-sniffing dogs on campus. She says it in the last sentence of the article. I can tell by the tone of the sentence.
5. I think that it is okay to use the dogs. We don't need drugs at our school. If kids have drugs, maybe they will keep them at home.

Using Questions and Responses in Paired Discussion Groups. After the students work individually to put their thoughts in writing, they move into paired discussion groups. They are directed to use the prompt questions and their written responses to aid in the discussion. To keep students focused and on task, Ms. Swartz asks students to add at least two additional points to their notes that are identified during the discussion. To hold students accountable, they switch from pen to pencil (or change ink colors) for this task. As students listen and write, they are revisiting the text a third time and are gaining insight from their partner's ideas or perspective. This step also ensures that students are active and responsible listeners. After talking with his partner, Olga, Arnold added the following notes to his paper:

1. No problems because a dog's sense of smell is nine times better than humans, and dogs are trained to sniff out drugs.
2. Since the student is in a public place their rights may be limited.
3. A student would think twice about bringing drugs into school knowing that a dog could sniff personal belongings. But if a dog was wrong and that student got in trouble, that could cause a big problem.

Finalizing Ideas and Opinions. After the partner discussion, a lively class discussion ensues. Students refer to their written thoughts collected during sustained silent writing and partner discussions and once again add to them as they express their ideas and listen to others. To conclude this lesson, Ms. Swartz asks the students to write again. This time, the prompt is "What do you now want to know, what questions do you still have, or what opinion have you formed about this issue?" Olga, disagreeing with her partner, wrote:

> I learned that this safety technique presents a problem with invasion of privacy. People who do drugs outside of school should not be punished for something they do in private, not at school. Students have the right not to be searched without cause. What is the board of education doing to protect students' privacy rights?

Writing to Learn in Science

Step into Antoinette Linton's biology class with pen and paper in hand and be prepared for writing to learn every day. Ms. Linton uses writing to learn as a metacognitive strategy that leads her biology students to think critically about the content presented. Entry slips help her students clarify what they think, consider what they have learned, and reflect on how their learning may contribute to their personal lives as critical readers and thinkers. These daily prompts may elicit a summary of the previous day's lecture or require students to think about the organization of information pertinent to their individual research topics. As her students assume responsibility to prepare for, organize, and document research, these writing prompts guide students' thinking processes and give relevance and structure to the unit.

Using Entry Slips as Writing Prompts. During her cancer research project, Ms. Linton uses entry slips to focus her students on the topic at hand. She knows that her students have many things on their minds each day—from tests in other classes to dances and football games. The first entry slip for her cancer research project invites students to respond to the prompt, "Write down what you know about cancer. You can include topics from texts, lecture, other sources, and what you already know. Just write freely, getting your thoughts and ideas down on paper. If you have questions about cancer, write those down, too." Excerpts of these initial student entries include:

- I don't know much about cancer. I just know that it can spread and sometimes there can be a cure.
- Cancer is bad cells that ceased to recognize signals to stop the growing process.
- There are different types of cancer. Some people die from it.
- It occurs when there are problems with the enzymes that control cell division.
- It's a disease that can kill you, because of bad enzymes and damaged genes.

Some students asked questions in their entry slips:

- Which is the most common cancer?
- Can an infection cause cancer?
- Is cancer more common in men or women?

Informing Instruction Through Student Responses. The students' responses provide Ms. Linton a view of what her students already know about the topic, and focus her subsequent lesson planning. Their responses inform instruction because Ms. Linton can clearly identify the students' background knowledge, including missing, misleading, correct, or incorrect information. She now knows, for example, that she must provide specific information about cancer therapy and the absence of a cure.

Another day, Ms. Linton's entry slip prompt read, "What do I need to know about cancer in order to complete my research paper?" The students must now consider future lectures, readings, and labs in the following way: "The information that my teacher is about to give me will make me successful in my end product, which is a research paper or a presentation. Before she gets started, I need to set up a structure so that I can manipulate the materials she is about to present." Juan's entry illustrates how he is taking responsibility to organize information.

> What do I need to know about cancer in order to complete my research paper?
> I need to find answers to a lot of questions, like . . .
>
> - How and why does it start?
> - How many people have it?
> - How can you prevent it?
> - How can you tell if you're infected or not?
> - What can result from an abnormal cycle of cell division?
> - What are the causes and the current medications?

Another day, the entry slip prompt reads, "What cancer research are you most interested in doing?" Excerpts of student responses included:

> - I found out that viruses can be causes of cancer. If I can do research, this is where I want to go. I would like to know more about HIV and AIDS.
> - I would like to learn more about breast cancer. My mom had breast cancer, but I didn't know much about it.
> - Cancer is the second leading cause of death in the U.S. The four most prevalent types of cancer are lung, colon, breast, and prostate. What are the drugs used for these cancers and do they work?

Helping Students Connect Information Through Writing Prompts. Writing to learn prompts give students the opportunity to connect information gathered from class lectures, readings, and their own queries about the topic from their previous entry slips. Students then make choices that interest them, but at a point where these choices are informed, based on a growing bank of knowledge on the subject. However, Ms. Linton does not always focus her entry slip prompts on science. One day the students entered the classroom to find this prompt, "When writing a research paper, what steps should you follow?" Responding to this, Carolina wrote:

> It should have an introduction, body paragraphs, and a conclusion. Before starting the paper, you must research first, then create an outline based on what you found out from your questions. That outline turns into a draft. We revise it and get a final product. Listing your references is also necessary.

Writing to Learn in Electives

It's November, and family and consumer science teacher Pam Dahlin is teaching about food-borne illnesses. She schedules this unit of instruction for the week preceding Thanksgiving, knowing that many of her students will be assisting in their family's kitchens to prepare the holiday meal. She has selected a passage of the textbook on the subject titled "Guidelines for Cooking Foods."

Figure 8.4 Student RAFT from family and consumer sciences.

Guidelines for Safe Food Preparation
1. Cook all foods completely. Don't overcrowd the oven.
2. Microwave cooking: Cover food, stir, or rotate. Follow recommended standing time.
3. Do not taste any animal products until after they are completely cooked.
4. Cook and reheat food to an internal temperature of 165°F.
5. Failure to follow all food safety rules will result in immediate firing from job!

"I know one of the ways I help myself understand is to turn a heading into a question. Let's call this 'What are the guidelines for cooking foods?' That reminds me of the purpose for this section. I should be able to answer it for myself at the end," she tells them. She often integrates the SQ3R questioning strategy in her shared readings.

After reading the passage to her students while modeling her thinking, she introduces a writing to learn activity. "We're going to do some RAFT writing, and this time you'll do it in groups of four." Ms. Dahlin's students have done RAFT writing several times this semester, so she doesn't need to teach the steps again.

"Here's your task. Your group is going to design a food safety poster for a new restaurant." She turns on the overhead projector to display their assignment:

R = You are the chef of a brand-new, fancy restaurant that will be opening next month. You're training your new employees about food safety and sanitation.

A = Your new employees.

F = A poster for the kitchen.

T = Guidelines for cooking foods safely.

Ms. Dahlin continues: "You can use your textbook, the Internet, and of course, each other's knowledge. The supplies to make the posters are on your tables." For the next 15 minutes, the groups work on their posters, consulting information sources and debating the wording. One group's poster contained the information shown in Figure 8.4.

Conclusion

Writing to learn "is a tool we can use to see how students are thinking about and understanding what they are doing and learning in the classroom" (Mitchell, 1996, p. 93). It differs from learning to write in purpose. Process writing is used by students to refine their pieces through editing and rewriting. In contrast, writing to learn serves as a way to activate prior knowledge, recall newly learned information, make connections to other concepts, and promote reflective questioning.

This instructional strategy is useful across content areas, in part because what students write about can be easily tailored to the subject. Prompts can be constructed to ask about declarative, procedural, or conditional knowledge. First, writing to learn allows students to think about the content at hand and to focus on the subject. Students are invited to compose their thoughts and take stock of their

WRITING

beliefs and opinions before engaging in discussion. This rehearsal of language is likely to be especially useful for English language learners, who benefit from the chance to order ideas before sharing them with others.

Second, writing to learn provides students with data that they can use later for essays or class assignments. Learning logs are especially useful for this because they create a record of previous learning, allowing students to see how the teacher assembled the conceptual framework of the unit. Finally, writing to learn provides teachers a glimpse inside the student's mind—a rare opportunity to assess a student's understanding of the content. These brief writing events can allow the teacher to witness each student's use of logic, reasoning, and information to arrive at solutions and apply concepts.

The strength of writing to learn lies in its intended audience. Process writing ultimately must find an outside audience to influence, persuade, and move, for that is "the power of the pen." Writing to learn has an audience of one—the writer. Teachers create a quiet space for students to engage in an internal dialogue that leads them on a journey of self-reflection. How often have you heard writers remark that they didn't know what they thought about something until they read what they had written? And so it is with writing to learn. When students discover that these writing events illuminate their own understanding, they discover the power *in* the pen.

Chapter 9

Taking Stock: Standards, Assessment, and High-Stakes Testing

How will you know if your students have learned anything? How will you know if your students can use the strategies you have taught them? Naturally, you will assess them using a variety of informal and formal assessments. It is the act of assessment that distinguishes teaching from learning, because it is the teacher's way of ascertaining whether learning has taken place (Fisher & Frey, 2007).

How will you and other stakeholders know if the students in the classes you teach do well compared with other students in the state? Your students will be tested using a variety of norm-referenced and criterion-referenced instruments. These formal assessments are used for accountability purposes at the local, state, or national level.

Of course, there are many types of assessments. Table 9.1 provides an overview of the various types of informal and formal assessments that teachers and schools use.

Students are assessed for a variety of reasons, including:

- diagnosing individual student needs (e.g., assessing developmental status, monitoring and communicating student progress, certifying competency, determining needs);
- informing instruction (e.g., evaluating instruction, modifying instructional strategies, identifying instructional needs);
- evaluating programs; and
- providing accountability information. (Lapp, Fisher, Flood, & Cabello, 2001, p. 7)

In this chapter, we will discuss the roles of informal assessment and formal testing as a means for answering the questions posed above. These practices form the

Table 9.1 Guide to Formal and Informal Assessments

Informal Assessments		
Type of Test	Purpose	Administration
Observation	Gathers information about a student's academic, behavioral, or social skills used in an authentic setting.	Teacher records observational data in anecdotal notes, journals, or daily logs.
Portfolio	Provides evidence of a student's academic growth through the collection of work samples.	Student and teacher select representative samples of student work for display in a binder or other organizer.
Inventory	Documents student use of specified skills during a single observation.	A commercially or teacher-produced form of observable behaviors completed by the teacher.
Conference	Involves the student in direct feedback to the teacher in a one-to-one discussion.	Often scheduled by teacher at regular intervals to gauge progress on more complex academic behaviors such as reading comprehension.
Self-assessment	Allows student to engage in reflective learning.	Students assess their own academic performance using an age-appropriate checklist of indicators.
Survey	Collects student feedback about interests, prior knowledge, or motivation about a topic.	Student completes a commercially or teacher-produced survey of items.
Formal Assessments		
Type of Test	Purpose	Administration
Standardized	Yields a student's academic performance ranking compared to a normed sample of students.	■ Schedule determined by state and local agencies; often yearly. ■ Tests are usually timed and have strict protocols.
Criterion Referenced	Measures a student's performance compared to a set of academic skills or objectives. Scores are reported as the proportion of correct answers.	■ Tests may be untimed or timed. ■ May be administered annually or more frequently.

bookends for teaching students to read for information because they serve as measures of progress and points for making instructional and programmatic decisions.

Classroom Assessment Practices

Assessments are the link between teaching and learning. This concept lies at the heart of teaching because our classrooms are based on learner-centered instruction. This means the teacher doesn't merely march lockstep through the content of a standards-based curriculum, but balances the content with the needs of the learner. These needs are identified through ongoing assessment that is linked to subsequent instruction. In this model, assessment and instruction are considered to be recursive because they repeat as students learn new content. In learner-centered classrooms, teachers first assess to establish what students know and do not know, then plan instruction based on this information. Next, they deliver the instruction they have designed and observe how learners respond. Based on these observations, educators reflect on the results and assess again to determine what needs to be taught next. A diagram representing this concept can be seen in Figure 9.1.

This model may sound as if it would take a lot of time to complete; in fact, effective teachers perform these complex tasks rapidly. In well-organized classrooms, informal assessment happens throughout the day as teachers use questioning, discussions, and assignments to measure progress. In addition, teachers administer assessments to monitor progress and formulate future instruction. The first step is selecting the correct assessments.

Selecting the Right Assessment

The usefulness of every assessment is dependent on a proper fit between purpose and type of assessment used. It is important to remember that every assessment is useful and not useful *at the same time*. Any given assessment is useful in the hands of a conscientious educator who understands the limitations of the tool being used. Any given assessment is useless if it is interpreted to show something it was not intended to show. You would be very suspicious of a doctor who ordered a chest x-ray when you were seeking help for a sprained ankle. There is nothing inherently wrong with a chest x-ray; it is simply the wrong test for the task. In the same regard, the type of reading or writing assessment selected must match its intended use.

Guillaume (2004) offers these considerations for selecting an assessment. Each assessment needs to be:

- tied to your stance on learning;
- driven by learning goals;
- systematic;
- tied to instruction;
- inclusive of the learner; and
- integrated into a manageable system. (p. 131)

Struggling Readers

SHOW WHAT THEY KNOW IN DIVERSE WAYS

For many readers who struggle, standardized paper-and-pencil tests mask their strengths. They often have test anxiety, a collection of bad experiences with tests, and a belief that tests are used against them. Students who struggle with traditional assessments involving literacy can often demonstrate what they know in alternative formats. For example, a student may be able to illustrate the life cycle of a butterfly, but not write about it. Another student might be able to quickly calculate baseball statistics, but not be able to read classic texts. This doesn't mean that students who find reading and writing difficult should be excused from formal assessment situations, but it does mean that teachers must develop and use alternative assessment formats to gain a better understanding of their students' conceptual understanding.

It's also important to note that different states use different accommodations and modifications to testing such that performance in one geographic region might look different from the same student's performance if tested in a different geographic region. The National Center on Educational Outcomes (http://education.umn.edu/nceo/about/) maintains a list of accommodations and modifications used in assessment situations. NCEO also provides information on alternative assessments, graduation requirements by state, assessments of English language learners, universal design in education, and standards.

TESTING

Figure 9.1   Relationship between assessment and instruction.

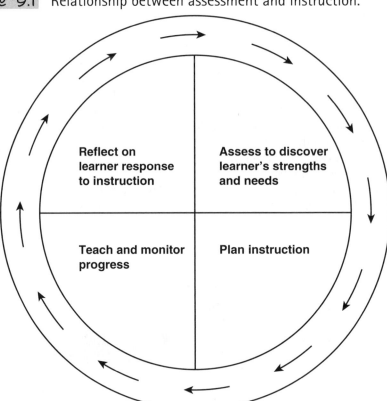

Tied to Your Stance on Learning. Every teacher brings a philosophy of education and a view of literacy to his or her practice. It is important to recognize how assessment choices fit into that perspective. For example, an educator who possesses a viewpoint of learning as a developmental phenomenon will be interested in assessment instruments that reflect benchmarks of developmental phases of learning. Teachers with a skills-based orientation will find skills measures to be useful.

Driven by Learning Goals. Assessments used should be consistent with state content standards for the grade level. As teachers we need to regularly assess students' understanding of the context and determine appropriate goals for students to master.

Systematic. Teachers select assessments that can be administered and analyzed in a systematic way at both the individual and class levels. Good assessments should contain data recording protocols that make it easy for the teacher to interpret the information at a later date. In addition, the teacher must determine how often assessments will be administered. Finally, each assessment should measure what it purports to measure (valid) and yield results that are consistent across administrations and assessors (reliable).

Tied to Instruction. Although this seems apparent, it is worth stating again. Assessment should be linked directly to instruction, either to determine what should be taught next (pretesting) or to check for understanding of skills or strategies that have just been taught (posttesting). Assessments that are not connected to instruction are likely to be frustrating for students because they appear purposeless, and inadequate for teachers because they do not provide relevant information.

Inclusive of the Learner. Assessments are intended to be completed in conjunction with the needs of the learner. Most of the assessments in this chapter are not completed in isolation by students, who then return the completed tests to the teacher. Instead, these assessments are designed to capture the work of children in the act of learning. Whether through listening to a student reading text or using a rubric to discuss a student's writing, these tools are intended to involve the learner in their own measures of progress. A position statement issued by the International Reading Association suggests that students "have a right to reading assessment that identifies their strengths as well as their needs and involves them in making decisions about their own learning" (International Reading Association, 2000, p. 7).

Integrated Into a Manageable System. No teacher can devote all his or her time to collecting and analyzing assessment data. The demands of assessment on the time available can become overwhelming and even crowd out equally valuable instructional time. Therefore, it is in the interests of the teacher to understand what each assessment does, then select the one that best fits the needs of the students, teacher, and curriculum. Having a collection of good, all-purpose assessments is preferable to administering overlapping assessments that do little to shed new light on a student's progress.

Types of Informal Assessments

There are a number of types of informal assessments commonly used in elementary classrooms to assess students' progress in learning to read for information. They include observations, portfolios, inventories, rubrics, conferences, self-assessments, and surveys.

Observations. Observations are perhaps the assessment tool most commonly used by teachers and identified by them as the most useful (West, 1998). There are several advantages to using observation as a tool for assessment:

- It focuses on student work in authentic learning situations (Frey & Hiebert, 2003).
- It mitigates some of the problems associated with formal testing, especially learner stress, because it occurs in the daily learning environment.
- It allows the teacher to obtain and analyze the information immediately, providing flexibility in instructional plans.

Observational notes can be difficult to collect if you don't have a system. Begin by identifying specific students you want to observe during a particular day, perhaps one to three students. If you select two or three students per day for targeted observation, you can collect notes on all of your students in under 2 weeks. Having said that, we also know that opportunities of observation sometimes arise serendipitously. The trouble arises when you make a note of something and then lose the

Figure 9.2 Clipboard for observations.

Addison, Melissa	Mohamed, Darif
Borrega, Luis	Norris, Andre
Chou, Ming	Penhas, John
Edwards, Michelle	Peveto, Chelsea
Estes, Diana	Quick, Lamoine
Grant, Ted	Roberts, Addie
Hoffman, Lydia	Reese, Dennis
Lazaroff, Megan	Tejada, Lourdes
Lincoln, Deasia	Uhl, Danny
McLain, Andy	Viotto, Marcus

Source: Language Arts Workshop: Purposeful Reading and Writing Instruction, by N. Frey and D. Fisher, 2006, Upper Saddle River, NJ: Pearson/Merrill/Prentice Hall. Used with permission.

note! To handle that problem, we create a clipboard of index cards, one for each student, at the beginning of the year. Each card contains pertinent information about the student. The cards are taped individually to the clipboard in a slightly overlapping fashion so that each card can be lifted. The student's name is written at the bottom edge of the card so it can be seen at all times. Anytime we write comments about a student on a sticky note, we place it on his or her card for later organization and filing. See Figure 9.2 for a diagram of this organizational system.

Although the act of reflective teaching is defined by a recursive cycle of teaching, observing, and reflecting, it is not realistic to think that any teacher could (or even would want to) record every observation. However, a simple observation form like the one in Figure 9.3 can assist a busy teacher in documenting meaningful observation data.

Portfolios. The term *portfolio* is used to describe a collection of student work that represents progress made over time (Tierney et al., 1998). Like an artist's portfolio, it is constructed by the learner in partnership with the teacher. Students are often invited to select a range of work, not just the most exemplary pieces, in order to represent their learning. The assembled portfolio is then used as a conference tool between parent, teacher, and student. Wilcox (1997) suggests that a portfolio of student work be organized around the following topics:

- *Reading artifacts* like reading journals and book reviews.
- *Thinking artifacts* that demonstrate the learner's process of understanding. Examples include notes, concept maps, and self-assessments.
- *Writing artifacts* like finished pieces and works in progress.
- *Interacting artifacts* that reflect work accomplished with peers. These might include reciprocal teaching sheets and written summaries of readings that have been collaboratively read through a jigsaw process.
- *Demonstrating artifacts* that represent public performance by the student, including oral reports, demonstrations, and lab experiments. (p. 35)

Inventories. An inventory of a store lists the items contained within the store. Likewise, skills inventories are lists of observable behaviors that can be easily identified and recorded by the teacher. These inventories most often come in the form of a checklist for easy transcription. An inventory can be commercially

Figure 9.3   Classroom observation form.

Name: _____   **Date:** _____

Time: From _____ **to** _____

Student observed working:

- Independently
- Collaboratively with _____
- Guided instruction with _____

Task observed:

Sequence of events observed:

Notes and reflections:

Abbreviations:
   S_1 = student being observed
   T = teacher
$S_2 - S_5$ = other students working with observed student

Source: Language Arts Workshop: Purposeful Reading and Writing Instruction, by N. Frey and D. Fisher, 2006, Upper Saddle River, NJ: Pearson/Merrill/Prentice Hall. Used with permission.

prepared, or it may be constructed by the teacher. A checklist of observable behaviors is especially useful when meeting with parents to discuss their child's progress.

Rubrics. Students often have difficulty predicting precisely what the teacher wants to see in an assignment or project. This is due in part to the difficulty teachers sometimes have in defining what they want. Rubrics are designed to clear up such confusions. These scoring guides are distributed and discussed in advance so that students are clear on what is expected. Rubrics are usually designed by the teacher, although many choose to develop rubrics with the class in order to prompt discussion about the characteristics of a good performance.

Conferences. Effective teachers routinely meet individually with students during the independent phase of instruction to discuss learning. These conferences are valuable because they are an opportunity to collect informal assessment information about a student. The information gathered during a conference on a student's learning provides authentic assessment data for use in planning future instruction.

Self-assessments. As we have discussed on several occasions throughout this book, the ability to self-assess is an essential skill for developing metacognitive awareness. You will recall that metacognitive awareness is the ability of a learner to describe how he or she best learns. In addition, it refers to a learner's ability to develop a plan for learning, then monitor and evaluate that plan (Kujawa & Huske, 1995). For example, a student of ours wrote, "I just wanted to let you know some of the skills I would like to work on. One of them is 'inference' or 'reading between the lines.' For example, I am very bad at answering questions in someone else's shoes such as 'What would this author say?' or 'Why was this piece written?'" One of the ways students develop metacognitive awareness is through the use of self-assessments. An example of a self-assessment for students working in groups appears in Figure 9.4.

Surveys. Assessment tools such as surveys can be an efficient way for a teacher to collect information about a large number of students in a short period of time. Surveys can be constructed on any topic and can measure student background knowledge or interest. Information collected from surveys can then be compiled to make instructional decisions. A reading survey for the beginning of the school year can be found in Figure 9.5.

An effective teacher uses a variety of assessments, including observations, portfolios of student work, inventories, rubrics, conferences, and self-assessments to monitor the progress of students and plan future instruction. Using a variety of assessment instruments, both formal and informal, provides the student with opportunities to more fully demonstrate his or her strengths in reading for information and reveal areas of continued need. When paired with informal assessments, the formal testing necessary for accountability purposes becomes more useful. It is not, however, without controversy.

Types of Formal Assessments

Like informal assessments, formal assessments are further distinguished by their purpose. Many are familiar with standardized assessments, sometimes called norm-referenced assessments. These are constructed using a large sample of

|Figure 9.4   Self-assessment of group work.

Name: _____			Date: _____		

Project: _____   Members of my group:

_____

_____

_____

Please rank yourself based on your contributions to the group. Circle the one that best describes your work.
5 = always   4 = almost always   3 = sometimes   2 = once or twice   1 = never

I completed my tasks on time.	5	4	3	2	1
I contributed ideas to the group.	5	4	3	2	1
I listened respectfully to the ideas of others.	5	4	3	2	1
I used other people's ideas in my work for the project.	5	4	3	2	1
When I was stuck, I sought help from my group.	5	4	3	2	1

Additional comments:

Source: Language Arts Workshop: Purposeful Reading and Writing Instruction, by N. Frey and D. Fisher, 2006, Upper Saddle River, NJ: Pearson/Merrill/Prentice Hall. Used with permission.

participants who are carefully included to reflect a larger population. Therefore, the sample is selected based on a host of demographic characteristics, including age, gender, socioeconomic status, and geographical location. The chief purpose of standardized tests is to evaluate programs and compare schools and districts. Many standardized tests are applied throughout the country, as they are not tied to the state content standards. An example of standardized test used in all 50 states is the National Assessment for Educational Progress (NAEP), which is used by the federal government to analyze broad trends in education. Other standardized tests that measure achievement include the Stanford Achievement Test and the Terra Nova.

Criterion-referenced tests measure students against an expectation, most often the content standards for the course. Sometimes called standards tests, these vary by state because they are derived from a common set of expectations. As with standardized assessments, they are also used to compare schools and districts within the state. Another example of a criterion-referenced test is the Gates-MacGinitie Reading Test (GMRT), which provides building-level data to make decisions about programs.

Formal assessments have been developed to be administered to students using a prescribed format concerning time, directions, and level of assistance. Most often, these assessments are given in conditions that do not reflect the ways in which students learned the tested skills. Most formal assessments include a

TESTING

Figure 9.5   Reading survey.

Name: _____   Date: _____

Please circle the answer that is best for you.

Reading Survey

When I am interested in a topic, I look for a book on the subject.

     Always   *Sometimes*   *Never*

I know how to find a book on the subject I am interested in.

     Always   *Sometimes*   *Never*

These are the things I like in an informational book (circle as many as you like).

     Photographs   *Colorful illustrations*   *Lots of interesting facts*

     Directions for making things   *Short chapters*   *Sidebars*

These are the kinds of things I read (check off all the ones you like).

Chapter books _____		Books with pictures _____
Web sites _____		Newspapers _____
Magazines _____		Textbooks _____
Reference _____		Biographies _____

These are the things I am most interested in reading about (check off all the things you like).

Science topics

- ☐ How things work
- ☐ The natural world
- ☐ Technology
- ☐ Weather
- ☐ Space
- ☐ Human body
- ☐ Other _____

Social studies topics

- ☐ Culture and language
- ☐ Exploration and conquest
- ☐ Government and economics
- ☐ Life long ago
- ☐ Life today and in the future
- ☐ U.S. history
- ☐ Our state
- ☐ Other _____

Mathematics topics

- ☐ Careers in mathematics
- ☐ Using math in everyday life
- ☐ Engineering
- ☐ Math puzzles
- ☐ Lives of mathematicians

The arts

- ☐ Dance
- ☐ Painting and drawing
- ☐ Athletics
- ☐ Sculpture
- ☐ Music
- ☐ Performance
- ☐ The lives of artists and musicians

---

lengthy testing protocol and student test booklets for collecting data. Protocols are the detailed directions for administering the test. Most formal assessment scoring is completed by the test publisher and the results are then reported back to the school and district, often several months later. Many of these formal assessments are used to measure school and district progress toward various state and national accountability targets. Formal assessments are often used to foster school return.

Concerns About the Uses of Formal Assessments

This approach to school reform through high-stakes accountability is not without its critics. Numerous educators have expressed dismay at the efficacy of achieving higher levels of student achievement through these means (Meier, Kozol, & Cohen, 2000; Ohanian, 1999). Alfie Kohn, a psychologist long involved with issues of education, has criticized the emphasis on accountability measures as a method that is ineffective for promoting reform and harmful to students and teachers whose anxiety about test results may actually impede performance (Kohn, 2000). These controversies are likely to remain throughout the next decade, and, as educators, we believe it is important to consider opposing viewpoints on matters of such importance. But we are also cognizant of the present realities faced by today's teachers. Students will be tested; teachers and schools will be evaluated according to student performance on these tests. Therefore, the remainder of this chapter will provide guidance for ensuring that students perform well on these accountability measures.

Addressing High-Stakes Tests

The use of formal assessments, with significant rewards or consequences attached to them, are part of the educational landscape. With the arrival of these high-stakes tests, teachers and schools are called upon to improve student performance. To address these expectations, several steps can be taken both in the short and long term. First and foremost, students must be motivated to do well on assessments. They must understand that the assessments they participate in matter.

The student's own perception, attitude, and positive disposition toward the test is essential. If students are to succeed on these assessments, they must view them as worthwhile, important, and achievable. To bring about such a positive outlook, it is essential that all school community members, especially the faculty, see the test as worthwhile, important, and achievable. Should the teachers discount, disparage, or exhibit significant anxiety over the tests, the impact upon student performance will be negative. Such teachers have, in effect, told students these tests are not important or that success on such tests is not possible. Given such an outlook by the teacher, students are not likely to put forward any significant effort into test taking, and will instead assume failure before beginning.

To create a positive and successful testing climate, the entire school should engage in a long-term campaign that addresses three major areas:

1. test format practice,
2. reading strategies instruction, and
3. student engagement in reading. (Guthrie, 2002)

As we look more closely at each of these areas, we must be careful not to allow the test practice to become the curriculum (Santman, 2002). In other words, we are not advocating that schools "teach to the test." Rather, we believe in teaching to the

TESTING

standards that are tested. When students are well versed in standards-based content, they are more likely to do well on the test. School is still about creating citizens who can participate in the democracy.

Additionally, we believe that students should be "test-wise." Consider the times in your adult life when you have been in a situation where the outcome could greatly affect your future. Perhaps it was giving testimony in a court case, or meeting with an Internal Revenue Service agent for an audit of your taxes. None of us would ever consider walking into such a high-stakes event without doing our best to prepare for the task. You've come by this wisdom from years of life experience. We believe that our students should also be wise about important events like standardized testing. The first step to being test-wise is to understand the format of the test. Like any genre, knowing the characteristics of the test assists the learner in understanding it.

Area #1: Test Format Practice

The worthiness of test format preparation depends upon how well it is infused into the curriculum, how connected it is to good general learning, and how it connects with effective literacy strategies (e.g., Duke & Ritchart, 1997). It is not enough, and may even be harmful to learning, if teachers simply find test items for their students to practice. Popham (2001) calls this type of practice "item-teaching" and believes that although it may improve student's scores, teachers cannot "infer that students can satisfactorily do other problems of that ilk" (p. 17). In other words, when teachers practice item-teaching they are preparing students only for specific test questions; little hope is provided that the learner has any fundamental understanding or can apply the concept to other areas.

Popham (2001) suggests that teachers instead be involved in "curriculum-teaching," whereby they focus upon specific content or skills that will later be tested, or as he states, "test-represented." According to Popham, curriculum-teaching "will elevate students' scores on high stakes tests and, more importantly, will elevate students' mastery of the knowledge or skills on which the test items are based" (p. 17).

Langer (2001) makes a similar point in her study of characteristics of literacy instruction in "beating the odds" schools. Langer identifies two quite different approaches to test preparation commonly practiced by teachers: separated or integrated. Test preparation can be treated either as a separate approach involving test practice and test hints or it can be directly integrated into the regular curriculum.

Schools that outperform their demographic counterparts often use integrated test preparation. In an integrated approach, teachers spend time "carefully analyzing test demands and reformulating curriculum as necessary to be sure that students would, over time, develop the knowledge and skills necessary for accomplished performance" (Langer, 2001, p. 860). This stands in contrast to Popham's (2001) item-teaching approach that is predicated on how well the teacher matches his or her direct teaching to the test questions featured on this year's exam.

In high-performing schools, teachers see tests as an opportunity to "revise and reformulate their literacy curriculum" (Langer, 2001, p. 860). Such teachers provide their students enriched course work by using the tests to go deeper into an understanding of literacy skills, strategies, and content. In the process, test preparation is seen not as an additional activity, but as one of many that ensure overall literacy learning (Langer, 2001).

To ensure that test format practice is integrated into the curriculum, we suggest that teachers focus on attitude, general test-wise skills, direction words, multiple-choice questions, and skills for reading passages.

Figure 9.6 Classroom poster.

> You too could become the next high SCORER!
>
> S—Schedule your time while taking the test.
> C—Use clue words to help answer questions.
> O—Omit difficult questions at first.
> R—Read questions carefully.
> E—Eliminate unreasonable choices.
> R—Review your responses.

Fostering a Test-Wise Attitude. As we have noted, students' attitudes toward the test may be one of the most important factors for success. We have all seen students use the answer sheet to make designs, clearly not paying attention to the test questions. Students sometimes refer to this as "Christmas treeing" the score sheet because the arrangement of bubbles on the scantron can be easily transformed into this holiday symbol. One schoolwide strategy is to use a mnemonic that the students can learn. The "High Scorer" posters remind students that the test is important and provides them with general information about test taking (see Figure 9.6).

These posters should be reviewed on a regular basis. Additionally, students should be asked to think about the following:

1. *Be prepared.* Get a good night's sleep and eat a good breakfast on test days.
2. *Relax.* It's normal to feel a little nervous. Some questions will be easy, others hard. Very few people get all of the answers right. Don't worry about information you don't know; just do your best.
3. *Think positively.* Tell yourself, "I'm going to do the best I can." Then do it.
4. *Practice your skills.* They will help you do your best work.

Regarding the answer sheet transformations that become works of art for some students: As the test sheets are collected and secured at the end of each test day, those with designs are noted. These budding Picassos are invited to meet with the principal to discuss the importance of test performance for the student.

General Test-Wise Skills. The following items comprise an overall approach from the start of testing when directions are read and questions can be asked, to the last few minutes of testing—when stray marks can be erased. The points suggest that the test taker begin the test with confidence and curiosity, tackle the questions systematically, and finish the test with diligence and attention to detail. Again, many of these are things that students have not been taught.

These skills should be reinforced in each class, especially when students complete teacher-created tests throughout the year.

1. Listen and read along with the teacher as he or she reads the directions to the test. Ask questions if you do not understand.
2. At the start of the test, quickly scan the pages and notice the types and number of questions—what's easy and what's hard. This will help you make the best use of your time.
3. Budget your time, making sure you allow enough time to answer all of the questions. Pace yourself. Watch the time. If you don't know the answer to a question, move on and come back to it later.
4. Answer the questions you know first. You will have time to read the others more closely the second time you go over the test. When you skip a question,

TESTING

mark your answer sheet so you won't use that space to answer another question. Keep an eye on the answer sheet to be sure you're marking the right space.

5. When you skip a question, be alert for answers or clues in other questions. Answers often pop up in other questions. In addition, as you take the test your background knowledge about the subject will become more active and make it more likely you will be able to figure out the harder questions later.

6. When you get to the end of the test, start over with the first question you skipped. Be sure to erase stray marks when you go back over the test. Complete the answer sheet correctly by filling in the bubbles completely and erasing any other pencil marks.

7. Do not change an answer unless you can prove your first answer is wrong. Your first instinct is usually correct.

8. During the last 2 minutes of the test, go back and fill in all blank answers with the same letter. If you leave an answer blank, you're guaranteed to get it wrong!

Direction Words. An important skill in reading for information is the ability to correctly interpret direction words. Success on each test item is dependent upon the clear understanding of exactly what the question is asking. If students do not take time to consider or do not know what the words mean in the question stem, there is little chance of success. Like the signal words associated with specific text structures these direction words signal the test taker to the task at hand. Extensive practice with these stems as part of the classroom's general pattern of instruction is essential.

Teachers must teach students to read the questions carefully and look for important direction words such as:

first step is	best answer is	the same as	refers to
most important	except for	most likely to	a fact
opinion	the purpose of	infer from	

Practicing with questions using these stems will allow students to arrive at, and become familiar with, the type of answer each stem is likely to require.

Additionally, there are common terms used on tests that students should understand. These terms can be incorporated into your vocabulary instruction. The following terms comprise a good start at understanding direction words:

- *Analyze.* Break the subject into parts and discuss the parts.
- *Approximate, estimate.* Make a reasonable guess.
- *Characterize, identify, explain, describe.* Name the characteristics that make something special.
- *Choose the best answer.* Select the answer that is most correct.
- *Examine.* Look carefully at similar answers as one will be a better choice.
- *Give the chronological order.* Give the time order.
- *Comment.* Give your opinion and support it with facts and examples.
- *Compare.* Tell how two or more things are similar and how they are different.
- *Contrast.* Tell how two or more things are different.
- *Discuss.* Tell all you can about the topic in the time available.

- *Evaluate.* Give evidence on each side of an issue, draw a conclusion from the evidence, and make a judgment about the topic.
- *Fill in the blank or complete the sentence.* If a list of possible answers is given, use the best word from the list. If not, use the word you know that best fits the meaning of the sentence.
- *Interpret.* Explain the meaning.
- *Justify.* Furnish evidence to support your answer.
- *Name, list, mention.* List the information that is asked for.
- *Put in your own words.* Rewrite complicated language in everyday English.
- *Rank.* List the information that is asked for in some special order, such as order of occurrence or chronological order.
- *Skim.* Glance through the passage quickly, looking for answers to specific questions.
- *State.* Give a short, simple answer. No discussion is necessary.
- *Summarize.* Briefly restate the passage, being sure to include the main points. Leave out small details. Your answer should be shorter than the original passage.
- *Trace.* Give major points in chronological order.

Multiple-Choice Questions. In addition to specific vocabulary suggestions for the words in the test directions, teachers should also address effective test-wise skills for multiple-choice questions themselves. The following considerations examine the choices the test taker must make between a variety of potential answers to discover which is the correct answer. Making choices between the correct answer and the attractive "distracters" is a matter of both knowledge about the question and knowledge about test taking. Figure 9.7 contains a checklist for creating assessment items, including multiple-choice items. This checklist can be used as a guide to creating assessment items that ensure students have test format practice.

1. Read all of the choices carefully. The people who write tests know that many people will not read carefully. Even if you are sure you see the right answer, read them all to be sure there is no surprise hiding at the end.

2. Don't get fooled by answers that seem to contain the exact words that appeared in the passage. Read those carefully to see if the context is correct.

3. Most of the time, there will be one or two obviously wrong choices. Ignore these and concentrate on the ones that might be right.

4. If you are sure that two of the answer choices are correct, the correct answer is usually "all of the above." Do not choose this answer unless you are sure that at least two of the choices are correct.

5. Watch for negative words in the instructions such as *no* or *not*. Watch out for trick questions! Some tests use the word *not* to fool you; stop and ask yourself what the question is really asking.

6. Absolute words, such as *none, all, never,* or *always,* usually indicate an incorrect choice. Very few things are absolute. Statements with words like *generally, some, often, usually,* or *most often* are more likely to be correct. Please note: Statements must be completely true to count as true. Statements with absolute words are often false.

Figure 9.7   Checklist for creating assessments.

All Items

☐ Is this the most appropriate type of item to use for the intended learning outcomes?

☐ Does each item or task require students to demonstrate the performance described in the specific learning outcome it measures (relevance)?

☐ Does each item present a clear and definite task to be performed (clarity)?

☐ Is each item or task presented in simple, readable language and free from excessive verbiage (conciseness)?

☐ Does each item provide an appropriate challenge (ideal difficulty)?

☐ Does each item have an answer that would be agreed upon by experts (correctness)?

☐ Is there a clear basis for awarding partial credit on items or tasks with multiple points (scoring rubric)?

☐ Is each item or task free from technical errors and irrelevant clues (technical soundness)?

☐ Is each test time free from cultural bias?

☐ Have the items been set aside for a time before reviewing them (or reviewed by a colleague)?

Short-Answer Items

☐ Can the items be answered with a number, symbol, word, or brief phrase?

☐ Has textbook language been avoided?

☐ Have the items been stated so that only one response is correct?

☐ Are the answer blanks equal in length (for fill-in responses)?

☐ Are the answer blanks (preferably one per item) at the end of the items, preferably after a question?

☐ Are the items free of clues (such as *a* or *an*)?

☐ Has the degree of precision been indicated for numerical answers?

☐ Have the units been indicated when numerical answers are expressed in units?

Binary (True-False) and Multiple-Binary Items

☐ Can each statement be clearly judged true or false with only one concept per statement?

☐ Have specific determiners (e.g., *usually, always*) been avoided?

☐ Have trivial statements been avoided?

☐ Have negative statements (especially double negatives) been avoided?

☐ Does a superficial analysis suggest a wrong answer?

☐ Are opinion statements attributed to some source?

☐ Are the true and false items approximately equal in length?

☐ Is there approximately an equal number of true and false items?

☐ Has a detectable pattern of answers (e.g., T, F, T, F) been avoided?

Matching Items

☐ Is the material for the two lists homogeneous?

☐ Is the list of responses longer or shorter than the list of premises?

☐ Are the responses brief and on the right-hand side?

☐ Have the responses been placed in alphabetical or numerical order?

☐ Do the directions indicate the basis for matching?

☐ Do the directions indicate how many times each response may be used?

☐ Are all of the matching items on the same page?

Figure 9.7 *Continued.*

Multiple-Choice Items

- ☐ Does each item stem present a meaningful problem?
- ☐ Is there too much information in the stem?
- ☐ Are the item stems free of irrelevant material?
- ☐ Are the item stems stated in positive terms (if possible)?
- ☐ If used, has negative wording been given special emphasis (e.g., capitalized)?
- ☐ Are the distractors brief and free of unnecessary words?
- ☐ Are the distractors similar in length and form to the answer?
- ☐ Is there only one correct or clearly best answer?
- ☐ Are the distractors based on specific misconceptions?
- ☐ Are the items free of clues that point to the answer?
- ☐ Are the distractors and answer presented in sensible (e.g., alphabetical, numerical) order?
- ☐ Has *all of the above* been avoided and has *none of the above* been used judiciously?
- ☐ If a stimulus is used, is it necessary for answering the item?
- ☐ If a stimulus is used, does it require use of skills sought to be assessed?

Essay Items

- ☐ Are the questions designed to measure higher-level learning outcomes?
- ☐ Does each question clearly indicate the response expected (including extensiveness)?
- ☐ Are students aware of the basis on which their answers will be evaluated?
- ☐ Are appropriate time limits provided for responding to the questions?
- ☐ Are students aware of the time limits and/or point values for each question?
- ☐ Are all students required to respond to the same questions?

Performance Items

- ☐ Does the item focus on learning outcomes that require complex cognitive skills and student performances?
- ☐ Does the task represent both the content and skills that are central to learning outcomes?
- ☐ Does the item minimize dependence on skills that are irrelevant to the intended purpose of the assessment task?
- ☐ Does the task provide the necessary scaffolding for students to be able to understand the task and achieve the task?
- ☐ Do the directions clearly describe the task?
- ☐ Are students aware of the basis (expectations) on which their performances will be evaluated in terms of scoring rubrics?

For the Assessment as a Whole

- ☐ Are the items of the same type grouped together on the test (or within sections or sets)?
- ☐ Are the items arranged from easy to more difficult within sections or within the test as a whole?
- ☐ Are items numbered in sequence, indicating so if the test continues on subsequent pages?
- ☐ Are all answer spaces clearly indicated and is each answer space related to its corresponding item?
- ☐ Are the correct answers distributed in such a way that there is no detectable pattern?
- ☐ Is the test material well spaced, legible, and free of typos?
- ☐ Are there directions for each section of the test and the test as a whole?
- ☐ Are the directions clear and concise?

Source: Adapted from *Measurement and Assessment in Teaching* (8th ed.), by R. L. Linn and N.E. Granlund, 2000, Upper Saddle River, NJ: Merrill/Prentice Hall. Used with permission.

TESTING

Test-Wise Skills for Reading Passages.   Just as the heart of a successful education is literacy instruction, the heart of successful test performance is reading comprehension. Strategies for reading for information have been the focus of this book. When testing is the issue, nothing can substitute for proven and engaging literacy instruction if students are to demonstrate test achievement. However, like the general test-wise skills discussed previously, we advocate for teachers to instruct students to do the following:

1. If the questions are based on a reading passage, read the questions first. Then you will know what to look for as you read. Don't read the choices yet; they will distract you.

2. After you have read the passage, read each question and answer the question in your head before you read the choices. If you know what kind of answer you are looking for, it will be easier to choose the right one.

Remember that these suggestions were not intended to be used 6 weeks before the test is given. The likelihood of successfully boosting achievement scores is diminished because without multiple opportunities to practice these techniques, students must rely on a confusing list of memorized, but not internalized, tips. For example, a student may ask, "Do I read the questions and the answers before the passage, or just the questions?" Instead, these strategies should be introduced and modeled at the beginning of the school year and used throughout the year on teacher-created tests and practice events. The goal is for students to see these standardized testing events as an extension of what they have done in the classroom.

Area #2: Reading for Information on Standardized Tests

Many of the skills for success on standardized tests are the same skills students need to be literate and are the focus of this book. Concerned educators should keep in mind that nothing can substitute for good instruction. Through direct instruction in reading strategies, teachers address the single most influential factor for improving student test performance (Feuer, Holland, Green, Bertenthal, & Hemphill, 1999). Preparing students for high-stakes tests through test format practice can be a highly effective activity, especially for students with little experience or familiarity with such tests. However, if test format practice is conducted for extended periods and to the exclusion of other instruction and content, students will score poorly (Guthrie, 2002). If done in isolation, test format practice provides students with few long-term gains. It is not in itself a well-rounded classroom practice.

An effective way to avoid the pitfalls of isolated test practice is to heed Langer's (2001) findings about "beating the odds schools." These high-achieving schools chose to emphasize curriculum improvement over separate and distinct test prep. Like Langer, our experience suggests that when schools adopt a set of instructional practices that work well across content areas, test scores increase (Fisher, 2001). When teachers across the campus begin to apply common literacy strategies in order to boost learning in their classroom, they are also employing an integrated approach to curriculum and testing. In other words, students learn to transport a set of strategies to new and novel situations.

Reviewing Types of Questions.   In thinking about the test format suggestion to read questions carefully, we can conclude that a great deal of instruction and practice must occur for students to be successful with this skill. Simply reading or reviewing the test format suggestions may bring about some awareness.

However, reviewing is not sufficient. Students must be provided practice, familiarity, and application of the suggestions if they are to use them on test days. Student practice with identifying the types of questions and corresponding answers and constructing their own questions will likely improve student test performance. After all, a test is itself a compilation of questions.

Accessing Prior Knowledge. Anticipatory activities can help students make use of their prior knowledge during test taking. Students adept at the processes readers use to enter a reading can gather information about the text and quickly identify features that stand out such as charts, pictures, and subtitles. Regular classroom use of the K-W-L process (Ogle, 1986) discussed earlier is particularly helpful because it creates some habits of mind useful for approaching unfamiliar text. We are not advocating that students construct a K-W-L chart to answer test questions. We are suggesting that frequent use of anticipatory activities models the practice of assessing what one knows and what one wants to know. It is especially useful for answering timed test questions. Anticipatory activities also keep students focused on the content so that their performance later is enhanced.

Building Knowledge and Fluency. The chapter on read alouds and shared reading may not seem connected to test taking at first glance, but consider the teaching that takes place during one of these events. During read alouds or shared readings, a teacher can model the fluent expression signaled by the content and the punctuation. Read alouds and shared reading can also build background knowledge and provide students with explicit instruction in the self-monitoring that goes on in the mind of a reader. Faced with an unfamiliar piece of text on a standardized test, a student exposed to these teaching events can apply the same strategies to better answer the questions associated with the passage.

Focusing Thinking and Recall. The notetaking and note making chapter can help teachers provide their students with skills to glean and prioritize main ideas quickly from the text. Notetaking enhances students' thinking by developing thought processes that eliminate extraneous details and instead focuses upon essential points. Note making skills are also helpful when taking standardized tests because students learn to glean information quickly from long text passages.

Representing Knowledge. Teaching students various ways to categorize information using graphic organizers can help them understand the graphs and charts that are frequently found on science and social studies tests. Through the use of graphic organizers, students become familiar with different types of text structures. Using graphic organizers will help students complete the test on time.

Understanding the Words on the Test. Comprehensive vocabulary instruction allows teachers to enrich their students' vocabulary, an essential and directly tested component of many standardized tests. Strategies for successful vocabulary instruction include transportable vocabulary skills such as prefixes and suffixes, semantic features of words, and multiple meaning words. Each of these areas of focus, as well as many others in the chapter, will pay dividends on accountability tests.

Assessing Content Knowledge. Writing to learn provides teachers with a way to check for student understanding of content. In addition, writing to learn helps students think about what they learned, how they learn, why the content is important, and what

TESTING

they still don't know. Regular writing to learn activities also provides students practice in analyzing the tests and the questions on the test for their underlying query.

Comprehension Strategy Practice. Finally, reciprocal teaching and other collaborative reading experiences help students perform better on tests because they have learned to read texts critically. Reciprocal teaching provides students with experience in comprehension skills as they discuss the parts of the text they know about, make predictions about the text, and ask questions of the text. In other words, reciprocal teaching provides students with the skills to tackle reading passages in confidence and with effectiveness.

In sum, the use of a set of strategies for teaching reading for information can serve the dual functions of good instruction and effective preparation for standardized tests. The ways of thinking inherent in these comprehension strategies are necessary to perform well on the test. Further, when students have multiple opportunities to apply these strategies across content areas and throughout the day, they become a part of their learning repertoire. Once internalized, they are able to use these strategies in testing situations.

Area #3: Student Engagement in Reading for Information

If students are to become better test takers, they must read more (Guthrie, Wigfield, Metsala, & Cox, 1999). Reading for knowledge, information, and pleasure is the essential endeavor of successful and contributing members of a literate society. To ensure that students do become fluent readers, teachers must encourage reading in every subject matter and classroom, as well as outside the classroom.

Engaging students in reading and addressing the challenges of high-stakes standardized tests is, for the school, a team effort. Test format awareness and employment of literacy strategies are good first steps. But, the work does not stop here. The use and enjoyment of reading as part of lifelong learning does not stop at the classroom door. The successful dissemination and use of effective literacy strategies is an ongoing endeavor both for students and their teachers.

Student enjoyment of reading can be fostered through a Silent Sustained Reading program (Fisher, 2004; Pilgreen, 2000). In such a program, the school sets a period of time each day devoted to reading. Everyone in the school from the principal to the clerical staff to the kindergarten students are provided time to read from books or other texts of their own choosing. As students watch their teacher model reading, they learn directly of the activity's pleasure and importance. When students are allowed to choose their own reading, the inherent interest in the material itself fosters better reading habits and ability. With students spending more time reading they become better readers, and better readers become better test takers. Of course, the genres of books available to students should include informational selections that provide students with further opportunities to explore their interests.

Using the Results of Informal and Formal Assessments

Conclusions can be drawn about a school's successes or failures by examining the assessment and test results and reviewing the wide variety of demographic and other data that accompany the results. These data-based decisions allow the school to directly confront the issues that matter (e.g., Chen, Salahuddin, Horsch, & Wagner, 2000). If low scores point to a weakness in specific content or a need for a change in instruction, steps can be taken to provide training in that area. If certain groups of students consistently score poorly, then steps can be taken to provide them with additional intervention and support. Without an awareness of what the tests indicate, the school will not likely address the needs of its faculty or students (Schmoker, 1996, 2001, 2006). For example, a group of faculty may meet to discuss test results. Their analysis may lead to an understanding that vocabulary was the most depressed area on the test. Upon further analysis, they may learn that multiple meaning words were the lowest score within the vocabulary domain. This finding could lead to changes in the curriculum across the school. The results from the next assessment could be used to determine if the curriculum change was effective.

A criticism of standardized tests is that by the time the results are posted 6 months later, the students have advanced to the next grade level and are no longer on the administering teacher's roster. This is true: Standardized tests are likely to be a poor source for obtaining meaningful information for designing next Monday's lesson. These curriculum decisions should be informed by the ongoing informal assessment data gathered by the teacher. However, standardized test results can be viewed as a snapshot of the entire student body. A photograph of all the students in the school is unlikely to be useful in pinpointing the attributes of a single student, but it can create a group portrait of the school at large. Similarly, close analysis of the results can illuminate areas of concern and strength.

A forum for discussing such concerns can diffuse defensive responses while assisting schools in getting down to the business of curriculum improvement. One such structure is a Total Quality Review committee, based on the Total Quality Management work of Edward Deming (2001). A TQR committee usually serves in an advisory capacity to the school's governance and is charged with analyzing data and making recommendations based on these results. The committee is typically comprised of representatives of all stakeholders, including noninstructional staff, parents, students, and community members, as well as teachers and administrators. By establishing such work groups, schools can make data-driven decisions without engaging in the "blame games" that sink many school reform efforts (Detert, Louis, & Schroeder, 2001).

A coordinated series of discussions to align curriculum to tested standards might also take place. The goal of such curriculum discussions would be to better prepare students for high-stakes tests and to allow teachers a reflective process to discern success. Learning about the content of tests will help ensure that it is covered in core subject matters. Reading across the curriculum is encouraged when test-relevant reading content is shared with teachers from different subjects. In such a process, effective strategies can be linked to important reading content, appropriate test format practice provided, and essential test vocabulary disseminated. A curriculum discussion cycle might take the following steps:

1. *Standards review:* course content alignment to test.
2. *Curriculum construction:* activities and tasks, scaffolding, materials and assessment events development, rubrics, integration of test questions, vocabulary and strategies suggestions.
3. *Curriculum delivery:* timelines for delivery, dates for key pieces (trigger events), schedules for test practice, development of common deliveries, and common student work submissions.

4. *Examination of student work and test scores:* reflective conversations regarding student work and tests results, group discussions of expected student performance, review of curriculum delivery.

Whereas the reported results of many formal assessments lag several months after students have taken them, informal assessment results do not. Many of these informal assessments, especially teacher-constructed tests, essays, and observations, can be utilized to foster conversation *among* teachers. The collective results of a group of students can be used to inform a group of teachers about what should be taught next, or retaught. This *feed forward* system complements feedback (providing students with information about their work) as it allows teachers to plan next steps in their instruction (Fisher & Frey, 2009).

The use of informal assessment data in a feed forward system usually involves teachers in course-alike groups who plan, administer, and analyze the results every 6 weeks. In many cases, these teachers also assemble to score these assessments together, especially when it involves a writing task. Through consensus scoring, the teachers calibrate their expectations with one another and discuss what the results tell them about what was taught effectively, and what was not (Fisher, Grant, Frey, & Johnson, 2007).

Conclusion

In this chapter, we have discussed the importance of informal and formal assessments for measuring progress in students' ability to read for information. Informal assessment should be ongoing and can include observations, portfolios, inventories, rubrics, conferences, self-assessments, and surveys. The choice of instruments should be driven by learning goals, linked to classroom instruction, and be systematic in administration and analysis.

Formal assessments, particularly standardized tests, have become increasingly important in this decade. We advocate an emphasis on test wisdom, where students receive integrated practice throughout the school year. Of particular value is test format practice, especially for students who are not familiar with the standardized test genre. As well, students must be taught to be strategic readers of information. Through implementation of effective literacy strategies, students are able to use the techniques of lifelong learners (e.g., Calkins, Montgomery, Santman, & Falk, 1998).

Equally important are the ways in which the entire school can increase student engagement in reading for information. If students are to read more, the school must find innovative ways to present students with informational texts. Providing important and relevant reading content might take place through a sustained silent reading program that allows for student self-selection.

Finally, ongoing faculty dialogue around literacy and literacy strategies is essential. Such faculty conversation can take many forms including staff development discussions, teacher literacy demonstrations, collegial coaching activities, and curriculum discussion cycles.

TESTING

References

Albright, L. K. (2002). Bringing the Ice Maiden to life: Engaging adolescents in learning through picture book read-alouds in content areas. *Journal of Adolescent & Adult-Literacy, 45*, 418–428.

Alfassi, M. (1998). Reading for meaning: The efficacy of reciprocal teaching in fostering reading comprehension in high school students in remedial reading classes. *American Educational Research Journal, 35*, 309–332.

Aliki. (1963). *The story of Johnny Appleseed*. New York: Aladdin.

Allington, R. L. (1983). The reading instruction provided readers of differing abilities. *The Elementary School Journal, 83*, 548–559.

Alvermann, D. E. (1988). Effects of spontaneous and induced lookbacks on self-perceived high- and low-ability comprehenders. *Journal of Educational Research, 81*, 325–331.

Alvermann, D. E., & Van Arnam, S. (1984, April). *Effects of spontaneous and induced lookbacks on self-perceived high and low ability comprehenders*. Paper presented at the annual meeting of the American Educational Research Association, New Orleans, LA. [ED246384].

Amer, A. A. (1997). The effect of the teacher's reading aloud on the reading comprehension of ESL students. *ELT Journal 1997, 51*(1), 43–47.

Anders, P. L., & Bos, C. S. (1986). Semantic feature analysis: An interactive strategy for vocabulary development and text comprehension. *Journal of Reading, 29*, 610–616.

Anderson, R. C., & Nagy, W. E. (1992). The vocabulary conundrum. *American Educator: The Professional Journal of the American Federation of Teachers, 16*(4), 14–18, 44–47.

Anderson, R. C., & Pearson, P. D. (1984). A schema-theoretic view of basic processes in reading comprehension. In P. D. Pearson, R. Barr, M. L. Kamil, & P. Mosenthal (Eds.), *Handbook of reading research* (pp. 255–292). Mahwah, NJ: Erlbaum.

Anderson-Inman, L. (1996). Computer-assisted outlining: Information organization made easy. *Journal of Adolescent & Adult Literacy, 39*, 316–320.

Andrews, S. E. (1997). Writing to learn in content area reading class. *Journal of Adolescent & Adult Literacy, 41*, 141–142.

Angelou, M. (1969). *I know why the caged bird sings*. New York: Bantam.

Armbruster, B., Anderson, T., Armstrong, J., Wise, M., Janisch, C., & Meyer, L. (1991). Reading and questioning in content areas. *Journal of Reading Behavior, 23*, 35–59.

Armstrong, T. (2009). *Multiple intelligences in the classroom* (3rd ed.). Alexandria, VA: Association for Supervisors of Curriculum Development.

Aronson, E. (1978). *The jigsaw classroom*. Beverly Hills, CA: Sage.

Asher, J. J. (1969). The Total Physical Response approach to second language learning. *Modern Language Journal, 53*(1), 3–17.

Atwell, N. (1998). *In the middle: Writing, reading, and learning with adolescents* (2nd ed.). Upper Montclair, NJ: Boynton/Cook.

Ausubel, D. P. (1960). The use of advance organizers in the learning and retention of meaningful verbal material. *Journal of Educational Psychology, 51*, 267–272.

Ausubel, D. P. (1978). In defense of advance organizers: A reply to the critics. *Review of Educational Research, 48*, 251–257.

Badger, R., White, G., Sutherland, P., & Haggis, T. (2001). Note perfect: An investigation of how students view taking notes in lectures. *System, 29*, 405–417.

Baker, S. K., Simmons, D. C., & Kame'enui, E. J. (1995). *Vocabulary acquisition: Curricular and instructional implications for diverse learners*. Technical report no. 13. University of Oregon: National Center to Improve the Tools for Educators.

Bangert-Drowns, R. L., Hurley, M. M., & Wilkinson, B. (2004). The effects of school-based writing-to-learn interventions on academic achievement: A meta-analysis. *Review of Educational Research, 74,* 29–58.

Barron, R. F. (1969). The use of vocabulary as an advance organizer. In H. L. Herber & P. L. Sanders (Eds.), *Research in reading in the content areas: First year report* (pp. 29–39). Syracuse, NY: Syracuse University Reading and Language Arts Center.

Beasley, W. (1982). Teacher demonstrations: The effect on student task involvement. *Journal of Chemical Education, 59,* 789–790.

Beck, I. L., & McKeown, M. G. (2001). Text talk: Capturing the benefits of read-aloud experiences for young children. *The Reading Teacher, 55,* 10–35.

Beck, I. L., McKeown, M. G., Hamilton, R. L., & Kucan, L. (1997). *Questioning the author: An approach for enhancing student engagement with text.* Newark, DE: International Reading Association.

Blachowicz, C. L. Z., & Fisher, P. (2000). Vocabulary instruction. In M. L. Kamil, P. B. Mosenthal, P. D. Pearson, & R. Barr (Eds.), *Handbook of reading research* (Vol. 3, pp. 503–523). Mahwah, NJ: Erlbaum.

Blanchfield, C. (Ed.). (2001). *Creative vocabulary: Strategies for teaching vocabulary in grades K–12.* Fresno, CA: San Joaquin Valley Writing Project.

Bloom, B. S. (1956) *Taxonomy of educational objectives: The classification of educational goals: Handbook I, cognitive domain.* New York: Longman.

Bloome, D., & Egan-Robertson, A. (1993). The social construction of intertextuality in classroom reading and writing lessons. *Reading Research Quarterly, 28,* 305–333.

Brandt, R. (1992). On Deming and school quality: A conversation with Enid Brown. *Educational Leadership, 50* (3), 28–31.

Brice, A., & Roseberry-McKibben, C. (1999). Turning frustration into success for English language learners. *Educational Leadership, 56*(7), 53–55.

Broaddus, K., & Ivey, G. (2002). Taking away the struggle to read in the middle grades. *Middle School Journal, 34*(2), 5–11.

Brooks, H. B., & Brooks, D. W. (1996). The emerging role of CD-ROMs in teaching chemistry. *Journal of Science Education and Technology, 5,* 203–215.

Brophy, J., & Good, T. (1986). Teacher behavior and student achievement. In M. Wittrock (Ed.), *The handbook of research on teaching* (3rd ed., pp. 328–375). New York: Macmillan.

Bruce, B. C. (1997). Current issues and future directions. In J. Flood, S. B. Heath, & D. Lapp (Eds.), *Research on teaching literacy through the communicative and visual arts* (pp. 875–884). Newark, DE: International Reading Association.

Bruner, J. S., Goodnow, J. J., & Austin, G. A. (1956). *A study of thinking.* New York: Wiley.

Buehl, D. (2001). *Classroom strategies for interactive learning* (2nd ed.). Newark, DE: International Reading Association.

Burke, J. (2002). Making notes, making meaning. *Voices from the Middle, 9*(4), 15–21.

Busching, B. A., & Slesinger, B. A. (1995). Authentic questions: What do they look like? Where do they lead? *Language Arts, 72,* 341–351.

California State Board of Education. (n.d.). *Grades nine & ten: English-language arts content standards.* Retrieved from http://www.cde.ca.gov/be/st/ss/enggrades9-10.asp

Calkins, L., Montgomery, K., Santman, D., & Falk, B. (1998). *A teacher's guide to standardized reading tests: Knowledge is power.* Portsmouth, NH: Heinemann.

Calweti, G. (Ed.). (2004). *Handbook of research on improving student achievement* (3rd ed.). Arlington, VA: Educational Research Service.

Carr, E., & Ogle, D. (1987). K-W-L plus: A strategy for comprehension and summarization. *Journal of Reading, 30,* 626–631.

Carter, C. J. (1997). Why reciprocal teaching? *Educational Leadership, 54*(6), 64–68.

Carter, T. A., & Dean, E. O. (2006). Mathematics intervention for grades 5–11: Teaching mathematics, reading, or both? *Reading Psychology, 27,* 127–146.

Caserta-Henry, C. (1996). Reading buddies: A first-grade intervention program. *The Reading Teacher, 49,* 500–503.

Cazden, C. B. (1986). Classroom discourse. In M. Wittrock (Ed.), *Handbook of research on teaching* (3rd ed., pp. 432–462). New York: Macmillan.

Cazden, C. B. (1988). *Classroom discourse: The language of teaching and learning.* Portsmouth, NH: Heinemann.

Chaucer, G. (1400/1985). *The Canterbury tales.* (D. Clark, Trans.). Oxford: Oxford University Press.

Chen, J., Salahuddin, R., Horsch, P., & Wagner, S. L. (2000). Turning standardized test scores into a tool for improving teaching and learning: An assessment-based approach. *Urban Education, 5,* 356–384.

Choldenko, G. (2004). *Al Capone does my shirts.* New York: Penguin.

Ciardiello, A. V. (1998). You ask a good question today? Alternative cognitive and metacognitive strategies. *Journal of Adolescent & Adult Literacy, 42,* 210–219.

Cobb, J. B. (1998). The social contexts of tutoring: Mentoring the older at-risk student. *Reading Horizons, 39,* 50–75.

Cofer, J. O. (1996). *An island like you: Stories of the barrio.* New York: Puffin.

Cohen, J. (1986). Theoretical considerations of peer tutoring. *Psychology on the Schools, 23,* 175–186.

Cohen, P. A., Kulik, J. A., & Kulik, C. C. (1982). Educational outcomes of tutoring: A meta-analysis of findings. *American Educational Research Journal, 19,* 237–248.

Cuervas, G. J. (1984). Mathematics learning in English as a second language. *Journal for Research in Mathematics Education, 15*(2), 134–144.

Cummins, J. (1980). The cross-lingual dimensions of language proficiency: Implications for bilingual education and the optimal age issue. *TESOL Quarterly, 14,* 175–187.

Cummins, J. (1980). The entry and exit fallacy in bilingual education. *NABE: Journal for the National Association of Bilingual Education, 4*(3), 25–60.

Cunningham, P. M. (2002). *Prefixes and suffixes: Systematic sequential phonics and spelling.* Greensboro, NC: Carson-Dellosa.

Cunningham, P. M., & Allington, R. L. (2003). *Classrooms that work: They can all read and write* (3rd ed.). Boston: Allyn & Bacon.

Curtin, E. (2005). Teaching practices for ESL students. *Multicultural Education, 12*(3), 22–44.

Daniels, H., & Bizar, M. (1998). *Methods that matter: Six structures for best practice classrooms.* York, ME: Stenhouse.

Darwin, C., & Quammen, D. (2008). *On the origin of species: Illustrated edition.* New York: Sterling.

Davey, B. (1983). Think aloud: Modeling the cognitive processes for reading comprehension. *Journal of Reading, 27*(1), 44–47.

Demi. (1997). *One grain of rice.* New York: Scholastic.

Deming, W. E. (2001). *Out of the crisis.* Boston: MIT Press.

Detert, J. R., Louis, K. S., & Schroeder, R. G. (2001). A culture framework for education: Defining quality values and their impact in U.S. high schools. *School Effectiveness and School Improvement, 12,* 183–212.

DeVorkin, D., & Smith, R. W. (2004). *The Hubble space telescope: Imagining the universe.* Washington, DC: National Geographic Society.

Dewey, J. (1938/1963). *Experience and education.* New York: Macmillan.

Diller, S. (2003). *Literacy work stations: Making centers work.* York, ME: Stenhouse.

Dillon, J. T. (1988). *Questioning and teaching: A manual of practice.* New York: Teachers College Press.

DiVesta, F. J., & Gray, S. G. (1972). Listening and note taking. *Journal of Educational Psychology, 63,* 8–14.

Dixon, C., & Nessel, D. (1983). *Language experience approach to reading (and writing): Language-experience reading for second language learners.* Hayward, CA: Alemany.

Dolch, E. W. (1936). A basic sight vocabulary. *The Elementary School Journal, 36,* 456–460.

Donovan, M. S., & Bransford, J. D. (Eds.). (2005). *How students learn: History, mathematics, and science in the classroom.* Committee on How People Learn: A Targeted Report for Teachers. Division on Behavioral and Social Sciences and Education. Washington, DC: National Academies.

Duke, N. K., & Ritchart, R. (1997). No pain, high gain standardized test preparation. *Instructor, 107*(3), 89–92, 119.

Dunning, S., & Stafford, W. (1992). *Getting the knack: 20 poetry writing exercises.* Urbana, IL: National Council of Teachers of English.

Durkin, D. (1978–1979). What classroom observations reveal about reading comprehension. *Reading Research Quarterly, 14,* 481–533.

Dye, G. A. (2000). Graphic organizers to the rescue! Helping students link—and remember—information. *Teaching Exceptional Children, 32*(3), 72–76.

Early, M. (1990). Enabling first and second language learners in the classroom. *Language Arts, 67,* 567–575.

Early, M., & Tang, G. M. (1991). Helping ESL students cope with content-based texts. *TESL Canada Journal, 8*(2), 34–44.

Echevarria, J., Vogt, M. E., & Short, D. (2004). *Making content comprehensible to English learners: The SIOP model.* Boston: Allyn & Bacon.

Egan, M. (1999). Reflections on effective use of graphic organizers. *Journal of Adolescent & Adult Literacy, 42,* 641–645.

Eggen, P., & Kauchak, D. (2001). *Educational psychology: Windows on classrooms* (5th ed.). Upper Saddle River, NJ: Merrill/Prentice Hall.

Elbow, P. (1994). *Writing for learning—not just for demonstrating learning.* Amherst: University of Massachusetts Press.

Ellis, D. (2000). *The breadwinner.* Toronto: Groundwood.

Enzensberger, H. M. (1998). *The number devil: A mathematical adventure.* New York: Metropolitan.

Erickson, B. (1996). Read-alouds reluctant readers relish. *Journal of Adolescent & Adult Literacy, 40,* 212–214.

Espin, C. A., & Foegen, A. (1996). Validity of general outcome measures for predicting secondary students' performance on content-area tasks. *Exceptional Children, 62,* 497–514.

Faber, J. E., Morris, J. D., & Lieberman, M. G. (2000). The effect of note taking on ninth grade students' comprehension. *Reading Psychology, 21,* 257–270.

Fancher, L. (1998). *The quest for one big thing.* New York: Hyperion.

Farley, M. J., & Elmore, P. B. (1992). The relationship of reading comprehension to critical thinking skills, cognitive ability, and vocabulary for a sample of underachieving college freshmen. *Educational and Psychological Measurement, 52,* 921–931.

Faust, M. A., & Glenzer, N. (2000). "I could read those parts over and over." Eighth graders rereading to enhance enjoyment and learning with literature. *Journal of Adolescent & Adult Literacy, 44,* 234–239.

Fay, L. (1965). Reading study skills: Math and science. In J. A. Figurel (Ed.), *Reading and inquiry* (pp. 92–94). Newark, DE: International Reading Association.

Fearn, L., & Farnan, N. (2001). *Interactions: Teaching writing and the language arts.* Boston: Houghton Mifflin.

Feuer, M. J., Holland, P. W., Green, B. F., Bertenthal, M. W., & Hemphill, F. C. (1999). *Uncommon measures: Equivalence and language among educational tests.* Washington, DC: National Academy Press.

Fisher, D. (2001). "We're moving on up": Creating a schoolwide literacy effort in an urban high school. *Journal of Adolescent & Adult Literacy, 45*, 92–101.

Fisher, D. (2004). Setting the "opportunity to read" standard: Resuscitating the SSR program in an urban high school. *Journal of Adolescent Adult Literacy, 48*, 138–150.

Fisher, D., & Frey, N. (2003). Writing instruction for struggling adolescent readers: A gradual release model. *Journal of Adolescent & Adult Literacy, 46*, 396–407.

Fisher, D., & Frey, N. (2007). *Checking for understanding: Linking teaching and learning.* Alexandria, VA: Association for Supervision and Curriculum Development.

Fisher, D., & Frey, N. (2008). *Word wise and content rich, grades 7-12: Five essential steps to teaching academic vocabulary.* Portsmouth, NH: Heinemann.

Fisher, D., & Frey, N. (2009). Feed up, back, forward. *Educational Leadership, 67*(3), 20–25.

Fisher, D., & Frey, N. (2010). *Guided instruction: How to develop confident and successful learners.* Alexandria, VA: ASCD.

Fisher, D., Brozo, W. G., Frey, N., & Ivey, G. (2011). *50 instructional routines to develop content literacy.* Boston: Pearson.

Fisher, D., Flood, J., Lapp, D., & Frey, N. (2004). Interactive read alouds: Is there a common set of implementation practices? *The Reading Teacher, 58*, 8–17.

Fisher, D., Frey, N., & Lapp, D. (2008). Shared readings: Modeling comprehension, vocabulary, text structures, and text features for older readers. *The Reading Teacher, 61*(7), 548–556.

Fisher, D., Frey, N., & Williams, D. (2002). Seven literacy strategies that work. *Educational Leadership, 60*(3), 70–73.

Fisher, D., Grant, M., Frey, N., & Johnson, C. (2007). Taking formative assessments schoolwide. *Educational Leadership, 65*(4), 64–68.

Fitzgerald, J., García, G. E., Jiménez, R. T., & Barrera, R. (2000). How will bilingual ESL programs change in the next millennium? *Reading Research Quarterly, 35*, 520–523.

Flake, S. G. (2004). *Who am I without him?* New York: Hyperion.

Fountas, I. C., & Pinnell, G. S. (2001). *Guiding readers and writers grades 3–6: Teaching comprehension, genre, and context literacy.* Portsmouth, NH: Heinemann.

Freedman, M. P. (2000). Using effective demonstrations for motivation. *Science and Children, 38*(1), 52–55.

Frey, N., & Hiebert, E. H. (2003). Teacher-based assessment of literacy learning. In J. Flood, D. Lapp, J. R. Squire, & J. M. Jensen (Eds.), *Handbook of research on teaching the English language arts* (2nd ed.), pp. 608–618. Mahwah, NJ: Erlbaum.

Frey, N., Fisher, D., & Everlove, S. (2009). *Productive group work: How to engage students, build teamwork, and promote understanding.* Alexandria, VA: Association for Supervision and Curriculum Development.

Frey, N., Fisher, D., & Gonzalez, A. (2010). *Literacy 2.0: Reading and writing in the 21st century.* Bloomington, IN: Solution Tree.

Fu, D. (2004). Teaching ELL students in regular classrooms at the secondary level. *Voices from the Middle, 11*(4), 8–15.

Gage, R. (1995). Excuse me, you're cramping my style: Kinesthetics for the classroom. *English Journal, 84*(8), 52–55.

Gajria, M., Jitendra, A. K., & Sood, S. (2007). Improving comprehension of expository text in students with LD: A research synthesis. *Journal of Learning Disabilities, 40*(3), 210–225.

Gambrell, L. (1983). The occurrence of think-time during reading comprehension instruction. *Journal of Educational Research, 77*(2), 77–80.

Gardner, H. (2006). *Multiple intelligences: New horizons.* New York: Perseus.

Gaustad, J. (1993). Peers and tutoring. *ERIC Digest, 79.* Office of Educational Research and Improvement. (ERIC Document Reproduction Service No. ED354608).

Giannangelo, D. M., & Bolding, R. A. (1998). Ethnocentrism, geography, and foreign guest speakers: An attempt to change attitudes. *Journal of the Middle States Council for the Social Studies, 122*–126.

Giesecke, D. (1993). Low-achieving students as successful tutors. *Preventing School Failure, 37*, 34–43.

Giles, G. (2002). *Shattering glass.* Brookfield, CT: Millbrook Press.

Gillet, J. W., & Temple, C. (1978). Word knowledge: A cognitive view. *Reading World, 18*, 132–140.

Gilman, C. P. (1997). *"The yellow wallpaper" and other stories.* New York: Feminist Press.

Gipe, J. (1978–1979). Investigation techniques for teaching word meanings. *Reading Research Quarterly, 4*, 624–644.

Glanz, J. (1999). Ten suggestions for teaching the Holocaust. *History Teacher, 32*, 547–565.

Glass, A. (1995). *Folks call me Appleseed John.* New York: Bantam Doubleday Dell.

Glencoe Science. (2007). *Focus on physical science: California 8.* New York: Author.

Good, T., & Brophy, J. (2002). *Looking in classrooms* (9th ed.). New York: HarperCollins.

Goodman, L. (2001). A tool for learning: Vocabulary self-awareness. In C. Blanchfield (Ed.), *Creative vocabulary:*

Strategies for teaching vocabulary in grades K–12. Fresno, CA: San Joaquin Valley Writing Project.

Gordon, W. J. J. (1961). *Synectics: The development of creative capacity.* New York: Harper and Row.

Grant, M. C., & Fisher, D. (2010). *Reading and writing in science: Tools to develop disciplinary literacy.* Thousand Oaks, CA: Corwin.

Graves, D. H. (1983). *Writing: Teachers and children at work.* Portsmouth, NH: Heinemann.

Green, J. (2005). *Looking for Alaska.* New York: Dutton Children's Books.

Gu, P. Y. (2003). Vocabulary learning in a second language: Person, task, context and strategies. *TESL-EJ, 7*(2), 1–25.

Gu, Y., & Johnson, R. K. (1996). Vocabulary learning strategies and language learning outcomes. *Language Learning, 46*, 643–679.

Guillaume, A. M. (2004). *K–12 classroom teaching: A primer for new professionals* (2nd ed.). Upper Saddle River, NJ: Merrill/Prentice Hall.

Guszak, F. J. (1967). Teacher questioning and reading. *The Reading Teacher, 21*, 227–234.

Guthrie, J. T. (2002). Preparing students for high stakes test taking in reading. In A. E. Farstrup & S. J. Samuels (Eds.), *What research has to say about reading instruction* (pp. 370–391). Newark, DE: International Reading Association.

Guthrie, J. T., Wigfield, A., Metsala, J. L., & Cox, K. E. (1999). Motivational and cognitive predictors of text comprehension and reading amount. *Scientific Studies of Reading, 3*, 231–256.

Haluska, R., & Gillen, D. (1995). Kids teaching kids: Pairing up with cross-grades pals. *Learning, 24*(3), 54–56.

Harmon, J. M., Wood, K. D., Hedrick, W. B., Vintinner, J., & Willeford, T. (2009). Interactive word walls: More than just reading the writing on the walls. *Journal of Adolescent & Adult Literacy, 52*(5), 398–408.

Hartman, D. K., & Allison, J. (1996). Promoting inquiry-oriented discussions using multiple texts. In L. B. Gambrell & J. F. Almasi (Eds.), *Lively discussions! Fostering engaged readings* (pp. 106–133). Newark, DE: International Reading Association.

Hautman, P. (2004). *Godless.* New York: Simon Pulse.

Head, M. H., & Readence, J. E. (1986). Anticipation guides: Meaning through prediction. In E. K. Dishner, T. W. Bean, J. E. Readence, & D. W. Moore (Eds.), *Reading in the content areas* (2nd ed., pp. 229–234). Dubuque, IA: Kendall Hunt.

Helfeldt, J. P., & Henk, W. A. (1990). Reciprocal question-answer relationships: An instructional technique for at-risk readers. *Journal of Reading, 33*, 509–514.

Henk, W. A., & Stahl, N. A. (1985). *A meta-analysis of the effect of notetaking on learning from lecture.* Paper presented at the 34th meeting of the National Reading Conference, St. Petersburg, FL. [ED258533].

Heron, T. E., Villareal, D. M., Yao, M., Christianson, R. J., & Heron, K. M. (2006). Peer tutoring systems: Applications in classroom and specialized environments. *Reading & Writing Quarterly, 22*(1), 27–45.

Herrold, W. G., Jr., Stanchfield, J., & Serabian, A. J. (1989). Comparison of the effect of a middle school, literature-based listening program on male and female attitudes toward reading. *Educational Research Quarterly, 13*(4), 43–46.

Hillis, M. R., & von Eschenbach, J. F. (1996). Varying instructional strategies to accommodate diverse thinking skills: Curriculum concerns. *Social Studies and the Young Learner, 9*(2), 20–23.

Holbrook, H. T. (1987). Writing to learn in the social studies. *The Reading Teacher, 41*, 216–219.

Holdaway, D. (1982). Shared book experience: Teaching reading using favorite books. *Theory into Practice, 21*, 293–300.

Howe, M. E., Grierson, S. T., & Richmond, M. G. (1997). A comparison of teachers' knowledge and use of content area reading strategies in the primary grades. *Reading Research and Instruction, 36*, 305–324.

Hurst, B. (2001). ABCs of content area lesson planning: Attention, basics, and comprehension. *Journal of Adolescent & Adult Literacy, 44*, 692–693.

Hyerle, D. (1996). *Visual tools for constructing knowledge.* Alexandria, VA: Association of Supervision and Curriculum Development.

International Center of Photography. (2003). *African American vernacular photography: Selections from the Daniel Cowin collection.* New York: Author.

International Reading Association. (2000). *Making a difference means making it different: Honoring children's rights to excellent reading instruction.* Newark, DE: Author.

Irvin, J. L., Lunstrum, J. P., Lynch-Brown, C., & Shepard, M. F. (1995). Enhancing social studies through literacy strategies. *Bulletin 91.* National Council for the Social Studies, Washington, DC.

Isdell, W. (1993). *A Gebra named Al.* Minneapolis: Free Spirit.

Ivey, G., & Broaddus, K. (2001). "Just plain reading": A survey of what makes students want to read in middle school classrooms. *Reading Research Quarterly, 36*, 350–377.

Ivey, G., & Fisher, D. (2006). When thinking skills trump reading skills. *Educational Leadership, 64*(2), 16–21.

Jacobson, J., Thrope, L., Fisher, D., Lapp, D., Frey, N., & Flood, J. (2001). Cross-age tutoring: A literacy improvement approach for struggling adolescent readers. *Journal of Adolescent & Adult Literacy, 44*, 528–536.

James, L. A., Abbott, M., & Greenwood, C. R. (2001). How Adam became a writer: Winning writing strategies for low-achieving students. *Teaching Exceptional Children, 33*(3), 30–37.

Janney, R., & Snell, M. E. (2000). *Modifying schoolwork: Teachers' guides to inclusive practices.* Baltimore: Brookes.

Jenkinson, E. B. (1988). Learning to write/writing to learn. *Phi Delta Kappan, 69,* 712–717.

Jiménez, F. (1997). *The circuit: Stories from the life of a migrant child.* Albuquerque: University of New Mexico Press.

Jiménez, F. (2000). *La mariposa.* New York: Houghton Mifflin.

Johnson, D. D., & Pearson, P. D. (1984). *Teaching reading vocabulary* (2nd ed.). New York: Holt, Rinehart & Winston.

Johnston, P. H. (2004). *Choice words: How our language affects children's learning.* Portland, ME: Stenhouse.

Jorgensen, C. M. (1998). *Restructuring high schools for all students: Taking inclusion to the next level.* Baltimore: Brookes.

Juel, C. (1991). Tutoring between student athletes and at-risk children. *The Reading Teacher, 45,* 178–186.

Kagan, S. (1992). *Cooperative learning.* San Juan Capistrano, CA: Kagan Cooperative Learning.

Katayama, A. D., & Crooks, S. M. (2001). Examining the effects of notetaking format on achievement when students construct and study computerized notes. *Learning Assistance Review, 6*(1), 5–23.

Keene, E. O., & Zimmermann, S. (1997). *Mosaic of thought: Teaching comprehension in a reader's workshop.* Portsmouth, NH: Heinemann.

Kellogg, S. (1988). *Johnny Appleseed: A tall tale retold.* New York: Morrow Junior Books.

Keys, C. W. (1999a). Language as an indicator of meaning generation: An analysis of middle school students written discourse about scientific investigations. *Journal of Research in Science Teaching, 36,* 1044–1061.

Keys, C. W. (1999b). Revitalizing instruction in scientific genres: Connecting knowledge production with writing to learn in science. *Science Education, 83,* 115–130.

Kiewra, K. A., Benton, S. L., Kim, S., Risch, N., & Christensen, M. (1995). Effects of note-taking format and study technique on recall and relational performance. *Contemporary Educational Psychology, 20,* 172–187.

Kiewra, K. A., Kauffman, D. F., Robinson, D. H., DuBois, N. F., & Staley, R. K. (1999). Supplementing floundering text with adjunct displays. *Instructional Science, 27,* 373–401.

Klein, M. L. (1988). *Teaching reading comprehension and vocabulary: A guide for teachers.* Upper Saddle River, NJ: Prentice Hall.

Knipper, K. J., & Duggan, T. J. (2006). Writing to learn across the curriculum: Tools for comprehension in content area classes. *The Reading Teacher, 59,* 462–470.

Kohn, A. (2000). *The case against standardized testing: Raising the scores, ruining the schools.* Portsmouth, NH: Heinemann.

Kolb, D. (1984). *Experiential learning: Experience as the source of learning and development.* Upper Saddle River, NJ: Prentice Hall.

Krull, K. (1995). *Lives of the artists: Masterpieces, messes (and what the neighbors thought).* San Diego: Harcourt.

Krull, K. (2000). *Wilma unlimited: How Wilma Rudolph became the world's fastest woman.* New York: Voyager.

Kujawa, S., & Huske, L. (1995). *The strategic teaching and reading project guidebook* (Rev. ed.). Oakbrook, IL: North Central Regional Education Laboratory.

Laden, N. (1998). *When pigasso met mootise.* San Francisco: Chronicle.

Landau, J., & Cameron, J. (1997). *Titanic* [motion picture]. United States: Paramount Pictures.

Landauer, T. K. (1975). Memory without organization: Properties of a model with random storage and undirected retrieval. *Cognitive Psychology, 7,* 495–531.

Langer, J. A. (1985). Children's sense of genre: A study of performance on parallel reading and writing. *Reading Research Quarterly, 2,* 157–187.

Langer, J. A. (2001). Beating the odds: Teaching middle and high school students to read and write well. *American Educational Research Journal, 38,* 837–880.

Lapp, D., Fisher, D., Flood, J., & Cabello, A. (2001). An integrated approach to the teaching and assessment of language arts. In S. R. Hurley & J. V. Tinajero (Eds.), *Literacy assessment of second language learners* (pp. 1–26). Boston: Allyn & Bacon.

Lapp, D., Flood, J., & Goss, K. (2000). Desks don't move—students do: In effective classroom environments. *The Reading Teacher, 54,* 31–36.

Larsen, J. D. (1991). Pay attention! Demonstrating the role of attention in learning. *Teaching of Psychology, 18,* 238–239.

Lee, C. (2000). Modelling in the mathematics classroom. *Mathematics Teaching, 171,* 28–31.

Leu, D. J., & Kinzer, C. K. (1995). *Effective reading instruction K–8* (3rd ed.). Upper Saddle River, NJ: Merrill/Prentice Hall.

Lewis, J. P. (2005). *Galileo's universe.* Mankato, MN: Creative Editions.

Li, X., & Li, Y. (2008). Research on students' misconceptions to improve teaching and learning in school mathematics and science. *School Science and Mathematics, 108*(1), 4–7.

Longfellow, H. W., & Bing, C. (1860/2001). *The midnight ride of Paul Revere.* New York: Handprint.

Lowry, L. (1994). *The giver.* New York: Laurel Leaf.

Lyman, F. T. (1981). The responsive classroom discussion: The inclusion of all students. In A. Anderson (Ed.),

Mainstreaming digest (pp. 109–113). College Park: University of Maryland Press.

Lytton, R. H., Marshall-Baker, A., Benson, M. J., & Blieszner, R. (1996, Spring). Writing to learn: Course examples in family and consumer sciences. *Journal of Family and Consumer Sciences, 88*, 35–41.

Manguel, A. (1997). *A history of reading*. New York: Penguin.

Manzo, A. V. (1969). ReQuest procedure. *Journal of Reading, 13*, 123–126.

Marlatt, E. A. (1995). Language through Total Physical Response. *Perspectives in Education and Deafness, 13*(4), 18–20.

Martinez, M., Roser, N. L., & Strecker, S. (1998–1999). "I never thought I could be a star": A reader's theatre ticket to fluency. *The Reading Teacher, 52*, 326–334.

Marzano, R. J., Pickering, D. J., & Pollock, J. E. (2001). *Classroom instruction that works: Research-based strategies for increasing student achievement*. Alexandria, VA: Association for Supervision and Curriculum Development.

Mastropieri, M. A., Leinart, A., & Scruggs, T. E. (1999). Strategies to increase reading fluency. *Intervention in School and Clinic, 34*, 278–283, 292.

McDermott, M. (2010). More than writing to learn. *The Science Teacher, 77*(1), 32–36.

McGuffey's Eclectic Spelling-Book. (1879). Rev. ed. New York: Wiley. (Modern reproduction)

McIntosh, M. E., & Draper, R. J. (1996). Using the question-answer relationship strategy to improve students' reading of mathematics texts. *Clearing House, 69*, 154–162.

McIntosh, M. E., & Draper, R. J. (2001). Using learning logs in mathematics: Writing to learn. *Mathematics Teacher, 94*, 554–557.

McKeown, M. G., & Beck I. L. (1999). Getting the discussion started. *Educational Leadership, 57*(3), 25–28.

Mehan, H. (1979). *Learning lessons*. Cambridge, MA: Harvard University Press.

Meichenbaum, D., & Biemiller, A. (1998). *Nurturing independent learners: Helping students take charge of their learning*. Newton, MA: Brookline Books.

Meier, D., Kozol, J., & Cohen, J. (2000). *Can standards save public education?* Boston: Beacon.

Merkley, D. M., & Jefferies, D. (2001). Guidelines for implementing a graphic organizer. *The Reading Teacher, 54*, 350–357.

Metzloff, A. N., Kuhl, P. K., Movellan, J., & Sejnowski, T. J. (2009). Foundations for a new science of learning. *Science, 325*, 284–288.

Mitchell, D. (1996, September). Writing to learn across the curriculum and the English teacher. *English Journal, 85*, 93–97.

Moore, D. W., Readence, J. E., & Rickelman, R. J. (1989). *Prereading activities for content area reading and writing* (2nd ed.). Newark, DE: International Reading Association.

Muncey, D. E., Payne, J., & White, N. S. (1999). Making curriculum and instructional reform happen: A case study. *Peabody Journal of Education, 74*, 68–110.

Myers, W. D. (2001). *145th Street: Short stories*. New York: Bantam Doubleday Dell.

Nagy, W. E., & Anderson, R. C. (1984). How many words are there in printed school English? *Reading Research Quarterly, 19*, 304–330.

Nagy, W. E., & Herman, P. (1985). Incidental vs. instructional approaches to increasing reading vocabulary. *Educational Perspectives, 23*, 16–21.

Nagy, W. E., & Scott, J. A. (1990). Word schemas: Expectations about the form and meaning of new words. *Cognition and Instruction, 7*(2), 105–127.

National Center for Educational Statistics. (2001). *International comparisons in fourth-grade reading: Findings from the progress in international reading literacy study (PIRLS) of 2001*. Retrieved July 19, 2006, from http://nces.ed.gov/pubs2004/pirlspub/

National Center on Education and the Economy. (2001). *Speaking and listening*. Pittsburgh, PA: Author.

National Council for Teachers of Mathematics. (2000). *Principles and standards for school mathematics*. Reston, VA: Author.

Nessel, D. (1988). Channeling knowledge for reading expository text. *Journal of Reading, 32*, 225–228.

Neuschwander, C. (1997). *Sir cumference and the first round table*. Watertown, MA: Charlesbridge.

Newell, F. M. (1996). Effects of a cross-age tutoring program on computer literacy learning of second-grade students. *Journal of Research on Computing in Education, 28*, 346–358.

New Webster's dictionary of the English language. (1981). New York: Delair.

Nichols, J. N. (1983). Using prediction to increase content area interest and understanding. *Journal of Reading, 27*, 225–228.

Nieto, S. (1992). *Affirming diversity: The sociopolitical context of multicultural education*. White Plains, NY: Longman.

No Child Left Behind Act of 2001, Pub. L. No. 107–110.

Ogle, D. M. (1986). K-W-L: A teaching model that develops active reading of expository text. *The Reading Teacher, 39*, 564–570.

Ohanian, S. (1999). *One size fits few: The folly of educational standards*. Portsmouth, NH: Heinemann.

Palincsar, A. S., & Brown, A. L. (1986). Interactive teaching to promote independent learning from text. *The Reading Teacher, 39*, 771–777.

Palincsar, A. S., & Herrenkohl, L. R. (2002). Designing collaborative learning contexts. *Theory into Practice, 41*(1), 26–32.

Pappas, T. (1991). *Math talk: Mathematical ideas in poems for two voices.* San Carlos, CA: Wide World Publishing/Tetra.

Pappas, T. (1993). *Fractals, googols, and other mathematical tales.* San Carlos, CA: Wide World Publishing/Tetra.

Paris, S. G., Cross, D. R., & Lipson, M. Y. (1984). Informed strategies for learning: A program to improve children's reading awareness and comprehension. *Journal of Educational Psychology, 76,* 1239–1252.

Paris, S. G., Wasik, B. A., & Turner, J. C. (1991). The development of strategic readers. In R. Barr, M. L. Kamil, P. Mosenthal, & P. D. Pearson (Eds.), *Handbook of reading research* (Vol. 2, pp. 609–640). Mahwah, NJ: Erlbaum.

Pauk, W. (2000). *How to study in college* (7th ed.). Boston: Houghton Mifflin College.

Pearson, P. D. (1985). Changing the face of reading comprehension instruction. *The Reading Teacher, 38,* 724–738.

Pearson, P. D., & Gallagher, M. C. (1983). The instruction of reading comprehension. *Contemporary Educational Psychology, 8,* 317–344.

Pearson, P. D., & Johnson, D. D. (1978). *Teaching reading comprehension.* New York: Holt, Rinehart and Winston.

Perie, M., & Moran, R. (2005). *NAEP 2004 trends in academic progress: Three decades of students performance in reading and mathematics* (NCES 2005–464). U.S. Department of Education, Institute of Education Sciences, National Center for Education Statistics. Washington, DC: U.S. Government Printing Office.

Peterson, A. (1996). *The writer's workout book: 113 stretches toward better prose.* Berkeley, CA: National Writing Project.

Pilgreen, J. (2000). *The SSR handbook: How to organize and manage a silent sustained reading program.* Portsmouth, NH: Boynton/Cook.

Pithers, R. T., & Soden, R. (2000). Critical thinking in education: A review. *Educational Research, 42,* 237–250.

Pittleman, S. D., Heimlich, J. E., Berglund, R. L., & French, M. P. (1991). *Semantic feature analysis: Classroom applications.* Newark, DE: International Reading Association.

Poe, E. A. (1849/1966). *Complete stories and poems.* Garden City, NY: Doubleday.

Poling, L. G. (2000). The real world: Community speakers in the classroom. *Social Education, 64*(4), 8–10.

Popham, W. J. (2001) Teaching to the test? *Educational Leadership, 58*(6), 16–20.

Prescott, H. M. (2001). Helping students say how they know what they know. *Clearing House, 74,* 327–331.

Price, R. D. (1978). Teaching reading is not the responsibility of the social studies teacher. *Social Education, 42,* 312, 314–315.

Purcell-Gates, V., & Waterman, R. (2000). *Now we read, we see, we speak: Portrait of literacy development in an adult Freirean-based class.* Mahwah, NJ: Erlbaum.

Pynte, J., & Prieur, B. (1996). Prosodic breaks and attachment decisions in sentence parsing. *Language and Cognitive Processes, 11,* 165–191.

Raphael, T. E. (1982). Teaching children question-answering strategies. *The Reading Teacher, 36,* 186–191.

Raphael, T. E. (1984). Teaching learners about sources of information for answering questions. *Journal of Reading, 27,* 303–311.

Raphael, T. E. (1986). Teaching children question-answering relationships, revisited. *The Reading Teacher, 39,* 516–522.

Raphael, T. E., & Au, K. H. (2005). Enhancing comprehension and test taking across grades and content areas. *The Reading Teacher, 59,* 206–221.

Rasinski, T, V., Padak, N. D., McKeon, C. A., Wilfong, L. G., Friedauer, J. A., & Heim, P. (2005). Is reading fluency a key for successful high school reading? *Journal of Adolescent-Adult Literacy, 49,* 22–27.

Rasinski, T., & Padak, N. D. (2005). Fluency beyond the primary grades: Helping adolescent struggling readers. *Voices from the Middle, 13*(1), 34–41.

Reinhard, J. (1998). *Discovering the Inca Ice Maiden: My adventures in Ampato.* Washington, DC: National Geographic Society.

Resnick, L. (1995). From aptitude to effort: A new foundation for our schools. *Daedalus, 124*(4), 55–62.

Richardson, J. S. (1997–1998). A read-aloud for foreign languages: Becoming a language master. *Journal of Adolescent & Adult Literacy, 41,* 312–314.

Richardson, J. S. (2000). *Read it aloud! Using literature in the secondary content classroom.* Newark, DE: International Reading Association.

Richardson, J. S., & Gross, E. (1997). A read-aloud for mathematics. *Journal of Adolescent & Adult Literacy, 40,* 492–494.

Richardson, J. S., & Morgan, R. F. (1994). *Reading to learn in the content areas.* Belmont, WA: Wadsworth.

Rieck, B. J. (1977). How content teachers telegraph messages against reading. *Journal of Reading, 20,* 646–648.

Robinson, D. H. (1998). Graphic organizers as aids to text learning. *Reading Research and Instruction, 37,* 85–105.

Robinson, F. P. (1946). *Effective Study.* New York: Harper & Row.

Robinson, F. P. (1996). *Effective study.* New York: Harper & Row.

Roehler, L. R., & Duffy, G. G. (1991). Teachers' instructional actions. In R. Barr, M. L. Kamil, P. Mosenthal, & P. D. Pearson (Eds.), *Handbook of reading research* (Vol. 2, pp. 861–883). Mahwah, NJ: Erlbaum.

Romero, F., Paris, S. G., & Brem, S. K. (2005). Children's comprehension and local-to-global recall of narrative and expository texts. *Current Issues in Education, 8*(25). Retrieved from http://cie.ed.asu.edu/volume8/number25/

Rosenshine, B., & Meister, C. (1994). Reciprocal teaching: A review of the research. *Review of Educational Research, 64*, 479–530.

Rothenberg, D., & Fisher, D. (2007). *Teaching English language learners: A differentiated approach.* Upper Saddle River, NJ: Merrill/Prentice Hall.

Routman, R. (2000). Teacher talk. *Educational Leadership, 59*(6), 32–35.

Sacks, O. (2001). *Uncle Tungsten: Memories of a chemical boyhood.* New York: Knopf.

Sams, C. R. II, & Stoick, J. (2000). *Stranger in the woods: A photographic fantasy.* Milford, MI: Authors.

Santa, C., & Havens, L. (1995). *Creating independence through student-owned strategies: Project CRISS.* Dubuque, IA: Kendall-Hunt.

Santman, D. (2002). Teaching to the test? Test preparation in the reading workshop. *Language Arts, 79*, 203–211.

Schmidt, P. R. (1999). KWLQ: Inquiry and literacy learning in science. *The Reading Teacher, 52*, 789–792.

Schmoker, M. (1996). *Results: The key to continuous school improvement.* Alexandria, VA: Association for Supervision and Curriculum Development.

Schmoker, M. (2001). *The results handbook: Practical strategies from dramatically improved schools.* Alexandria, VA: Association for Supervision and Curriculum Development.

Schmoker, M. (2006). *Results now.* Alexandria, VA: Association for Supervision and Curriculum Development.

Scieszka, J. (1995). *Math curse.* New York: Viking.

Shakur, T. (1999). *The rose that grew from concrete.* New York: Simon & Schuster.

Shanahan, T., & August, D. (Eds.). (2006). *Developing literacy in second-language learners: Report of the National Literacy Panel on Language-Minority Children and Youth.* Mahwah, NJ: Erlbaum.

Simon, S. (2006). *The brain.* New York: HarperCollins.

Smith, F. (1998). *The book of learning and forgetting.* New York: Teachers College Press.

Smith, R. J., & Otto, W. (1969). Changing teacher attitudes toward teaching reading in the content areas. *Journal of Reading, 12*, 299–304.

Somyürek, S., Atasoy, B., & Ozdemir, S. (2009). Board's IQ: What makes a board smart? *Computers and Education, 53*(2), 368–374.

Soto, J. (2005). Understanding the Human Genome Project. Using stations to provide a comprehensive overview. *The American Biology Teacher, 67*(8), 475–484.

Spielvogel, J. (2003). *World history: Modern times.* New York: Glencoe/McGraw-Hill.

Spires, H. A., & Stone, P. D. (1989). The directed notetaking activity: A self-questioning approach. *Journal of Reading, 33*, 36–39.

Sprenger, M. (1999). *Learning and memory: The brain in action.* Alexandria, VA: Association for Supervision and Curriculum Development.

Stahl, N. A., King, J. R., & Henk, W. A. (1991). Enhancing students' notetaking through training and evaluation. *Journal of Reading, 34*, 614–622.

Stanovich, K. E. (1986). Matthew effects in reading: Some consequences of individual differences in the acquisition of literacy. *Reading Research Quarterly, 21*, 360–407.

Stauffer, R. G. (1969). *Teaching reading as a thinking process.* New York: HarperCollins.

Steinbeck, J. (1939). *The grapes of wrath.* New York: Viking.

Sternberg, R. J., & Williams, W. M. (2002). *Educational psychology.* Boston: Allyn & Bacon.

Stowe, H. B. (1852/1983). *Uncle Tom's cabin or life among the lowly.* New York: Bantam.

Struble, J. (2007). Using graphic organizers as formative assessment. *Science Scope, 30*(5), 69–71.

Tang, G. (2001). *The grapes of math.* New York: Scholastic.

Taylor, C. (1992). *The house that crack built.* San Francisco: Chronicle.

Taylor, R. T., & McAtee, R. (2003). Turning a new page to life and literacy. *Journal of Adolescent & Adult Literacy, 46*, 476–480.

Templeton, S. (1992). Theory, nature and pedagogy of higher-order orthographic development in older children. In S. Templeton & D. Bear (Eds.), *Development of orthographic knowledge and the foundations of literacy: A memorial festschrift for Edmund H. Henderson* (pp. 253–278). Hillsdale, NJ: Erlbaum.

Tharp, R. G., & Gallimore, R. (1989). *Rousing minds to life: Teaching, learning, and schooling in social context.* New York: Cambridge University Press.

The Freedom Writers (with Gruwell, E.). (2001). *The freedom writers diary: How a teacher and 150 teens used writing to change themselves and the world around them.* New York: Doubleday.

Thomas, E., & Robinson, H. (1972). *Improving reading in every class: A sourcebook for teachers.* Boston: Allyn & Bacon.

Thompson, D. N. (1998). Using advance organizers to facilitate reading comprehension among older adults. *Educational Gerontology, 24*, 625–638.

Thoreau, H. D. (1849/1965). *Civil disobedience.* New York: HarperCollins.

Thorkildsen, T. A., & Nicholls, J. G. (2002). *Motivation and the struggling to learn: Responding to fractured experience.* Boston: Allyn & Bacon.

Thorndike, E. L., & Lorge, I. (1944). *The teacher's word book of 30,000 words*. New York: Teachers College, Columbia University.

Tienken, C. H., Goldberg, S., & DiRocco, D. (2009). Questioning the questions. *Kappa Delta Pi Record, 46*(1), 39–43.

Tierney, R. J., Clark, C., Wiser, B., Simpson, C. S., Herter, R. J., & Fenner, L. (1998). Portfolios: Assumptions, tensions, and possibilities. *Reading Research Quarterly, 33*, 474–486.

Trelease, J. (2006). *The read-aloud handbook* (6th ed.). New York: Penguin.

Twain, M. (1890). In G. Bainton (Ed.), *The art of authorship: Literary reminiscences, methods of work, and advice to young beginners, personally contributed by leading authors of the day* (pp. 85–88). New York: D. Appleton and Company.

Vacca, R. T., & Vacca, J. L. (1998). *Content area reading: Literacy and learning across the curriculum* (6th ed.). New York: Longman.

Val, L. B. (2003). *Through the lens: National Geographic greatest photographs*. Washington, DC: Author.

Vandergrift, L. (2006). Second language listening: Listening ability or language proficiency. *Modern Language Journal, 90*(1), 6–18.

Vandergrift, L., Goh, C. C. M., Mareschal, C. J., & Tafaghodtar, M. H. (2006). The metacognitive awareness listening questionnaire: Development and validation. *Language Learning, 56*(3), 431–462.

Vanderwood, M. L., McGrew, K. S., & Flanagan, D. P. (2001). The contribution of general and specific cognitive abilities to reading instruction. *Learning and Individual Differences, 13*, 159–188.

Venezky, R. (1982). The origins of the present day chasm between adult literacy needs and school literacy instruction. *Visible Language, 16*, 113–136.

Vygotsky, L. S. (1978). Mental development of children and the process of learning. In M. Cole, V. John-Steiner, S. Scribner, and E. Souberman (Eds. and Trans.), *Mind in society: The development of higher psychological processes*. Cambridge: MA: Harvard University Press.

Wade, S. E., & Moje, E. B. (2000). The role of the text in classroom learning. In M. L. Kamil, P. B. Mosenthal, P. D. Pearson, & R. Barr (Eds.), *Handbook of reading research* (Vol. 3, pp. 609–628). Mahwah, NJ: Erlbaum.

Wajnryb, R. (1990). *Grammar dictation*. Oxford, England: Oxford University Press.

Walsh, J. A., & Sattes, B. D. (2005). *Quality questioning: Research-based practice to engage every learner*. Thousand Oaks, CA: Corwin.

Wang, J. (1996). An empirical assessment of textbook readability in secondary education. *Reading Improvement, 33*, 41–45.

Warger, C. (2001). *Five homework strategies for teaching students with learning disabilities*. ERIC/OSEP Digest E608. Washington, DC: Clearinghouse on Disabilities and Gifted Education.

West, K. R. (1998). Noticing and responding to learners: Literacy evaluation and instruction in the primary grades. *The Reading Teacher, 51*, 550–559.

Wheeler, A. E., & Hill, D. (1990). Diagram-ease. Why students misinterpret diagrams. *Science Teacher, 57*, 58–63.

Wigfield, A., & Eccles, J. S. (2000). Expectancy-value theory of achievement motivation. *Contemporary Education Psychology, 25*, 68–81.

Wilcox, B. (1997). Writing portfolios: Active vs. passive. *English Journal, 86*(6), 34–35.

Wills, C. (1995). Voice of inquiry: Possibilities and perspectives. *Childhood Education, 71*, 261–265.

Wimer, J. W., Ridenour, C. S., & Thomas, K. (2001). Higher order teacher questioning of boys and girls in elementary mathematics classrooms. *Journal of Educational Research, 95*(2), 84–92.

Winter, J. (1998). *My name is Georgia*. San Diego: Harcourt Brace.

Woodward, J. (1994). The role of models in secondary science instruction. *Remedial and Special Education, 15*, 94–104.

Worthy, J. (2002). What makes intermediate-grade students want to read? *The Reading Teacher, 55*, 568–569.

Wright, E. L., & Govindarajan, G. (1995). Discrepant event demonstrations. *Science Teacher, 62*(1), 24–28.

Zamel, V. (2000). Engaging students in writing-to-learn: Promoting language and literacy across the curriculum. *Journal of Basic Writing, 19*(2), 3–21.

Zollman, A. (2009). Students use of graphic organizers to improve mathematical problem solving communications. *Middle School Journal, 41*(2), 4–12.

Index

Note: Tables and figures are indicated by *t* and *f*.